**TOURISM AND CULTURAL CHANGE**
*Series Editors*: Professor Mike Robinson
Cultural Change, Leeds Metropolitan University, Leeds, UK
and Dr Alison Phipps, *University of Glasgow, Scotland, UK*

# The British on Holiday
## Charter Tourism, Identity and Consumption

Hazel Andrews

**CHANNEL VIEW PUBLICATIONS**
Bristol • Buffalo • Toronto

**Library of Congress Cataloging in Publication Data**
A catalog record for this book is available from the Library of Congress.
Andrews, Hazel.
The British on Holiday: Charter Tourism, Identity and Consumption/Hazel Andrews.
Tourism and Cultural Change: 28
Includes bibliographical references and index.
1. Tourism–Great Britain. 2. Travelers–Great Britain. 3. British–Travel–Spain–Majorca.
4. Visitors, Foreign–Spain–Majorca. 5. Resorts–Social aspects–Spain–Majorca. 6. Majorca
(Spain)–Description and travel.
I. Title.
G155.G7A65 2011
910.941–dc23 2011015782

**British Library Cataloguing in Publication Data**
A catalogue entry for this book is available from the British Library.

ISBN-13: 978-1-84541-183-1 (hbk)
ISBN-13: 978-1-84541-182-4 (pbk)

**Channel View Publications**
UK: St Nicholas House, 31-34 High Street, Bristol BS1 2AW, UK.
USA: UTP, 2250 Military Road, Tonawanda, NY 14150, USA.
Canada: UTP, 5201 Dufferin Street, North York, Ontario M3H 5T8, Canada.

Typeset by Datapage International Ltd.
Printed and bound in Great Britain by Short Run Press Ltd.

# Contents

# Acknowledgements

Many people have contributed to the making of this book, not least the many tourists who I engaged with during my fieldwork, and I am particularly grateful to them for their cooperation. In addition, numerous residents and employees of tourism in Magaluf and Palmanova supported the fieldwork process. I'd especially like to thank Glenn, both Brians, Liam and Jason, Janet, Silvia and David, Liz, Mick and Sheila, Rachel, Dennis and Natalie, Tony and Raoul, Paco and Pedro, and Miguel. I'd also like to thank Unijet, and the managers of the Hotels Son Maties and Cala Blanca. A special thank you to Tony Pallicer who provided invaluable information, useful contacts, generous hospitality and help during all of my sojourns in Mallorca. I thank Professor Jackie Waldren for providing support and advice during the early days of my fieldwork. Thanks also to colleagues at the Universitat de les Illes Balears for their support during my visit in 2009.

A very special thank you to Professor Tom Selwyn for his many years of support, continued interest, guidance, inspiration and commitment to me from the inception of this work to its completion. Thank you also to Professor Graham Dann for his support and detailed reading of my work in the earliest days of the project.

I am grateful for the support offered by the then University of North London for my doctoral bursary, and additional financial assistance from the Radcliffe-Brown Memorial Fund and the British Federation of Women Graduates, all of which supported my early research. I am also grateful to the Faculty of Education, Community and Leisure at LJMU for allowing me a sabbatical in order to progress the writing of this book.

Thank you Les for all your help and unfailing support and to Ella and Marc for being the wonderful children you are. Lastly, I'd like to thank both my mum and dad who laid all the foundations that have made my work and life possible. This is for you.

# Chapter 1
# *Introduction*

## Introduction

This book is an ethnography of British[1] charter tourists in the resorts of Palmanova and Magaluf on the Mediterranean island of Mallorca. Although ethnographic techniques of enquiry have increasingly been brought to bear on the subject of tourism in recent years, this remains an under-used research method in tourism studies, with full-scale ethnographies being few and far between. Simultaneously, studies of charter tourists are largely and curiously absent from the tourism studies literature. There are exceptions, but none specifically related to British tourists or based on in-depth ethnographic enquiry.

At the same time, the use of tourism to explore issues of everyday social concern, tourism as a mirror to understanding the issue in the wider social world is also under explored. Outside the canon of business concerns, the study of tourism has tended to focus on its impacts, in terms of costs and benefits, host–guest relations, economics and development studies. All of these remain pertinent and important areas of enquiry, couched as they often are in terms of trying to address issues of power imbalance, exploitation of resources and the degradation of local peoples and their cultures. However, the concentration on the 'out there' that such concerns demand, misses the opportunity to reflect on 'what's here'. That is, what can this particular practice of mobility tell us about the nature of the home world?

The purpose of this chapter is to lay the foundations on which subsequent discussion takes place. The ethnographic detail on which my argument rests results from several periods of participant observation among the predominately British tourists who holiday in Magaluf and the conjoining resort of Palmanova, between 1998 and 1999 and a return visit in the autumn of 2009. I begin by describing the setting in which the study takes place or what Bourdieu (1993) terms the 'field of action'. From here, I move on to consider the importance of the trope of travel and how it reflects ideas about the need to journey in search of a better or more satisfactory life. I then move on to briefly outline the theoretical

1

background that has shaped social science discussions about tourists and the nature of tourism.

## The Field of Action

The island of Mallorca is situated off the east coast of the Spanish peninsula, in the north-west Mediterranean, and is the largest of the Balearic Islands (Figure 1.1). Tourism provides the main source of income for the Balearics. The development of tourism as an economic activity began at the start of the 20th century with rapid expansion underway by

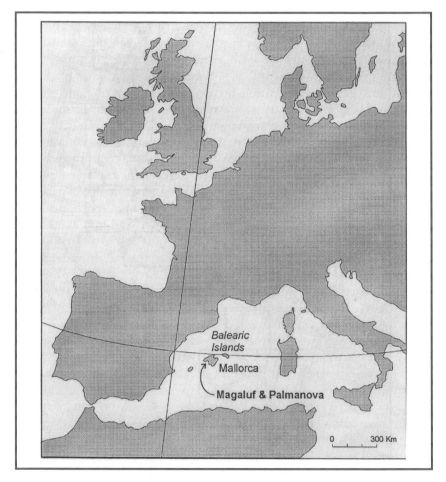

**Figure 1.1** Location Map

the 1950s and 1960s. By the mid 1970s, the islands were well established as mass tourism destinations, receiving 8 million annual visitors by 1995 with 6 million visiting Mallorca (Bardolet, 1996). Statistics show an ongoing increase, so that in 2005 the Balearics received in excess of 11 million tourists, 8 million of which went to Mallorca.[2]

Magaluf and Palmanova are in the municipality of Calvià, which is in the south-west of the island. They are two of six coastal resorts in the municipality. The other resorts are Illetes, Peguara, Portal Nous and Santa Ponça. The two main inland towns are Calvià and Capdella. Although Palmanova and Magaluf can be understood as two separate places in terms of name, there is no neat spatial division between them as they run into each other. They were among the first resorts to witness tourism development, with two hotels in place by 1930 (Selwyn, 1996b). Such has been Calvià's success with tourism that in 1996 the municipality was the richest in Spain and one of the richest in Europe (Selwyn, 1996b). The Spanish National Institute of Statistics reported that in July 2008, Calvià was the lead municipality for bed occupancy in the whole of Spain.[3] Over time, the local authority has made many improvements to the physical structure of the two resorts, e.g. building a promenade that runs alongside nearly the full length of the beaches. This makes it possible to walk from one end of Palmanova to the far end of Magaluf, almost without interruption. Other initiatives include the removal of high-rise block hotels, the establishment of the post of Tourism Ombudsman within Calvià Council and traffic calming measures in the form of a way-one system. The extent to which the municipality has endeavoured to address environmental concerns and ensure the sustainability of the resorts has won it awards. Further, as far as possible, the council has pursued a policy that separates residential and tourist facilities from each other. The two resorts, then, are in place to serve tourists' needs in terms of accommodation, places to eat, shops, entertainment facilities and so on. However, the functioning of the resorts is underpinned by the relationship between the hotels and the tour operators. The hotels are dependent on the tour operators to supply the tourists. For example, in 1998, the head of the local hotel association advised me that 'the relationship between the hotels and the tour operators is the most important and the most important tour operator is Thomsons'.

Magaluf and Palmanova are predominately 'British'. There are several reasons why I make this claim. Firstly, the majority of tourists staying in the resorts derive from one of the four nations of the UK. This includes a very wide geographical spread from Cornwall to Aberdeen and everywhere in between. However, from my observations and encounters, a large proportion of the tourists hailed from the north-east of England, Manchester and surrounding areas. Secondly, the majority of the tourists arrive as part of an organised holiday led by one of the UK's leading tour operators, First Choice and Thomson. These companies also employ British workers as their representatives in the resorts. Such is the dominance of British operators that whole hotels are given over entirely to their business. Thirdly, the main language of communication is English. This is, in part, because of the sheer number of native English speakers present. Among these are members of an expatriate community, many of whom are involved in the tourism industry, seasonal British workers and the tourists themselves. The use of the English language relates to café-bar menus, television programmes and newspapers, including those derived from the UK and the locally produced *Majorca Daily Bulletin*. Fourthly, the food and drink available caters to British tastes, with the provision and sale of imported British milk, bread, meat, breakfast cereals and beers. It is often possible to buy an imperial pint and to spend pounds sterling. Fifthly, Britishness is displayed in an overt way, such as in the flying of the Union Jack flag (Figure 1.2). It is also evident in more subtle forms, through the choices and dispositions enacted by the tourists. In addition, the mediators of the tourists' experiences exploit a sense of national identity and the

**Figure 1.2** Flying the Union Jack

dangers posed by the other. They draw attention to points of difference and risks associated with being in the presence of 'the other'. As well as being British, I also categorise the tourists visiting the two resorts as predominately white, heterosexual and working class. Very few tourists holiday alone, but rather with friendship and kinship groups, the former often being single sex.

As already noted, Magaluf and Palmanova, although separate resorts, merge into one another. The whole area is bounded inland by a motorway running between the resort of Andraitx further to the west and the capital Palma to the east, and the edge of the land and sea form a natural perimeter. The distinctive character of Magaluf is one of a 'party' destination with its numerous café-bars and nightclubs that attract a youthful tourist in the style of Club 18–30. It is also underpinned by ideas of self-gratification in all sorts of ways, both alimentary and sexual. Such is the extent of the latter that it has earned the resort the nickname 'Shagaluf'. The main road in Magaluf, Punta Balena, is dominated by numerous shops that sell a wide range of goods, from souvenirs and postcards to clothes and jewellery. Many of the shops are packed tightly together, and the numerous stands exhibiting wares outside many of the shops give an impression of variety and choice. Mixed in with these shops are café-bars, nightclubs, amusement arcades and 'fast food' outlets, e.g. KFC and Burger King.

Palmanova exhibits some of the characteristics of Magaluf, but as I have elsewhere observed, 'it is considered by many of the tourists who stay there to be slightly more "upmarket", with some people referring to the "badly behaved" tourists in Magaluf as "animals"' (Andrews, 2006: 222). It is the case that Palmanova has fewer nightclubs and attracts fewer tourists looking for a Club 18–30 style holiday. Even if such tourists were accommodated in Palmanova, they would be more likely to concentrate their activities in Magaluf, which provides more of the facilities they are looking for. Thus, Palmanova tends to attract greater numbers of older people and family groups. However, in reality, neither resort can be demarcated in any exclusive way based on tourist typology. Both places exhibit similar characteristics that make them landscapes driven by the promotion and action of various forms of consumption (Andrews, 2006).

In both resorts there are numerous activities that tourists can participate in. Among these are sunbathing, hiring a moped, paragliding, riding an inflated banana; or, if staying in a hotel, games and activities led by hotel entertainers. There are numerous tours and excursions organised by tour operator representatives (reps), which are also available through local travel agencies. These include, for example, tours to the east of the island to visit the underground caves, excursions to markets based in Inca and Andraitx and general island tours to admire the scenery. Further, there are organised trips to night-time entertainment venues both inside and outside the resorts, and tour operator rep-marshalled bar crawls around Magaluf.

I continue the discussion by considering the broader framework of touristic action and the importance of the trope of travel.

## The Trope of Travel

Baudelaire (1970: 99–100) comments, 'it seems to me that I would always be better off where I am not, and this question of moving is one of those I discuss incessantly with my soul'. Baudelaire's words find resonance across cultures and time. The idea of journeying elsewhere for a better life, referred to by Baudelaire, finds resonance in many cultural expressions across different societies and throughout history. What all the stories tend to share is that the places to which the traveller journeys are legendary, secret, often mythical and magical. In addition, they offer the promise of freedom from the complications of life, the strife and struggle of everyday existence, and will take the voyagers closer to their origins, to a life in which they can discover their true nature.

Such stories are reminiscent of the promises offered by 'mainstream' religions. A better life cannot be found in the quotidian earthly world, but exists outside its realms. Paradise, Eden, Heaven, all offer an existence of non-suffering, total fulfilment, peace and happiness. The desire to travel for a better life has existed both metaphorically, in, e.g. life as a journey, as well as literally in the form of pilgrimage, for hundreds of years (Coleman & Elsner, 1995).

The sense of loss, or movement from one state to another, has been explored in theories found in the earliest days of sociology. For example, both Tönnies (1957 [1887]) and Durkheim (1933) draw attention to differences between the structural relations found in the pre-modern world and those found in the modern world. The pre-modern world is, for Tönnies, characterised by the features of Gemeinschaft and for Durkheim that of 'mechanical solidarity'. The attributes that Tönnies and Durkheim both accord these earlier forms of society are based on ideas of the collective and group bonding due to emotional face-to-face ties. Tönnies' Gesellschaft and Durkheim's 'organic solidarity' see the erosion of close kinship and community links due to the rise of the individual resulting from the changes wrought by the processes of industrialisation and urbanisation. The binary opposition that is established presents an argument for a difference between the here and the there; the now and then; or the now and the next. It is the relationship between these sets of dualisms that gives rise to the questions: What is different? What is there? What is it about these other places that makes them seem so alluring or able to satisfy that which is missing in the here? Further, if it is necessary to travel somewhere else to seek those elements absent from the home world,[4] is this contradiction at the heart of the touristic impulse? Does tourism provide a contrast with the world of home? Does it supply the associated freedoms from and reconciliation of the discontents of the home world? If the journey to elsewhere is a return to or discovery of a true self, then what is the true self that is being sought?

These questions are particularly pertinent to the tourists of Magaluf and Palmanova. The idea of difference pervades the tourist experience and yet what is presented in these two resorts is a world reminiscent of home. If a sense of self is being sought by these tourists, then it is one that is constructed within the context of a national identity that bemoans a lost past overtaken by external forces. In effect, in the words of one informant, 'England isn't England anymore'. In order to understand such a perspective, the next section outlines those forces that are argued to impinge on a sense of national identity in the UK.

## You Can't Call a Sausage a Sausage Anymore

At the end of September 2002, the UK Food Standards Agency revealed new labelling measures for meat products including sausages and burgers. The rules that came into effect in January 2003 are linked to a European directive concerning the contents of meat produce. A report in the *Guardian* explained, '[t]hat means a sausage previously described as containing 44% pork and 6% beef will have to be re-labelled as 32% pork, with added pork fat, pork rind, beef fat and beef connective tissue' (http://www. guardian.co.uk 21/11/03). The news was also announced on the BBC Radio 4 Today programme. It was suggested that because the directive from Europe aimed to increase the meat volume in sausages, the British would no longer be able to call 'their' sausages 'sausages', due to their high fat and gristle content. The discussion that ensued included suggestions that this ruling was yet another example of European Union intervention in British life.

The new labelling standards for meat products are among some of many similar perceived interferences in British life by the European Union. The threats to British sovereignty, independence and global importance have been well documented (e.g. Lunn, 1989; Cesarani, 1996;

Cinnirella, 2000; Powell, 2002; Triandefyllidon, 2002). Many of the perceived intrusions are connected with food, e.g. the ban on British beef exports and the introduction of metric measurements to replace imperial measures in the purchase of food and drink. These actions are seen as an attack on the way the 'British' do things, and, as such, an assault on their very identity. For example, during my 2009 fieldwork in Mallorca, the signing of the Lisbon Treaty by the Czech Republic was greeted in the *Daily Express* newspaper by the headlines: 'Britain the End'.

At the same time, other changes have occurred in Britain, largely associated with political events of the 1980s and the encouragement of neo-liberal free-market economics by Thatcherism. Coupled with this ideology was an attack on the manufacturing base of the British economy (Seabrook, 1996). The removal of much of Britain's production capabilities and the selling of public utilities had a two-fold effect. Firstly, the whole way in which people related to their work changed. The idea of a job for life was removed, and support from a broader community, in the form of a welfare state, was eroded. As Bauman (1997a: 39) comments, now there are 'no visible collective, joint agencies in charge of the global societal order. The care for the human plight has been privatized, and the tools and practices of care deregulated'.

The selling of public utilities placed consumption firmly at the centre of society. The provision of these items no longer functioned for the common good, but was 'up for grabs' by individuals and open to capricious market forces for 'best deals' and 'good prices'. Being able to consume and to take part in the great share sell-off began to speak about who the British were. Not to be part of this bonanza was to be a non-participant, an outsider. The situation was compounded by high unemployment and a lack of work opportunities. Without the means of accumulating wealth to participate in the market '[r]egardless of the reasons for their unemployment, they are derided as misfits, reproached for sloth, dubbed anti-social and stigmatized as spongers' (Bauman, 1997b: 25).

Thatcher famously claimed that 'there is no such thing as society'.[5] In doing her best to undermine it, her policies caused points of collectivity to change. That is, if people cannot produce, then they must consume. The ability to consume requires money and not to have it becomes a mechanism for exclusion. Therefore, in order for individuals to show that they belong to the 'in-group', they must be a consumer. The problem associated with this scenario is that because the items for consumption are ever changing, it becomes increasingly difficult to establish a stable sense of self. The result is increased uncertainty and accelerated individualism.

Further, Seabrook contends that Thatcherite economics entered into human relationships:

> Market values, applied with relentless rigour to the outer circumstances of our lives, also invade and colonize the spaces within, so that even our most intimate relationships and profound involvements with others are now governed by emotional and psychic economics. (Seabrook, 1996: 186–187)

There is much in the post-World War II history of the UK that suggests that a sense of identity is not something that is either easy to create or retain.

The free market with the attendant emphasis on consumption practices is now well established. It is not the intention to over-emphasise the Thatcher era as a specific historic marker because many of the features characteristic of her administration are ongoing processes. However, in many respects, her period in office does provide a hiatus in which ideas of the collective were undermined, as Seabrook (1996, 1997) and Bauman (1997a, 1997b, 2002) contend. It is against this backdrop that consumption gained in significance. For example, writing about the USA, Brown (2000) notes that consumer rights were promoted as a way of placating the citizenry and of regulating behaviour in the face of diminished welfare rights after World War II. The idea that consumerism can somehow compensate for loss in support from elsewhere, or be used as a means to pacify, links it with childhood. As Stearns (2001) notes, consumerism is used increasingly to appease children and forms part of the socialisation process.

A perceived sense of loss, the threat of outside influences, the undermining of the welfare state and an erosion of traditional forms of collective identities (e.g. unions) give rise to the suggestion of insecurity in the sense of self and nation. At the same time, however, it is precisely these issues from which ideas of national identity can be seen to draw. As Brown notes,

> [t]he nationalist myth of permanent, fixed, homeland community, derives its emotional power... from the anxieties generated by the fragility of the self, the ego, in the face both of the complex ambiguities inherent in relationships with the external modern world, and also of the disintegrative incoherence of the inner, psychological world. (Brown, 2000a: 24)

The nationalist myth is infused with references to an imagined past, a perception of what life used to be, an ideal often linked to childhood and finding refuge in the mother. Sceats (2000: 5) contends that the idea of the desire to be reunited with the maternal figure is a fantasy of return 'to the wholly fulfilled infant at the breast, or even *in utero.* This might almost be said to be the ur-longing, a desire to be reunited with the block off which we are a chip'. In this scenario, the nation, which at one time could be depended on to provide for basic needs, is symbolically a maternal figure. As Cusack (2003: 7) suggests, '[w]omen in particular have been used as cultural markers of the nation's identity... strongly associated with the family and tradition'.

At the beginning of this chapter, I suggested that there appears to be an over-arching desire for many in the Western world to achieve a different life from that which they already inhabit. The accomplishment of this goal can only ever be reached in a place other than home. Inherent in such an analysis are questions pertaining to the nature of ideas of the self in suggesting that one's true nature lies elsewhere. The conditions of modernity said to account for a sense of alienation are thought to be exaggerated in the post-modern world, which, in the case of Britain, is compounded by loss of Empire, changes in work patterns, the installation of the free market and an uneasy relationship with the European Union.

If the home world cannot provide a sense of identity or security, it becomes necessary to look for the self elsewhere. Tourism products are presented as something different and as offering an escape from the everyday. Yet, in this exodus from the quotidian, what is the nature of the self that the tourist is led to discover? This book examines this question in relation to a relatively understudied group of tourists: British working-class charter tourists.

The discussion that follows will contextualise the debate further by outlining the ways in which questions relating to the tourist and tourist motivation have been approached within the anthropological and sociological literature to date. It begins by providing the framework in which the social science study of tourism has taken place and notes that although key to an understanding of the subject of tourism, empirical-based studies of tourists were largely absent from the discussion.

## Where are the Tourists?

In his overview of the way in which international tourism has been studied in the social sciences, Crick (1989: 314) identified three key themes: (1) the political economy of tourism; (2) tourism in relation to meanings, motives and roles; and (3) images of tourism as a force in socio-cultural change. All three categories can be examined in their own right; but it is the nature of the tourism system that they will inevitably inter-link or interact with one another. However, in the anthropological literature on tourism, it is the impacts on tourist destinations and the 'host' cultures that have received the most attention (see, e.g. Abram *et al.*, 1997; Boissevain, 1996; Smith, 1989).

In terms of the second of Crick's groups, he contends that this is an understudied area in which questions pertaining to what tourists say about their experiences, what they learn and why they go overseas, have not been asked. This, he claims, is because 'tourists themselves are not the object of study' (Crick, 1989: 326), and where the tourist has been considered, '[w]e have, for the most part, taxonomies of tourist types and vague generalizations' (Crick, 1989: 330).

Crick's tracing of the social science approach to tourism was used as a foundation by Selwyn (1994) for assessing the current state of affairs concerning the anthropology of tourism. Selwyn's analysis identifies six main components of the anthropology of tourism, of which tourists are a key group. To have one group – the tourists – understudied leaves a gap in the literature. However, since Crick and Selwyn made their observations, the situation has changed. It will become apparent that there is now a body of literature that examines more closely the experiences and performances of tourists. The following begins by tracing the theoretical foundations to their discussion.

### They're on a sacred journey to the authentic

With regard to the tourist, Selwyn (1994) highlights a problem that has contributed to discussions of tourist motivation – how should the tourist or tourists be classified or how should tourist motivation be understood? I will begin by outlining the main contributors to these debates.

My starting point is MacCannell's (1976) seminal text, *The Tourist*. In this, he expounds on some ideas explored in an earlier work (MacCannell, 1973) in which he considers the nature of 'tourist spaces'. He claims that the basis of the tourist experience is like that of a religious or sacred journey. The tourist experience, he attests, is concerned with a search for authenticity because everyday life in the home world is characterised by inauthenticity. The notion of a quest for authenticity is continued in *The Tourist*, in which MacCannell suggests that the authenticity of the tourist experience is also related to structural relations in society; interpretations of which owe their conceptual lineage to Durkheim's study of primitive religions. Tourism, MacCannell (1976: 7) argues, is a way of organising the tourist, of bringing her/him into 'a relationship with the modern social totality'; of providing an authentic experience. For MacCannell, the tourist is then in search of cultural productions, sights that are viewed and visited in much the same way as religious sites or relics might be visited on a pilgrimage.

The idea that tourism is akin to a religious pilgrimage finds support in the work of Graburn (1989). He argues that tourism operates in a similar way to ritual in that, like a sacred ceremony, it is seen as transcendent and set apart from everyday reality. For Graburn (1989: 27), the tourist emerges from the end of their holiday a different person, feeling that they have been transformed, returning home as a 'new person' and ready to be reincorporated into the everyday world of home.

MacCannell's and Graburn's attempts to meta-theorise tourism and tourist motivation do not necessarily fit that well with what tourists in Palmanova and Magaluf are doing. The degree to which these tourists might be argued to be taken out of their everyday world is questionable. On a spatial level, they are removed and separated from the home world. However, the degree to which this might be seen as sacred or special is contentious. For some tourists, their holiday experience was the first time they had flown or it was their first visit to Mallorca. For others, it was their 18th or 19th visit to the island, suggesting that it was part of their routine. Indeed, two informants had always taken their holiday in the same hotel in Palmanova and at the same time every year.

An examination of the data, however, shows that there are aspects of tourists' activities that would fit the sacred journey paradigm. For example, buying new clothes, or setting aside special clothes, for the holiday and then, once on holiday, purchasing souvenirs that might be understood to occupy the place of religious relics. One man, describing his wife's preparation for their vacations, states, 'before we leave she cleans everything, clean sheets. When we get back she'll wash and iron all our holiday clothes and put them in the spare room ready for our next holiday'.

The signalling of Britishness in the two resorts, however, hardly lifts the tourists from the world of the profane. These tourists, in a way that is similar to the Japanese tourists described by Graburn (1987), also keep the home world in mind. At a time before the widespread use of mobile phones, queues at public telephone boxes in Magaluf and Palmanova, to phone home were a common sight most evenings. Sending postcards home, purchasing British newspapers and watching British news reports on satellite television all serve to keep the tourists, in part, mentally, if not physically, in the UK.

I will demonstrate that what the tourists encounter is a constructed landscape based on particular ideas of Britishness. In so doing, it contradicts MacCannell's idea of authenticity. That is, MacCannell suggests that authenticity lies in encounters with the other, that tourists seek something absent from the home world that can be re-discovered in 'exotic' locations and with 'exotic' people. The tourists in Magaluf and Palmanova did not, on the whole, express much interest in encountering the foreign other, rather the opposite: encounters with otherness were largely in the form of other British tourists.

Rather than an outward search for the 'something' missing in their lives, the tourists look backwards – not only to where they originated (in spatial terms), but back to a construction of British identity that is rooted in the past. British food and drink are looked for and the other is kept at bay in the rejection of locally produced food and water. There are exceptions; some repeat visitors do penetrate back areas, becoming friends with locals they encounter from year to year. In some cases, the penetration is complete when tourists become part of the back stage themselves through, for instance, marriage. In addition, tourists do not always reject the other outright, for example, some will sit and watch Flamenco dancing (although this is not a Mallorcan custom) and sample local food and drink.

MacCannell's (1976) ideas concerning markers are applicable in Magaluf and Palmanova. Tour operators direct tourists to attractions. Mallorca and its resorts are marked by their representation in holiday brochures and television holiday programmes. The whole of Palmanova and Magaluf appear to be constructed primarily around serving the needs of tourists. The resorts are staged, with an ideal of a particular type of Britishness. Being presented with Britishness rather than otherness means that authenticity is not found in the other. Where it may be said to exist is in ideas of the self, of having a 'good time' (Brown, 1996: 38) or the hot authenticity (Sewlyn, 1996a) of feelings and sensations. This assertion also calls into question Urry's (1990, 2002) assertion that the gaze is the main organising force of tourism.

## They're gazing at difference

Both MacCannell and Graburn argue that tourism is a form of sacred experience that is in opposition to the home world. This dichotomous relationship is also explored by Urry, although from a different

perspective. Contrary to MacCannell, Urry (1990: 11) contends '[i]t...
seems incorrect to suggest that a search for authenticity is the basis for
the organisation of tourism'. Instead, he claims that tourism is driven by
a socially constructed gaze, a way of looking at and seeing the world and
that central to the tourist experience is the idea of difference: 'The tourist
gaze is directed to features of landscape and townscape which separate
them off from everyday experience' (Urry, 1990: 7).

Prima facie, the idea that tourists to Magaluf and Palmanova are
getting something different is indisputable. Sets of binary oppositions can
easily be established, e.g. home/away, work/recreation, hot/cool and
dry/wet. Many of the tourists understand their experience as something
different. Bob's response to my questions about what made him come on
holiday was 'there's not really much to say other than the sun... the
climate. It's a change of routine, a break from what you normally do, it
doesn't really matter where you go'. Another informant replied to the
same question, 'it's just something different'.

The problem with Urry's (1990, 2002) idea as it applies to Magaluf and
Palmanova is that in many respects there is not much that is actually
different. English is the common language, imported UK food stuffs are
offered for consumption, British television programmes and newspapers
are all readily available. The whole emphasis is so much on a particular
construction of national identity that rather than difference, the tourists
are placed at the very heart of being British.

That tourists go sightseeing is also indisputable and so too is the idea
that the gaze is socially constructed and directed. Tourists are offered
particular packages for touring the island or participating in certain
entertainment activities. During one of the former excursions, tourists are
directed as to at which point they should take photographs. The tourist
gaze in Magaluf and Palmanova is primarily directed towards other
tourists, they are made spectacles of by self and others in some of the
games played. Urry, however, over-emphasises the gaze in privileging
sight above the other senses. In Magaluf and Palmanova, people *feel* their
holiday as burnt skin, being too hot, being drunk, feeling sick, smelling
vomit, falling over, dancing and hearing too much noise.

What the theories discussed thus far have in common is a tendency to
meta-theorise about tourists. They are seekers of authenticity, a sort of
pilgrim, or gazers on sights of difference. Moving away from this 'one
size fits all' approach is the work of Cohen (1974, 1979a, 1979b) and his
insistence that there are a number of categories of tourists that are
indicative of the individual's place in the home world, and it is to these
I now turn.

## They're children playing in paradise

To consider tourism as a form of pilgrimage in the way that MacCannell describes it, is to understand it at a deep, structural level within society, which according to Cohen (1979b: 22) is inadequate because 'different modes of touristic experiences of the alienated individual can be distinguished'. These are diversionary, recreational, experiential, experimental and existential. In addition, on the question of authenticity, Cohen (1985: 292) opines that 'many attractions are so lightly staged, and their inauthenticity is so easily recognizable, that one has to assume that tourists must be inordinately stupid or naïve to accept them seriously as authentic'. This understanding of attractions as staged is an element of tourism as play.

The category of recreational tourist is used by Cohen to explore the weaknesses of the analogy between tourism as pilgrimage/ritual in modern society and the role of pilgrimage and ritual in traditional societies. He suggests that the comparison is too generalised and that the transcendence brought about by non-secular activities can only be playfully imagined: '[r]ecreational tourism… permits a playful outlet to modern man's [sic] longing for Reality, without endowing the object of his longing with ontological substance and thus threatening the modern, secular world view' (Cohen, 1985: 300).

There is much game playing in Magaluf and Palmanova. I will demonstrate that this allows the expression of a particular type of Britishness without being a threat to the home world. In many respects, the tourists appear like children. As Dann (1989, 1996a) notes, there is much in tourism to suggest that tourists are like children, 'one is not surprised to encounter the phenomenon of regression' (Dann, 1996a: 104). Examples of child-like behaviour include game playing, the use of toys, dressing up and the emphasis on fun. In Magaluf and Palmanova for instance, activities on the beach might revolve around game playing. In addition, games are organised by hotel entertainers during the day and playing games becomes a feature of the entertainment at night. Games may involve the use of toys, such as bats and balls, as well as larger props, e.g. riding an inflated device in the shape of a gigantic banana. Tourists 'dress up' to go out at night and dress up to enact gender reversals as either men or women (although it is predominately men in drag). Having a good time is emphasised by bar DJs, hotel entertainers and tour operator representatives.

That tourist promotional literature plays on some basic child-like needs, such as warmth, security and protection, has been noted by

Dann (1989); for example, by stressing the theme of Mother Nature, which is represented in the appearance of land features. Such physical forms include mountains, pyramids and domes, all of which are argued, by Dann, to resemble mammary glands. An example of reassurance comes in the form of an advertisement for the Hilton hotel chain, which proclaims 'serving hamburgers and apple pie "just like mom used to make"' (Dann, 1989: 6). Signs of 'cooking like mum/mom' are a feature in Magaluf and Palmanova. References to mother are not connoted in signs of breasts, in the way that Dann suggests, but categorically and 'in the face', with the abundant appearance of actual breasts represented on postcards, aprons, ornaments and the exposure of real breasts during some entertainment. Here, the breast symbolises taking the tourist child to the bosom or heart of the nation. Here, the tourist child can have a one to one, intimate relationship with its (nation) mother in which that nation is white and heterosexual. The reality of the home world for many of the tourists is one in which they are forced out of their homes, as these become centres for particular groups of the immigrant community, and some politicians are perceived to be 'Paki lovers'. For example, two respondents explained how they had moved from Southall, London, because, in their minds, it had become dominated by Asians. An interpretation of this view is that the respondents are being denied the bosom of the mother nation, pushed aside by the other, which is seen to be increasingly encroaching on 'their patch'. In addition, the nature of the mother is being changed by increasing Europeanisation and alterations to the welfare state.

Tour operators and their reps also fulfil a parenting role. They guide, inform and constrain tourists as much as possible. They act like parents in the attempts they make to socialise the tourists. For example, giving advice to tourists at welcome meetings.[6] This counsel may take the form of how to take care in the sun. However, the meetings' main purpose is to sell the tourism operator-run excursions (Andrews, 2000). What Dann (1996a: 2) suggests is that 'the language of tourism attempts to persuade, lure, woo and seduce millions of human beings, and in so doing, convert them from potential into actual clients'. So, for example, during welcome meetings, tourists are reminded of the 'foreign-ness' of their position and encouraged to stay within the fold of the known tour operator. In order to do this, tourists, like children, need to be socialised, to learn the language of the new place. The tour operators are on hand to supervise this experience.

In Magaluf and Palmanova, therefore, the tourists can sup at the nation's teat as much as they like, as consumption of any form – food, drink and sex – are a central part of the fun. In this atmosphere, the tourists can be 'politically incorrect' as, for example, the British stand-up comedian, Roy Chubby Brown, who entertains on television. Through the games played and the subsequent use and references to the body, the tourists can appear to be sexy (or fantasise about it), be winners and feel important. Not knowing when to stop is a feature of childhood. The reminder of this appears in some of the video footage in the bars in which babies are shown, having over eaten, regurgitating their food.

The game playing, however, has an edge to it, an underpinning of violence subtly stated; but nevertheless there. At one entertainment venue, women can be admonished for not exposing their breasts and tourists of both genders humiliated in the games played. Not abiding by the rules brings punishment in the tour operator organised bar crawls. In addition, penalties for spilling a drink are administered in some bars. Spilling drinks is about not having control, again, reminiscent of childhood. The contradictions evident in this game playing are that tourists are encouraged to get drunk but are then punished for the behaviour that inebriation brings. The emphasis on fun disguises the brutality of the punishment. Delighting in the mockery and punishment of tourists is sadistic.

The tension that exists is that, on the one hand, the tourist as child is encouraged to let go, lose control and express thoughts and feelings that might be interpreted as sexist and/or racist, and thus disapproved of in the home world. On the other hand, the sense of freedom that this lack of constraint inculcates only becomes replaced by another set of controls: the spatial layout and construction of the resorts; the attempts made by the tour operators, hotel entertainers and bar and nightclub DJs to exert control over the tourists; as well as the realisation by the tourists that they cannot do entirely as they please.

It is not the case that the tourists in Magaluf and Palmanova are re-created or transformed as the tourism as pilgrimage paradigm would suggest; but, rather they can 'let it all hang out'. Not only does this include the ripples and folds of their skin on the beach, but also their behaviour. Selwyn (1994) argues that

> [i]n short the stuff of tourism is the stuff of myth... like myth, [it] provides tourists with a language which seems, if only momentarily, to address and to resolve the problems and contradictions of everyday life "back home". (Selwyn, 1994: 29)

The contradiction that many tourists in Magaluf and Palmanova feel they face is that to be British does not require being white and eating

sausages. In the resorts, the tourists encounter these aspects of Britishness in a pronounced way, e.g. the rejection of foreign food and water
and the engagement with a past based on vanquishing and expelling the
other. As such, tourists express a sense of who they are based on their
understandings of normative gender and ethnic divisions, which do not
necessarily reflect the structure of the world they perceive they inhabit in
the UK. Momentarily, tourists in Magaluf and Palmanova may feel a
reprieve from the pressures of life back home to conform to a way of
being that they would rather resist. This might be articulated in the
language of 'getting away from it all', 'having a break', 'not dealing with
bills' and 'something different', but it is hardly an inversion. Rather, it is
an aspect of identity finding a means of expression.

Only one of Cohen's classifications of tourists has been explored here,
that of recreational tourism. I am not attempting to apply the category
outright to the tourists in Palmanova and Magaluf, as the danger is that
people become reduced to a type rather than allowing the intricacies and
deviances of their behaviour to be studied. The focus on this type is
because, in this instance, it appears to be the most useful of Cohen's
categories. It is the most appropriate category because Cohen's (1979b)
classifications are based on where the spiritual centre of the tourists is
said to lie and in the case of the recreational tourist the centre is in the
home world. The actions, dispositions and words of the tourists in
Magaluf and Palmanova indicate that there is a strong identification with
the home world. The signs and symbols that characterise the landscapes
of Palmanova and Magaluf refer to a world outside Mallorca, to largely
that of the UK. Where I diverge from Cohen is when he suggests that the
activities 'possess no deeper meaning' (Cohen, 1979b) than simple
recreation. My findings suggest that tourists' experiences in Magaluf
and Palmanova have meaning deep at the heart of what it means to be
British. Further, the analyses can illuminate relationships that go beyond
those found within the holiday to those in the home world, with the
European Union, and beyond.

Another concept that Cohen (1982) has considered and links directly
with ideas explored in the opening of this chapter is the idea of Paradise.
To return to the question 'what are we missing in our lives that tourism
promises to satisfy?' part of the answer appears to lie in fulfilling promises
of a paradise-type vision. That is, in the search for a satisfied life of peace,
happiness and fulfilment, the traveller ventures towards paradise.
According to Cohen (1982: 24), the individual in mass tourism concerned
only with recreation and diversion travels towards a '"paradisiac"
illusion', which has been constructed by the tourism industry. Irrespective

of whether tourists' experiences of Magaluf and Palmanova fit with the ideas of paradise that they may hold, the resorts are places constructed by the tourism industry to attract tourists to them and in the socialisation processes once in the resort.

The term 'paradise' implies forward movement, as in a journey towards, but if the concerns of the tourists are considered – those that are based around perceived increased numbers of immigrants and inter-ference from 'Europe' – then the future at home does not propel them towards a better life. Rather, this better life is located in a past and an ideal world. It is one in which 'Britannia Ruled the Waves', where there were few ethnic minorities and the influence of the European Union was not felt. The resorts of Palmanova and Magaluf, especially the latter, refer backwards to past military glories as suggested in the names of some of the facilities. Currently, the tourists' paradisical longings can be satisfied by the sun and warm weather. As one tourist exclaims, 'this is fucking marvellous'. For others, a sense of freedom is available that, if not exactly paradisical, fits into notions of satisfying a fantasy. In the words of another tourist, 'we call this fantasy island'. Another aspect that links Palmanova and Magaluf to paradise is the idea of plenty and the removal of want. Food is available 24 hours a day, as is alcohol; and so is the heightened awareness of the availability of sex, and, if so desired, with a number of different partners. The sensual world of the tourist can be completely and utterly satisfied – that, at least, is the promise.

At the same time, however, paradise can become a nightmare. As Cohen (1982: 22) attests, the other is not just about paradise, but 'has another, malignant but fascinating aspect, finding its fullest expression in the symbol of Hell'. There is a price to pay for the indulgence that the total gratification of food and drink desires brings. The darker side is the vomit of drinking too much alcohol, the explosion of the body into a mass of fat, as shown on postcards, and even possibly the transformation of the tourists into pigs as they are depicted on souvenirs. That the holiday does become a form of nightmare for some tourists is evident in the desire expressed by some to go home. They found the weather too hot, were sick of the food or they could not get any sleep because of the noise. Again, one could follow Cohen's (1982) interpretations, that the tourists are willing participants, the architects of their own heaven or hell on Mallorca. Having said that, however, they build with the materials they are given and able to engage with, and these are provided, as Cohen also contends, by the tourism industry.

The foregoing discussion has outlined the main theoretical approaches to understandings of tourists and has examined their applicability to the present study. Within the discussion of the different approaches taken by MacCannell, Graburn, Urry and Cohen, parallels and similarities may be drawn – reference, for example, to the sacred, difference, authenticity. However, what all of these theories have in common is that none are based on empirical evidence. The next section brings into focus studies that have engaged directly with tourists' experiences.

## Speaking to Tourists

As I have suggested, the socio-anthropological approach to tourists has been shaped by a number of key theorists who have presented valuable insights into the nature of tourism. However, all are lacking a dialogue with actual tourists. The purpose of this section is to provide an overview of the contributions made by those commentators who have interacted with tourists.

Although the ethnographic material on tourists is scant, there have been some attempts made to study tourists in this manner, including the work of Wagner (1977) and Passariello (1983); the documentary film *Cannibal Tours* by O'Rourke (1987); van den Berghe's (1994) *Quest for the Other*; work by Selänniemi (1992, 1999); Hanefors (2001); and Harrison's (2003) *Being a Tourist*. However, none of these have been directly concerned with British tourists. Contributions to the study of this nationality have been made by Carr (1998), Wickens (2002), Desforges (2000) and Palmer (1999, 2003). The current ethnographic study in Mallorca considers British tourists and their relationship with the representations of Britishness that they encounter in Magaluf and Palmanova. Not only does it contribute to an understanding of the social processes at play in creating this identity, which Palmer (1999) calls for, but it also illuminates the subject of package tourists and takes the context of national identity abroad. At the same time, I examine the emotions, the feelings (as Palmer [2003] does) of the tourists, which links the discussion to the practice of tourism suggested by Crouch *et al.* (2001).

The point raised by Crouch *et al.* (2001) takes forward the importance of understanding tourists from the point of view of what they do and say. This marks a move away from a concentration on the textual that the earlier social science theories foregrounded and, instead, highlights the performative nature of tourism. Ideas of tourism and performance have now become mainstream in the tourism studies literature (e.g. Coleman & Crang, 2002; Bruner, 2005), along with ideas of embodiment (e.g. Morgan *et al.*, 2005; Andrews, 2005; Pocock, 2006). What this focus allows is a move away from overarching theories of tourists to more nuanced and micro-level scales of theorising. Such engagement provides depth and insight into the understanding of tourists and their behaviour, both within the context of their holiday taking and the wider world.

## Summary

The purpose of this opening chapter has been to set the scene both in terms of the background against which the ethnography is set and with regard to the main socio-anthropological tourism literature. The rest of the book will proceed in the following way.

Chapter 2 will build on some of the key issues that have been established in the introduction and demonstrate the close and inter-twined relationship between the three concepts in the chapter's (and book's) title: nation, identity and consumption. In so doing, it will briefly outline the theoretical lineage to which my interpretations are indebted.

Chapter 3 begins by considering the importance of studying the nature of tourism spaces. As such, the chapter explores how the symbolic landscape constitutes the social construction of a tourist place. It concentrates specifically on the names ascribed to café-bars, giving a detailed and in-depth examination of the associated meanings and myths attached to these names. As well as discussing theoretical approaches to the study of place making, it details an important aspect of the research method – the onsite mapping of the tourism facilities.

In Chapter 4, I explore how the landscapes are consumed as sites of economic activity and consumption. I examine how the consumption practices and the performances of the tourists are related to the social constructions of national identity inherent in the names explored in Chapter 3. I will demonstrate that these consumption practices firstly enact and perform the identities presented to them in the place names, and secondly the ways in which the choices exercised feed into and contribute to other aspects of the social construction of identity.

Chapter 5 begins by exploring the centrality of the body to tourists' experiences. The ethnographic detail begins with an approach to the body that considers the appearance and dressing of the body as representations of the wearer. In particular, I draw attention to the representation of women in the two resorts and how they are situated as items of consumption.

The theme of the body is continued in Chapter 6, using a phenom-enological approach that allows the embodied nature of tourists' experiences to be explored. Thus, it goes beyond the body as representation to a concentration on the use of the body and the feelings and sensations associated with practice. In so doing, it picks up again on the threads of Chapter 4 in which the spaces of the tourist resorts are examined for their enactment of the 'Britishness' signalled in some of the place names in the resorts.

Literal consumption as it relates to food and drink is examined in Chapter 7. It brings together the other two key areas of space and the body by showing, firstly, how what is consumed in the form of food and beverages helps to create a sense of place. It proceeds with the idea that the practice of consumption and what is acceptable to ingest is linked to understandings of identity and fears of incorporating the other. In this respect, it is closely allied with the creation of ideas of nation. It also becomes important in terms of gendered constructions of identity as the role of women as providers of nourishment is examined with particular reference to the female breast. As such, it links to the body. In elaborating on how elements of the tourism industry feed into ideas of otherness, it examines the way in which tourists themselves become objects of consumption practices by the tourism industry.

The concluding chapter will provide an overview of the material in the preceding chapters. It will reiterate the points about understandings of 'Britishness' and the link between constructions of identities (with particular reference to national identity) and practices of consumption. The chapter will re-examine, in light of the ethnographic evidence presented, the question of the tourist in relation to the existing main theoretical approaches found in social science studies of tourism and the value of tourism in approaching key issues within the social sciences. The conclusion will firmly establish the link between nation, identity and consumption and draw a final conclusion about the meaning, understanding and constructions of 'Britishness' in this context.

## Notes

1. I want to note the difficulty inherent in discussions of ideas of Britishness or British identity, particularly given that it is often the case that the terms English and British, United Kingdom and Britain are conflated to cover all of the countries and separate identities that make-up these concepts. Thus I recognise that Scottish, Welsh, Irish and English identities are involved, but that within this is a complex intersection of the different groups, which can also be extended to regional identities. However, Cinnirella notes '[t]here has often been a preoccupation with the nation as a collective historical subject in the British Isles, which includes the perception of the need for a continuous national (often English) history' (2000: 60). A similar point is also noted by Palmer (2003: 428). From a methodological point of view in Magaluf and

Palmanova it is not easy to disaggregate the individual 'nations' or regions unless these were clearly identified by the tourists concerned, and where possible these identities are reflected in the book. However, there is a need to think about the tourists collectively and thus the terms British, Britain and UK are used for discussion purposes.

2. On WWW at http://www.mallorcaweb.co./news/2006/01tourism-balearic-islands-2005. Accessed 15.10.08.

3. On WWW at http://www.euroweeklynews.com/news/10888.html. Accessed 15.10.08.

4. The concept of 'home' is itself complex (Morley, 2000). In this context, it refers to the normal place of dwelling or the origin of the tourists. However, in discussions with tourists it becomes evident that the idea of home often relates to nostalgic perceptions of what used to be. In this respect, 'home' becomes more like Heimat, which 'is a mythical bond rooted in a lost past, a past that has already disintegrated' (Morley & Robins, 1993: 7).

5. This is an oft-attributed quote to Margaret Thatcher, which has become somewhat clichéd. The quotation in full reads:

> I think we've been through a period where too many people have been given to understand that if they have a problem, it's the government's job to cope with it. "I have a problem, I'll get a grant". "I'm homeless, the government must house me". They're casting their problems on society. And you know, there's no such thing as society. There are individual men and women, there are families. And no government can do anything except through people, and people must look after themselves first. It's our duty to look after ourselves and then, also, to look after our neighbours. People have got their entitlements too much in mind, without the obligations. There is no such thing as entitlement, unless someone has first met an obligation. (http://www.dollynet.freeserve.co.uk/thatcher.htm, accessed March 2004).

6. Those meetings where the tour operator representative introduces himself/herself to tourists at the start of their holiday with the purpose of imparting practical information, but primarily to sell tour operator organised excursions and activities.

## Chapter 2
# Nation, Identity and Consumption

## Introduction

The purpose of this chapter is to outline the lineage of the broader theoretical framework that underpins the discussion in this book. In so doing, I will also introduce the key nuclei around which my arguments are structured. That is, questions of identity as they are constructed, experienced and expressed through space, the body, and food and drink. The theoretical foundations of my work are eclectic. I am of the view that theories provide tools that enable the unpacking of the social world, which entails the utilisation of different perspectives to understand and interpret the data to hand.

## The Symbolic World

The influence of Durkheim (1915) can be observed in the earliest social science discussions of tourists. Indeed, MacCannell (1976: 2) noted of his French fieldwork data, that the 'interpretations kept integrating themselves with a line of enquiry begun by Émile Durkheim in his study of primitive religion'. In this book, the symbolic world of the tourists is used to understand how they may distinguish themselves from articulations of the other through expressions of identity, as symbolised in, for example, the food consumed by tourists, understandings of the body and the names ascribed to places in the resorts.

The theoretical lineage associated with the importance of imbuing objects with value above their functional purpose can also be followed in the work of Mauss (1954) and Lévi-Strauss (1969 [1962]). With regard to the latter, the importance of the individual as *bricoleur* is evident when considering the idea that tourism allows an ordering and, therefore, an understanding of the world manifesting as a form of language.

A key element of this book is the idea that tourists are bricoleurs, that they make sense of their world, and who they are in Magaluf and Palmanova, from the signs of Britishness they encounter in the two resorts. This approach implies that the landscape is read for the pre-existing meanings present in the symbols that represent underlying structural relations. The importance of these structures is not to be undervalued. However, I go beyond this approach by moving from the textual into the sensual and phenomenological world of embodied and performing tourists.

The theoretical underpinning that has been discussed so far relies on the notion of externalising thoughts, concepts and feelings. In this approach, we project emotions and ideas onto objects, so that they take a material form and can be more readily seen and understood. Such an approach has formed the basis of much work in structural anthropology (e.g. Douglas, 1966; Tambiah, 1969). By accepting that the relationship between the internal and external world is mediated through signs or symbols, the role of the anthropologist in trying to decipher and interpret symbols becomes clear. In this regard, Geertz (1973: 9) proposes that the 'doing' of ethnography is about providing an account of social discourse through which a culture can be analysed by 'sorting out the structures of signification'. The analysis of symbols can therefore be used to relate to society at large and the fine detail recorded as the 'thick description' of ethnography is the actuality and intricacy of a wider world of 'mega-concepts', such as modernisation, integration and conflict (Geertz, 1973: 23). The question of identity and the narrative of a particular type of Britishness relate to what I identify as the mega-concepts of consumption and nationalism.

Although a foundation in Durkheimian sociology implies a structural analysis that assumes an *a priori* set of structures, such an approach is not a prerequisite for examining symbolic landscapes. Rather, they can also be understood as part of a process of identity and meaning making in which individuals have an active part. As such, the contextual aspect of where symbols are interpreted and how they are then used is important (Geertz, 1973). A similar point is also made about identity as Tapper (2008: 101) reminds us: 'identities, ethnic and other, are flexible, negotiable, multiple and always situational'. Further, Brück (2001: 655) contends, 'people always have the resources to produce alternative interpretations of a context ... Hence, the relationships, events, and places that constitute the self can be strategically evoked in a highly contextual and contingent realization of selfhood'.

In order to understand the symbolic world of the tourists, there is a need to understand the place that the symbols occupy in the narratives of the people concerned. Indeed, Urban (1989) observes that the advertising images used in tourism 'narrate' the consciousness and memory of the traveller. As such, it becomes necessary to refer back to the generating market to understand the symbolic meanings of particular symbols and how these travel with the tourists and gain significance at their subsequent destination.

Symbols are a means of communication to both self and others about the world and form a type of language or grammar that comprises a system of messages (Barthes, 1993 [1957]). Barthes has written on a range of objects and events among which are the essays *Steak and Chips* and *Striptease*, and most notably in connection with tourism, *The Blue Guide* (1993 [1957]) and *Eiffel Tower* (1983). The role of semiotic analysis is to identify the connotations and try to understand from where they come and what they might mean. Signs, then, are like symbols. Both stand for something else, both are imbued with meaning and thus socially constructed. The meaning usually has resonance within particular contexts and is open to interpretation. That is, meanings afforded to a sign or symbol are not fixed, quite simply they mean different things to different people at different times. They are not *a priori*, but are negotiable, given meaning to by the actors involved in their construction and ongoing interpretation as part of lived experience.

I examine, therefore, the signs and symbols of Britishness within a particular context. At the same time, I listen to the meaning making of the main protagonists – the tourists – as they use the symbolic discourse to construct their sense of identity in the world of the foreign destination. The other is not simply the Spanish (or Mallorcan) other, but also the other tourists. If tourism and the language of signs is based around the creation of myths (Levi-Strauss, 1964; Selwyn, 1996), then I contend that the use and manipulation of signs and symbols, within the resorts of Palmanova and Magaluf, are concerned with creating, if only temporarily, a particular mythology of being British. Further, I suggest that the tourists are complicit in this by not only engaging with the signs and symbols, but also in living out the expectations attached to the myths and perpetuating them further.

The idea that the tourists themselves have some kind of involvement in creating the meanings of the signs and symbols, or continuing the mythologies attached to them, shifts the focus of the theoretical boundaries underpinning my argument. The move is away from *a priori* classifications to a world that is understood through lived experiences. The theoretical pathway followed in this respect is derived from phenomenology and forms the subject of the next section.

## The Phenomenological World

The purpose of taking a phenomenological approach is to shift away from the world as object to the world as it is experienced. To illustrate the theoretical shift, an example from tourism proves useful. For instance, Urry (1990) has tried to understand tourist motivation from the perspective of gazing on difference. This stance positions the sights of difference as objects. However, there is no sense of how the tourists engage with the attractions other than to look at them. Privileging sight over all the other senses also distances the tourists, both literally and metaphorically, from their experience.[1] Thus, the world as object leaves aside feelings and sensations. Tourists' experiences in Magaluf and Palmanova are not only based on what they see, but also on what they hear, smell and feel. Not to address these features of their behaviour would leave a whole part of who the tourists are unexamined.

The concentration on the gaze in early tourism studies was noted by Veijola and Jokinen (1994). Urry (1999) also acknowledges the issues concerned with emphasising sight in his later discussion of the role of smell in the experience of leisure spaces. Considering other senses moves the study of tourism into the realm of ideas of embodiment, a shift noted by Crouch (1999b, 2001). In addition, Dann and Jacobsen's (2002) consideration of olfaction in relation to spa tourism demonstrates that other senses have long been of importance.

The phenomenological perspective is taken from the writings of Merleau-Ponty (1962) in *The Phenomenology of Perception*. Merleau-Ponty (1962) suggests that understanding of the world is derived from experiencing it, and this is understood through the senses: '[t]he world is not what I think, but what I live through'. It is less concerned with causation and more with description. Thus, rather than trying to get to the bottom of some kind of reality or truth with which people attempt to engage, understanding is derived from seeing the world as that which is perceived and created by people's engagement with the world.

In the discipline of anthropology, the way in which attempts to overcome the subject–object dualism that structuralism favours and Merleau-Ponty resists is through the concept of embodiment. As Csordas (1990: 7) notes, 'the paradigm of embodiment has as a principal characteristic the collapse of dualities between mind and body, subject and object'. A useful example is found in Gell's (1996) insightful text, *Reflections on a Cut Finger*, in which he notes that the taboos on auto-cannibalism (e.g. nail biting, licking one's own blood) in Umeda society reflected the taboo on eating self-killed game. Similarly, children and neophytes must observe a taboo on eating a particular fish with red markings that are thought to resemble the markings sometimes worn by those groups of people that is the children and neophytes. Thus, it is only through experience that perception comes about. In terms of tourism, such an approach to the study of the tourist is found in the work of Crouch *et al.* (2001: 254), who note, '[b]eing a tourist is to practise. By practice we mean the actions, movements, ideas, dispositions, feelings, attitudes and subjectivities that the individual possesses'.

In this book, the symbolic world of the tourists is easily identifiable. However, to understand how these become or are the self of the tourists, it is necessary to examine the tourists' intentional acts. For example, the idea of the holiday as 'freedom' is embodied and becomes the self in the unbuckling and disrobing of the body in Magaluf and Palmanova. In this respect, the tourists are given agency. This may appear to be at odds with earlier discussions suggesting that the tourists' experiences are created and controlled by key mediators, and that the tourists arrive at destinations that are characterised by pre-given structures.

A useful way of approaching this is through the concept of *habitus*. The meaning of the term identified here is derived from the work of Mauss (1979 [1950]) and its further development in discussions by Bourdieu (1979, 1990, 1977). The underlying principle is trying to elucidate how the external environment is differently absorbed or interpreted by members of a particular social group. According to Bourdieu, people are born into their class *habitus*; they learn manners and attitudes from a pre-existing world. The manners and attitudes make up the cultural capital of the class and individual who is born into it. Importantly, these manners and attitudes become embodied, they are a way of *being in the world*. A way of being in the world is not necessarily fixed. Indeed, people can change deportment, voice and manners.

The notion of change has been further explored by Jackson (1989: 129, italics in original) in the idea of a 'disrupted *habitus*'. In Jackson's (1989: 129) example of an initiation ceremony, the disruption of the environment 'lays people open to possibilities of behavior [sic] which they embody but ordinarily are not inclined to express'. Thus, *habitus* is ongoing and negotiable, and peoples' place in the world, or their perception of the world, begins with them.

In the case of the tourists in Palmanova and Magaluf, they experience a disrupted environment, they are not in their *habitus* of home. Following Jackson, the tourists are now open to new possibilities of being, or of allowing 'somatic' disposition to come to the fore (Andrews, 2009b). This also accords well with Cohen's classification of the recreational tourist who, he argues, is open to latent possibilities of being through tourism. In the case discussed here, I argue the possibilities are concerned with expressions of Britishness. The tourists live out the *habitus* of Britishness and, in so doing, create a Magaluf and Palmanova of their own image, often perpetuating, playfully or otherwise, the attendant mythologies. However, because it is a world of possibilities, those whose purpose it is to economically benefit from the presence of the tourists, seek to mediate and control the direction this takes. Hence, the efforts of tour reps at welcome meetings and on bar crawls to socialise the tourists (Andrews, 2000). The degree to which the tourists respond is based on the level of ontological insecurity they feel in the new setting in which they find themselves.

One way of understanding tourists is through the spaces they inhabit. In the Durkheimian sense, space is a way of categorising and differentiating between territories. Such an approach is a defining tenet of Anglo-French social anthropology. Much work has been concerned largely with spatial order and organisation (cf. Bourdieu, 1973). In addition, as Corsín-Jiménez (2003: 140) notes, space is what people do, not only where they are. It is not a fixed category but an instrument and dimension of peoples' sociability, a condition of social relationships. A similar argument is forwarded by Crouch (2001: 63, emphasis in original), who notes, 'rather than spatialities being prefigured in representations and contexts through which human subjects encounter space ... they may be developed *in practice*, ontologically, discursively made sense and felt in an embodied way'.

One method of reconciling the given world (the categories, the signs and symbols and attachments of place and landscape) with that of the living world is through Lefebvre's (1991) three-fold analysis of space in *The Production of Space*. For Lefebvre, space is socially produced. He challenges the idea that space is *a priori* a container of action, arguing that it is produced through the dynamic convergence of three different spatial elements that give insights into the nature of social relationships. The three aspects of space that Lefebvre outlines are: (1) spatial practices, (2) representation of space and (3) representational space.[2]

The first, *spatial practice*, refers to the 'facts' of space, i.e. its physical or natural form. It is linked to the production and reproduction of specific places and spatial ensembles. As such, an area may be developed for a particular activity or purpose. Thus, an area is understood or perceived to be a site of or for a particular economic activity, thereby becoming a reflection of economic relations.

The second aspect, *representations of space*, refers to formal abstractions. It is mental or conceived space. This is the space of the professionals, of planners, policy makers, scientists and designers. Here, space is constructed and formalised around ideological discourses on space that is manifest in symbolic works, e.g. maps.

The third aspect, *spaces of representation*, is concerned with the world of the senses. This is social or cultural space, a discourse of space and the embodiment of the other two aspects, which is how space is directly lived through symbols. For Lefebvre (1991: 33), it is the space in which resistance to the hegemony of spatial practice and representations of space can be acted on as he links it to 'the clandestine or underground side of social life'. It is through this lived experience of space that changes can be wrought and thus it is these spaces that 'provide the focus for identity' (Meethan, 2001: 37). My main concern is with representations of space and spaces of representation, or 'conceived' and 'lived space'.

What Lefebvre's triad offers is a possibility of becoming, that is, it is the actors in the spaces of representation who create the space by resisting (or accepting) the codes and hegemonic inscriptions of space. Crouch and Lübbren (2003: 11) make a similar point in their observation in relation to tourism and visual culture, which they suggest 'may be considered processes, processes of knowledge, experience and identities, and examples of processes of individual becoming rather than merely being'.

Although working in different ways, parallels may be drawn with the concept of *habitus*. Lefebvre is concerned with the way in which space is produced in terms of its structuring by 'experts' and the practice of people. *Habitus* assumes a pre-structured world that is lived-out in practice. It also offers an opportunity for transformation and becoming because people can (if one accepts that they are born into a particular *habitus*) resist or accept the embodiment of their class.

In the discussion of the symbolic world, it was noted that Geertz (1973: 23, emphasis in original) suggests that it is in the fine detail of ethnography that the mega-concepts with which social scientists are concerned 'can be given the sort of sensible actuality that makes it possible to think not only realistically and concretely *about* them, but, what is more important, creatively and imaginatively *with* them'. Two aspects of social life stand out in the two resorts and form the mega-concepts of this work. The first is concerned with the construction of national identity and the second with consumption activities. It is to these that I now turn.

## Consuming Britishness

Two mega-concepts have been identified in relation to social life in the resorts of Palmanova and Magaluf. The first is based on identity; constant reference to who people are, is made by the mediators of the tourist experience and is evident in the activities and voices of the tourists. The identities constructed and displayed occur at different levels in the form of, e.g. age and gender. However, the most notable category of identity is that of national identity, which is constantly referred to in the everyday undertakings of the tourists, e.g. where they eat, what they eat, how they use their bodies and the ways in which they traverse the spaces of the two resorts and other parts of the island.

The second prominent feature of social life is that of consumption. The ability to consume links with fantasies of an imagined better life found elsewhere, it is in contrast to a world of want. In the resort, the tourists are encouraged to have whatever they desire and in as large a quantity as wanted. The feeling of satisfaction that the act of consumption seeks to supply is often thwarted in the practices of the tourists. Encouraged by both the mediators of their experiences and their own expectations, the tourists regurgitate (i.e. are physically sick, especially following a heavy bout of drinking) consumption items and raise the need to begin again.

The encoding of the resorts with signs of Britishness indicates that one of the levels[3] of identity etched onto the landscape and acted out by tourists is that of a national identity. Alongside this, other layers of identity exist based on age, gender (which is overtly sexualised), region or town, or city of origin in the UK. In addition, distinctions are made based on which of the two resorts is being visited, or the difference between the behaviour of the self and other tourists.

Nationality and sexuality are the most immediately obvious forms of identity expressed. There is much emphasis on sexual expression through imagery, expectations (Magaluf as 'Shagaluf') and, for some, practice. Parker *et al.* (1992) suggest that nationalism and sexuality are two of the most powerful discourses that shape identity in the modern world. They state '[w]henever the power of the nation is invoked ... we are more likely than not to find it couched as a *love of country*: an eroticized nationalism' (Parker *et al.*, 1992: 1, emphasis in original). I will demonstrate that the identity of Britishness that is being carved out in the two resorts is firmly linked to one of 'normative' sexual relations based on heterosexuality and that the holiday period is a time of heightened sexual and gender awareness.

That the nation is sexualised becomes most evident in the representation of the breast. A multi-vocal symbol, its role is complex. On the one hand, it links into notions of intercourse and sexuality as it is displayed for titillation and the object of male attention. On the other, it becomes desexualised in its role as the nourishing mother and symbol of the nation. The prevalence of images of the breast, the presence of the Union Jack flag[4] appearing like a brand or logo to sell commodities, alongside British TV programmes and the names ascribed to café-bars, all serve to keep the identity of the tourists as British in mind. In this respect, they link to the imaginings of a nation. Such material expressions of identity belong in the realm of the imagined community described by Anderson (1991). He claims that 'in the modern world everyone can, should, will "have" a nationality, as he or she "has" a gender' (Anderson, 1991: 5). Nationality stems from the nation and it is the entity of the nation that is described as imagined. 'It is *imagined* because the members of even the smallest nation will never know most of their fellow-members, meet them, or even hear of them, yet in the minds of each lives the image of their communion' (Anderson, 1991: 6). Thus, if the Union Jack is taken as a symbol of Britishness, depicting it alongside a picture of a plate of the fry-up gives that dish a nationality, it becomes conceived as British and something that the British eat.[5]

Gellner (1983: 138) claims that nationalism is a distinct form of patriotism, which relies on groups that are 'culturally homogenous, based on a culture striving to be a high (literate) culture'. The aspect of striving that Gellner refers to has resonance in the resorts of Palmanova and Magaluf. The games played by tourists as part of the hotel entertainment introduce an element of competition in which some of the tourists participating attempt to be the best.

Both Gellner (1983) and Anderson (1991) have noted that capitalism, industrialisation and nationalism have had a symbiotic relationship. Taking the cue from semiotics that 'the entire field of social behaviour which constitutes the culture ... might *be* a language' (Hawkes, 1977: 32, emphasis in original), then all the objects on which ideas are externalised and fixed also form a language that perpetuates and enables capitalism and nationalism in the same way as the written and spoken language referred to by Gellner and Anderson.

Nationalism, like religion, provides a link both to the past and to the future. The sustainability and legitimisation of nationalism is due to the creation, or use, of tradition. It is often the case that certain sets of practices that are presented as having longevity or of emanating from the 'dawn of time' have, in reality, relatively recent histories – they are 'invented' (Hobsbawm, 1983: 1). Thus, a national identity requires a link to a past (real or mythical), particular symbols thought, or imagined, to be peculiar to a distinct group, which are learnt or understood by that group in the manner of a language.

Here I return to myth as a key issue. Samuel and Thompson (1990: 14–15) contend that 'the most powerful myths are those which influence what people think and do: which are internalized, in their ways of thinking, and which they pass on consciously or subconsciously to their children and kin, their neighbours, workmates, and colleagues'. To return to the very beginning of my argument, I suggested that the longing for elsewhere for some British people is based on an under- standing of a UK that has passed, and that this is alluded to in Magaluf and Palmanova by reference to past military 'glories', the most recent, at the time of my fieldwork, being the Falklands War.[6] As Cesarani notes:

> the compulsive reference back to Britain's "finest hour" and the round of wartime anniversaries in the 1990s all focus on an England that was white. The [second world] war is taken to evoke the British at their best, the qualities of Churchill's "island race." This is mythological nonsense, but it helps construct a sense of nation and nationality that excludes the bulk of post-1945 immigrants. (Cesarani, 1996: 69)

Further implications that arise from these assertions are of longevity and rights of belonging, both of which are related or tied to a specific space, a bounded territory. The concept of the nation can act to exclude the other (as the example from Cesarani illustrates); but as Anderson (1991) contends, it is also the source of inspiration for cultural products and self-sacrifice – dying for the nation is not unlike dying for religion. Looking to the past for a sense of self strongly links national identity with heritage and nostalgia. In the case of the former, questions are what can people recover from the past that tells them who they are? and what is passed on that relates to their being in the world? For nostalgia, it is looking to the past in a romanticised way that suggests that it was somehow better than the present. Thus, in the face of organic solidarity and Gesellschaft-like societies, the erosion by modernity of a binding sense of community gives the individual a ready urge to look to the past for that sense of the whole that remains unsatisfied in the present.

The term 'banal nationalism' was coined by Billig (1995: 6) to consider 'the ideological habits which enable the established nations of the West to be reproduced'. Underpinning this, he argues that nationalism, or ideas of the nation, are reproduced on a daily basis 'in a banally mundane way'

(Billig, 1995: 6). In Magaluf and Palmanova, there are constant references to the idea of nationhood through signs and practices pertaining to everyday life: not only do national flags appear in the literal sense, but the act of flag waving is manifest in, for example, the signalling of British identity in the food eaten and the sports pages of British daily papers available for purchase.

Palmer (1998) uses banal nationalism to explore the ways in which the nation is experienced in everyday life. Her analysis concentrates on three areas: the body, food and landscape. All three, she notes,

> are aspects of our contemporary material world, they help to define "us" and in so doing contribute to both our individual and collective identities...the sense of identity that comes from the foods we eat and the uses we make of our bodies is not communicated in isolation, it is part and parcel of our physical surroundings. (Palmer, 1998: 183)

References to food suggest that identity, in part, is made through acts of consumption and it is this that I now focus on.

In the anthropology of tourism, the discussion of consumption has largely been based on the issue of commoditisation (Selwyn, 1996a). The foundation for this approach is Greenwood's (1989 [1977]) paper on the Basque Alarde festival. This perspective places the tourist as a consumer of others, a theme also brought to the fore in one of the earliest tourism ethnographies in the form of O'Rourke's (1987) documentary film *Cannibal Tours*. The discussion of commoditisation has had much mileage in the tourism studies literature and has been strongly linked with issues of authenticity (e.g. Cohen, 1988; Halewood & Hannam, 2001; Cole, 2007). Meethan (2001: 5) argues that 'the processes of commodification ... are in fact central to the whole basis of tourism'. While he makes a pertinent point, there are other characteristics of consumption relevant to tourists' experiences. Selwyn (1996a), for example, points the way towards an understanding of the use of consumption practices in the creation of identity, when he argues that the depiction of the tourists in *Cannibal Tours* reveals more than a cynical set of relations based on commodity exchange for financial purposes, but shows a concern for social organisation.

The theoretical lineage in this respect is indebted to the work of Veblen's (1925 [1899]) *A Theory of the Leisure Class*. His main contention is that class divisions can be identified by the ability to 'waste time' (i.e. not spent in productive labour), and the ability to buy goods beyond 'basic needs'. As such, consumption can be considered a 'class marker'. This links the discussion directly to Bourdieu (1979). Consumption practices are indicative of class divisions. It is not just that which is physically ingested by the body that counts as consumption, but all items of culture that are used as a means of expression of the self, and by corollary as a mark of identity difference from the other. This wider view of consumption practices returns the discussion to the creation of identity and the expression of the relationship between the external and internal world in the form of representation. That is, the projection of the internal onto external objects.

Similar observations have been made by Baudrillard (1988), who argues that consumption is one of the chief basis of social order, a means by which internal classifications arise, and a system by which behaviour and groups are coded. As such, consumption practices act as a means of communication in society. In Palmanova and Magaluf, the choices exercised in terms of consumption practices, for example, the preference for 'British' products in the form of imported food and drink over local varieties, signifies a rejection of the foreign other in favour of incorporating a familiar self.

Baudrillard (1988) extends his argument by suggesting that the social activity of consumption acts as a part of the socialisation process. As such, it is linked to industrial society and capitalism because of what he describes as the mystification of the liberty and sovereignty of the consumer. That is the rhetoric of 'freedom, individual and choice', which accompanies the economic system of late capitalism and, by corollary, democratic processes that lead to a situation in which 'the freedom of choice is imposed' (Baudrillard, 1988: 39). To link this to national identity, in his discussion of the development of landscaped gardens in England, Franklin (1989) notes the association between gardens with ideas of liberty. The idea of freedom was seen as a feature of British national identity that contrasted with the French. In more contemporary times, the ability to consume is linked to ideas of freedom.

In Magaluf and Palmanova, tourists are under pressure to consume. This has a practical purpose. The holiday is an intense, relatively short-lived experience (discounting memory and post-holiday feelings) in which those who construct the experience wish to maximise their profits from the tourists in the minimum amount of time. The numerous shops seemingly offer choice and abundance and many items are flagged as bargains. Food and drink are on tap 24 hours a day, and ideas of flowing beer are portrayed in some postcards, as well as the emphasis on consuming ever more, which is played out in the bar crawl games organised by the tour operators. However, these games also pick up on the idea of force suggested by Baudrillard, as people are coerced into spending and consuming, which extends beyond food and drink to other objects and to each other.

The mystification that Baudrillard refers to is present in the idea of the holiday as a time of freedom; my data suggest the opposite. In addition, the apparent abundance of choice of restaurants and souvenir shops does not fulfil their promises because much of what is on offer is the same. In short, there is little 'product differentiation'. People are free to choose, but the idea of choice becomes redundant when the options are largely uniform and unvarying. Indeed, fashion in clothing for example, which might well be seen as a method of self-expression, innovation and progression, in reality requires conformity and homogeneity. Not only does the 'product' of Magaluf and Palmanova not offer much from which to choose, but the expectation of people to behave in a particular way, to conform, is also evident. Bar crawls are one such example, but so too are the tourists who get annoyed with their travelling companions who do not wish to enter into the great consumption fest, and get labelled as 'boring' and 'kill joys'.

This chapter has been concerned with laying the theoretical foundations of the proceeding discussion. Two strands have been identified. The first is a symbolic world that is understood through an analysis of the signs and symbols present in a given social setting; food, body parts and place names all fit into this domain. However, I have noted that this is a limited approach and does not allow the range of senses and emotions that also make up aspects of identity to be fully appreciated. Thus, there is a need to think about the phenomenological world of the 'feeling of doing' (Crouch, 2001: 62). In order to try and understand the relationship between these two 'worlds', the concepts of *habitus* and the social production of space have been discussed to show the link between structure and practice. In terms of the present ethnography, two themes emerge that fit well with this approach. The first is national identity. Palmanova and Magaluf resound with symbols of Britishness and the tourists are brought into a pre-ordered world. However, it is through their consumption activities (and others) that they engage and manipulate these symbols and feel and express (or reject) them as part of their own identity. In order to understand who the tourists in Magaluf and Palmanova are, how they are as tourists and as British (in this context), I focus on three aspects of social life – space, the body, and food and drink. The rest of the book is concerned with the ethnographic detail – the thick description – of the findings of the research along with their analysis and interpretation.

## Notes

1.  Falk (1994: 10) notes, '[I]n the Western tradition, from Plato to Kant and after, the higher position is granted to the distant senses, especially the eye'.
2.  Sometimes translated as 'spaces of representation'.
3.  This is referred to as a level of identity because people have multiple identities based on roles that they may fulfil, e.g. mother, bus driver or student.
4.  Selwyn claims (personal communication) that this is the incorrect term for this flag, and that it refers to the flag flown from the jack mast of a sailing ship. However, Brewer (1988) refers to the Union Jack as 'the national banner of Great Britain and Ireland'. He states that the use of the word Jack has often been interpreted as referring to King James as the original unifier, but that it actually refers to the French *Jacque*, a surcoat emblazoned with the St George's cross. Given that the flag is colloquially known as the Union Jack, it will be referred to in this manner in this book.
5.  To take Geertz's assertion that a concept must have meaning within the society in which a symbol appears and Urbain's suggestion that tourism images narrate the consciousness of the traveller, during the summer of 2003, an advert appeared on the London Underground for Garfunkels restaurant. It depicted a plate of sausages and mash in the middle of a Union Jack.
6.  There are, of course, more recent conflicts, but during the time of my initial fieldwork, these had not yet occurred and were not manifest during my visit in 2009.

## Chapter 3
# Symbolic Landscapes of Tourism

## Introduction

The starting point of the ethnographic detail is space.[1] To understand tourists' experiences in Magaluf and Palmanova, it is necessary to understand the resorts as places, how they look, their layout and structure. This is because, as Crouch *et al.* note,

> space ... at least in part, is constructed and signified by the tourist. Moreover ... space is a medium through which the tourist negotiates her or his world, tourism signs and contexts, and may construct her or his own distinctive meanings. (Crouch *et al.*, 2001: 254)

With such an approach it is possible to discuss how space is embodied or lived through the actions of tourists. The theoretical framework that informs the discussion of the ethnographic material is based around Lefebvre's (1991) tri-partite formulation of the production of space. I wish to start, however, by exploring why space is an important area of enquiry.

## The Value of Space

An understanding of space is essential for three reasons: firstly, how spaces are classified leads to their divisions along the lines of social practices (cf. Simmel, 1950 [1903]). Secondly, space is important because it enables an understanding of social relationships, as they are inscribed in space and, as such, contribute to the processes producing a particular space (Lefebvre, 1991: 129). Thirdly, a consideration of space is important in terms of methodology. As Kent (1995: 459) suggests, 'ethnographers miss crucial data by generally ignoring the use of space and architecture'. However, work by Bender (1993, 2001), Chambard (1980) and Low and Lawrence-Zúñiga (2003) has ensured that space and place are central to anthropological discussion. I follow Chambard's (1980) example and map the resorts (Appendix). The mapping exercise also follows Crick's (1994) and van den Berghe's (1994) examples within tourism studies; both use maps to aid the analysis of their respective field sites. The process of mapping allowed me a grounding in the field (Andrews, 2009a) and proved to be a rich source of data.

Through an analysis of the symbolic significance of landscape, Selwyn (1996) has also examined the creation of social relations in tourism. Using Israeli walking tours as an example, he discusses the encoding of the space with a particular set of values and meanings derived from a dominant political ideology, which speaks of a wider set of social relations. Similarly, in his discussion of the Kabyle House, Bourdieu (1973) also relies on an interpretation of the symbolic nature of its space. Bourdieu's claim is that the way in which the different spaces of the house are inscribed with meaning reproduces social relations, thereby helping to ensure social order. Both Bourdieu's and Selwyn's analyses fall into the representation of spaces, to use Lefebvre's term. Representation of space is the dominant space in society and is 'tied to the relations of production and to the "order" which those relations impose, and hence to knowledge, to signs, to codes and to "frontal" relations' (Levebvre, 1991: 33).

In describing the acts of shepherds in naming features of the landscape in which they graze their sheep, Gray (2003) draws on the work of the geographer Douglas J. Porteous (1990: 72 in Gray, 2003: 236) to claim that the naming of places by shepherds 'tames' the natural environment of the hills, and in so doing acts in 'transforming them into places where they feel at home' (Gray, 2003: 237). Part of the analysis of the spaces of Palmanova and Magaluf also involves the way in which the spaces are named.

The names of the facilities available to tourists give insight into the dominant ideological discourses present in the two resorts. The constant reference to the UK and Britishness and the connotations of specific signs, shape the understanding of what it means to be British. However, this is a representation of space and so, according to Lefebvre (1991: 38), forms only part of the production of space. Another element is how space is practiced in the everyday, as Bender (1993a: 1) notes, '[l]andscapes are created by people – through their experience and engagement with the world around them'. According to Hirsch, landscape is composed of a foreground and background of social life. The former refers to 'the way we now are' or 'concrete actuality of everyday social life' and the latter 'the way we might be' (Hirsch, 1995: 3) – the perceived potentiality. Magaluf is inscribed with signs of Britishness and through engagement and enactment with these signs, the world of the tourists is made. For example, a rhetoric of war and militarism is repeated throughout Magaluf in the names of café-bars and in performances such as Pirates

Adventure. Participation in Pirates Adventure by the tourists and the responses to the performance by some of them, e.g. aggressive behaviour following the show, is an embodiment of the ideas being represented. The representation becomes practiced and makes the space. As Corsín Jiménez says,

> the world happens with us and, in choosing what set of practices we will enact and engage in, we are also choosing what world we want to live in. Through our engagements with and in the world, we become the spaces to which we have invested our practices. (Corsín Jiménez, 2003: 140)

However, Merrifield (1993: 523) notes that representational or lived space, although open to possibilities, 'is the dominated, passively experienced space that the conceived, ordered, hegemonic space will intervene in, codify, rationalize and ultimately attempt to usurp'. Thus, in Magaluf and Palmanova the nature of the space is subject to those who attempt to mediate the tourists' experiences and reinforce the codifications of space. The tour operator representatives (reps), hotel entertainers and bar DJs all fall into the category of encoders of Magaluf and Palmanova. An example discussed in the ethnography examines the way in which the reps supply reminders of the spatial differences between the resorts and the home world, e.g. temperature and time differences, the dangers of drinking local water and the presence of the foreign other.

## The Significance of Café-bar Names in Palmanova and Magaluf

Before continuing with the discussion of place names, I want to note the importance of making maps in gathering my data. The production of maps was central to the evolution of my work on space (Andrews, 2009a). The maps I drew in the field provided an opportunity for reflection as well as being a schematic representation of the resorts. Working with the maps post fieldwork, the names of the facilities were categorised according to what the names seemed to represent (Table 3.1). So 'comic' is a class because several of the café-bars are named after famous British comedians or refer to comedy programmes, e.g. Del Boys Pub and Benny Hills Party Pub. The category 'birds' is derived from establishments that use birds in their name. As in most cases of classification, the categories are necessarily discrete and some names fall into more than one class.

**Table 3.1** Categorisation of facilities' names in Magaluf and Palmanova

| Comic | Military/heroes | Familiar British | Cosy England | National/regional/ethnic identity | Royalty | Birds | Mythology/fantasy |
|---|---|---|---|---|---|---|---|
| Nutters | Bar Trafalgar | Arfur's | The Local British Pub | Windsor | Windsor | Mucky Duck | Robin Hood |
| Popeyes Fun Pub | Popeyes Fun Pub | Windsor | Coach and Horse Inn | Britannia Pub | Kings Arms | The Green Parrot | Fantasy Island Bar |
| Jokers Pub | The Three Musketeers | Fred's Fish and Chips | The Cottage Pub | Bar Piccadilly | Prince William | Roosters Fish and Chips | Robinson Cruseo |
| Benny Hills Party Pub | Duke of Wellington | Hard Times | The White Rose | O'Malleys Irish Tavern | Queens Bar | | Casanovas |
| Peter Sellers Disco Fun Pub | Robin Hood | Ministry Club | Mail Coach | Big Ben | The Rose & Crown | | Camelot Pub |
| Del Boys Pub | Captains Arms | The Office | The Oak | The Tartan Arms | Lady Diana | | Oasis Pub |
| Crazy Daisy's Disco | Lord Nelson | Talk of the Town | Horse Shoe Bar | Eastenders | Diana Beach Bar | | Abracadabra Pizzas |
| Poco Loco | Linekar's | Uncle Tom Pub | The Plough | Dudley Tavern | | | Golf Fantasia |

**Table 3.1** (*Continued*)

| Comic | Military/heroes | Familiar British | Cosy England | National/regional/ethnic identity | Royalty | Birds | Mythology/fantasy |
|---|---|---|---|---|---|---|---|
| Chaplin's Bar | The Falklands (Las Malvinas) | Belt Up | Uncle Tom Pub | City Lights (Ref to London) | | | The White Horse |
| Café Bar Mr Bean | The Tartan Arms | Pickwick Pub (claims to be oldest in Magaluf) | Pickwick Pub (claims to be oldest in Magaluf) | Scots Corner | | | |
| Bananas | Heroes Disco | Eastenders | British Chippy | Tokio Joes | | | |
| Banana Joes Fun Pub | Kings Arms | Soul Train/Car Wash | Dudley Tavern | Tee Pee | | | |
| Cheeks Fun Pub | Prince William | Arthurs Alcohol (est 1984) | The Rose & Crown | Sospan Fach | | | |
| | Tom Browns on the Beach | Natalies Snack Bar | Gardens Café | Molly's the Yorkshire Lass | | | |
| | Tom Browns Good Food Inn | The Underground | The Willows | The Underground | | | |
| | Tom Browns in the Town | Cutty Sark | The Welcome Inn | Geordie Pride | | | |
| | Geordie Pride | Karen's | | Cork & Cardiff | | | |

**Table 3.1** (*Continued*)

| Comic | Military/heroes | Familiar British | Cosy England | National/ regional/ethnic identity | Royalty | Birds | Mythology/ fantasy |
|---|---|---|---|---|---|---|---|
|  | Pirates | Roger's Bar |  | Big Ben Silver |  |  |  |
|  | The White Horse |  |  | Jimmy's Tam from Glasgow |  |  |  |
|  |  |  |  | O'Grady's Sports Bar |  |  |  |
| Nutters | Bar Trafalgar | Arfur's | Coach and Horse Inn | Windsor | Windsor | Mucky Duck | Robin Hood |
| Popeyes Fun Pub | Lord Nelson | Windsor | The Local British Pub | Britannia Pub | Kings Arms | The Green Parrot | Fantasy Island Bar |

The facilities listed represent a fraction of those on offer in Palmanova and Magaluf and refer mainly to café-bars and nightclubs (see maps for locations). They have been selected because their names appear to be incongruous with Spain or Mallorca. Other names are chosen because they are considered to represent or provide insight into the nature of the holiday experience, or at least the imagined nature of that experience. For example, the hotels Bermudas and Jamaica conjure up ideas of an exotic, paradise-like other. The names of the establishments are not to be taken as indicative of ownership or management. Rather, they can, in part, be seen as an understanding of the market they are trying to attract. In this way, they might initially be comprehended as appealing because of their associations with notions of the exotic or because they are familiar, as in the case of The Red Lion or The White Horse for example. However, it would be somewhat reductionist to leave the analysis there. Following a semiological approach, I begin my analysis with military and heroic names.

## Military and heroic names

A group of names that appears to be particularly striking is that which relates to military conflict and the evocation of heroes. The importance of discussing this group of names lies not only in the number of them but because of the way that they link the tourists to a past that is based on 'kinship ties' (Palmer, 1999: 477).

The names Bar Trafalgar, the Duke of Wellington and the Lord Nelson can all be seen to relate to each other in their shared significance during the Napoleonic wars of the early 19th century. Nelson and Wellington have a place in the military folklore of Great Britain.[2] The significance of the battles in which they were involved has been acknowledged by the incorporation of the place names into the actual landscape of London in the form of Trafalgar Square and Waterloo Station. Both men have also been glorified by the erection of statues in their honour. The significance to the construction of identity that these features represent is the observation that narratives of nationalism that rely on the past are used to create ideas of identity in the present (Carter et al., 1993). While there is an establishment named from the French side – a shop called Napoleon – its significance is less potent given its location in the more internationally 'flavoured' Palmanova. The names of the bars and the monuments serve as reminders of past British military might and greatness. They also perform another purpose, in that they masculinise the landscape of Britain. Their transference to Magaluf also serves to masculinise that landscape. Discussion of the ways in which landscape can be gendered has been ongoing (e.g. Aitchison, 1999; Andrews, 2009b; Bondi, 1992; Edensor & Kothari, 1994). The dominance of male heroic figures and the virtual absence of women figures de-values the latter's roles in historical events.

The military theme of the place names in Magaluf is continued in the presence of The Captains Arms, The Tartan Arms and The Kings Arms; the second half of the names referring to weapons and heraldry. In terms of The Prince William, it has a more complex set of associations. There is William of Orange's battles in Ireland, William the Conqueror's invasion of 1066, and the son of Charles, Prince of Wales, who like his father has connections with the armed forces. This position is shared with Charles's younger son Harry, who by 2009 had made it onto the map of the resorts in the name ascribed to a smaller fast food establishment located next door to The Prince William pub.

The Prince William is significant in other respects. Its location is geographically hard to define in that some people proclaim, despite its postal address, that it is in Torrenova rather than either Magaluf or Palmanova. However, the club 18–30 brochure lists it as a bar in Magaluf (1999). In many ways, it symbolises much of what Magaluf is about in terms of a holiday for a group of young people. It is the starting point of many of the tour operator rep organised bar crawls, which are often characterised by excessive and rowdy behaviour. It is also next door to Hotel Teix, which is also used for Club 18–30 style holidays. The reference to non-peaceful pursuits and the latent aggression associated with the game playing on bar crawls places the lived experiences of the tourists within the context of a landscape constructed along conventional, violent, masculine lines, which speak of the possession of territory and the achievement of a superior position resulting from bloody confrontation.

The idea of armed conflict is continued in the name of a general store, called The Falklands. The shop's name is displayed next to the Union Jack, along with the flags of Scotland and Sweden. The sign that appears on the shop in 1998 and 1999 hides another (just visible in Figure 3.1) that calls the shop Las Malvinas (the Argentinean name for the Falklands). The name The Falklands is still visible in 2009.

The importance of the Falkland Islands in the British psyche gained in significance as a result of the 1982 war with Argentina regarding their ownership. The presence of the name The Falklands brings a more contemporary focus to the militarism that is evident in Magaluf. Its presence links together the much older disputes of the Napoleonic wars

**Figure 3.1** The Falklands shop sign

to the present because there is a common thread of conflict. The Falklands shop is situated at the west end of Punta Balena, marking the beginning of a road that is infamous for its unruly behaviour. Not only does the presence of the name Falklands indicate possession, but also one that is predicated on aggression.

In Palmanova and Magaluf there is a layering of the facilities in a physical sense, that is accommodation might be above shops or café-bars, which are themselves above other types of facilities. There is, however, another form of layering and that is in the laying down of representations of Britishness onto a surface that is Spanish or Mallorcan. So, for example, both The Tartan Arms and The Kings Arms are on Punta Balena. Thus, there is an imposition of Britishness onto Spain. There is a renaming of the space, which the presence of the sign The Falklands over a sign reading Las Malvinas also suggests. The naming of places in a British fashion is reminiscent of colonialism and empire in which British names laid claim to territory. Like the statues of Nelson and Wellington, the significance of the Falklands has been temporarily incorporated into the British landscape. The World's End pub on Marylebone Road, London, at one time depicted the Falklands as the fifth continent (Selwyn, 2002, personal communication). The Falklands is incorporated into the wider landscape of Britain in the annual war dead Remembrance Day services every November.

The significance of the Falklands is referred to elsewhere in the resorts. For example, entertainment in one Palmanova hotel features a comedian who presents himself as having 'entertained the troops in the Falklands'. The sort of imagined community (Anderson, 1991) that references to the Falklands evoke is continued in the content of the comedian's performance. He initially refers to ethnic divisions by asking the audience if they come from Scotland, Wales, England or Ireland. He goes on to makes further divisions by asking for Southerners and Northerners, etc. People respond by cheering to the name of their country or region. He then proceeds to re-establish unity by making reference to an other in the form of telling jokes about the Japanese based on stereotypical notions about Japanese body size. He also tells jokes about women and, by way of illustration of 'how times have changed', he quips 'they don't get married these days, they have a "love child" instead'. Thus, the audience is brought up to date. A social commentator, who has his authority from the Falklands conflict, serves to remind the audience of their ethnic origins and differences and further adds to the ethos promoted in the resorts of conventional heterosexual relationships and the role of women within that. Although it is likely that many in the audience may not find themselves in the same moral framework[3] alluded to by the entertainer, they nevertheless laugh heartily at his jokes.

The celebration of military victories is also evident in The White Horse. White horses carved into hillsides are a feature of the English landscape (Odhams, 1961). The one found at Uffington is said to have been made to commemorate the victory by Alfred over the Danes at Ashford in 871, during the reign of Ethelred 1 (Brewer, 1988). Other figures, some of which are believed to be ancient, are also cut into the land. Many have been lost, but by 1950, of the figures that survived, 16 were horses. Twentieth century additions have included: World War I regimental badges in Wiltshire, a crown in Kent and an aeroplane near the town of Dover to acknowledge Bleriot's flight across the English Channel (Simpson & Roud, 2000). Regardless of the origins of the carvings, many have a military association. However, although a conquering of sorts, Blériot's crossing of the channel was not a military victory. Even though Blériot was French, his mastery of the skies was appreciated. In addition, Gruffudd (1991) argues that English national identity is located 'in the skies' as much as in the land. The patriotic propaganda of World War II referred to the symbolism of the sky and aerial combat. In Magaluf and Palmanova, the skies are occupied by planes full of tourists journeying to and from Mallorca, and on a lower level by the paragliding activities available to the tourists, and in the light aircrafts trailing banners advertising some of the nightclubs, e.g. The Car Wash and BCM advertise their respective venues in this manner.

Among the grouping of names associated with the military and heroes is Robin Hood. Hood, a semi-mythological figure, relates to medieval English history. He is usually depicted as a dispossessed Earl fighting on the side of the good and the just. Not only is Robin Hood a defender of establishment rules, he is also the protector of the poor. His attempts at a redistribution of wealth, feed into notions of fair play, a characteristic associated with British national identity. There are different stories of Robin Hood. In some cases, he is interpreted as a remnant of the Saxons standing in defiance against Norman oppressors (Brewer, 1988). However, the fact (or fiction) that he was operating outside of what were seen as unfair laws imposed by the 'evil' Prince John accords him a liminal status in that his social position as Earl of Huntingdon is suspended in the absence of King Richard. Similarly, tourists find themselves in a liminal position in that they are in the presence of much that is British, but the laws and the attached due processes are absent. Hood is also a figure associated with knowing how to have a good time; his depiction in films about his adventures shows feasts and ale drinking. In addition, he is associated with the corpulent Friar Tuck whose body size is a signifier of generosity, satisfaction and self-indulgence. Regardless of the accuracy of Hood's existence as he is portrayed in popular cultural representations, the character has become 'a symbol of gallantry, patriotism, freedom, and justice' (Simpson & Roud, 2000).

Underpinning much of the foregoing discussion is the idea of heroism and it is also one that is bound up with machismo: heroes on the field of battle and heroes on the side of justice and fair play. This idea is summed up in the naming of one nightclub as Heroes. It is also further added to by a bar called Lineker's (re-named The Red Lion in 2009), which is housed in a white building with a large red sign on it. There is a motif of a football player in striking position, just about to kick a ball. The picture looks as if it has been cut from a Union Jack. Above the bar are Lineker's apartments. The bar is clearly associated with the England national football team. The internal space of the venue is decorated with photographs of individual English football players, including one of Paul Ince with blood pouring from a cut on his face, a display of heroism and survival in the face of violent conflict. Further, one Northern Irish informant advises that he would not watch any of the games in the bar because of its connection with England, and he feared being attacked. The bar is also obviously connected with Gary Lineker, a football hero in his own right. Since he stopped playing football, he has, in various guises, appeared regularly on British television, making him a well-known figure in the popular imagination.

The key aspect to emerge from the discussion so far is that of a space inscribed with British names that are masculine and based on the possession or acquisition of territory. At the same time, they exhibit loyalty and deference to leaders. In turn, this is associated with ideas pertaining to British national identity based on strength in adversity, a sense of fair play and winning, with the attachment of superiority, derived from the ultimate competitive environment of war. These names are not isolated because they link to other encodings in Palmanova and Magaluf that relate to different aspects of constructions of Britishness, e.g. notions of heritage and ethnicity. The next section will demonstrate how the ideas of possession, masculinity and militarism are performed by the tourists, beginning with an exploration of Pirates Adventure, one of the top evening entertainment attractions for the British on Mallorca.

## Pirates Adventure

The foregoing discussion demonstrates how the space of Magaluf is inscribed with meaning that relates it to a British military history and how these names also identify aspects of British identity. The purpose of the proceeding analysis is to explore the way in which some of these ideas become actualised in touristic practice. I begin by discussing Pirates Adventure, which in turn allows other themes to emerge, relating to the emotional and performative dispositions of the tourists.

Pirates Adventure is located in the south-west of Magaluf on Camí De Sa Porrassa (Figures 3.2–3.6). Pirates Adventure is a themed, night-time entertainment show aimed at a primarily British audience. Tickets are sold by all the major British tour operators, as well as independent travel agents in Palmanova and Magaluf. In addition, tourists come from resorts located in other parts of the island, arriving at the venue by the coach load.

There are two Pirates Adventure performances: Adult Pirates and Family Pirates. The following is based on four visits during the summer of 1998, three to Adult Pirates and one to Family Pirates. Although the main story line stays the same for both shows, there are some differences between the two performances. These include the starting time, which is

**Figure 3.2** Outside Pirates Adventure

earlier for Family Pirates than for Adult Pirates, there is an absence of profanities in the Family show and some of the audience participation games are different.

The Adult Pirates show begins at 11.30 pm, but a queue to get into the venue has already started to form by 10.15 pm. The doors open at 10.45 pm. As the queue moves towards the entrance, each person is given a strip of material depicting a skull and crossbones and the wording 'pirates'. Everyone has their (group) photograph taken with a Pirate. The photographs are presented for purchase later in the evening.

Inside the building it is dark and hot. It consists of a large open space with a stage on one side. Seating is around tables that can accommodate

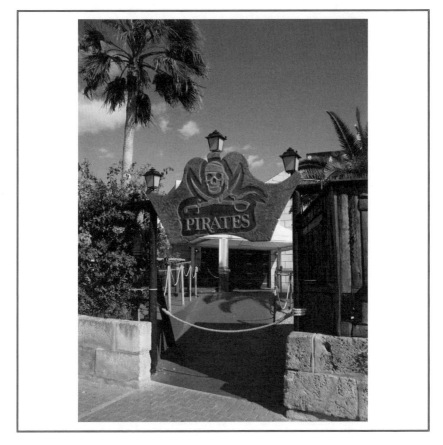

**Figure 3.3** Outside Pirates Adventure

ten people and run adjacent to the stage. The seats and tables are arranged in sections with gangways separating them. There is a further seating area on a balcony. The tables are set with a jug of sangria, ten oval plastic plates, forks and drinking cups, all white and plastic. As everyone is being seated and waiting for the show to begin, more merchandise is offered for sale including plastic silver swords and black pirate scarves decorated with a skull and crossbones.

The acceptance of the strip of material on the way in and any subsequent purchase of a souvenir serves to bring everyone into the same realm. The strip of material offers a shared experience of Pirates Adventure in the

**Figure 3.4** Outside Pirates Adventure

outward display of a sign of where the tourists are. The other memorabilia, including the tourists' own photographs, also serve to fix the tourists within the context of the event and enable them, too, to be pirates.

Before the show starts, the audience is divided into four groups based on one of the 'British' pirates – Blackbeard, Captain Scarlet (the only lead woman pirate), Barbarossa and Sir Francis Drake – who visits his/her section in the audience to give instructions about who should be cheered for, as well as how to get more sangria and beer. On one visit, my table is in Sir Francis Drake's team. He tells us 'I'll be looking after you tonight' and gets us to practice chanting for him. He does this at each table in his section.

**Figure 3.5** Outside Pirates Adventure

**Figure 3.6** Pirates Adventure

At one point before the show starts, many of the tourists who had purchased the plastic souvenir swords, are banging the hilts on the tables and singing 'Vindaloo'[4] (Figure 3.7). The song serves to create a sense of community through the acknowledged sharing of a particular type of food. The reference to a hot curry also marks the character of the English. The ability to digest highly spiced food acts as a form of distinction between the binary oppositions of strong/weak and winner/loser (Andrews, 1999). In this respect, the heroic nature of the British[5] discussed in the place names is enacted in the recognition and consumption of food associated with the UK.

The show opens with the character of Captain Darling (on other occasions Sir Henry Morgan leads the opening act) advising the audience: 'if you are easily offended, if you don't like blue things or swearing, piss off, you know where the door is'. He also makes some safety announcements for the running of the performance and then encourages everyone to shout in response to their UK place of origin. This is followed by setting the scene for the story. Opening a treasure chest said to be full of Moroccan gold and jewellery, the compere raises a crown above his head. He points to the back wall of the theatre and

**Figure 3.7** Tourists singing Vindaloo at Pirates Adventure

advises that it depicts the battleground of the last battle with the French in which they were defeated. The picture (a painting, cartoon-like in character) depicts a sea and sand vista with a treasure chest and a number of skulls littered on the beach. Every time the French are mentioned the audience boos and any mention or the appearance on stage of the French pirate Jacques Laffite, he is referred to as 'that evil French Bastard'. In Family Pirates he is called a 'French Pillock' or 'French Poof'. Among other comments is: 'we don't want the French here do we?' In one show, the audience is told that Laffite could be a German.

The show's next step involves audience participation – a member from each pirate team on stage playing the 'Yes/No' game, led by Captain Darling. The game's object is to answer all the questions put by Darling without using the words 'yes' or 'no'. The winning prize is a bottle of champagne. During the game, the male participants are often vilified and the appearance of the women players commented on. In the family version of the game, the contestants are still adults, but when they are tripped up the audience is told to shout 'adios', after a count of three. There is a sense of fun, but there is also a notion of humiliation at the expense of the contestants. The playing of this game at the very beginning of the show serves to instil ideas of competition between audience members overseen and controlled by the comperes. The sharing of enjoyment in the put-down of the contestants makes the audience complicit in the aim of the story of the show, which is not just about defeating the 'French Bastard', but also humiliating him.

The show opens proper with the 'English' pirates celebrating their victory over the French, the wrecking of their ship – La Hispaniola – and the capture of the treasure. The performance involves acrobats juggling fire torches, twirling the fire around and caressing their bodies with the lighted torches. Sir Francis Drake balances hot coals on his tongue. The twirling flames come close to the audience and people wince back, there is a sense of danger. Captain Scarlet is the object of the other captains' attention as they attempt to kiss her. At one point, two of them come close to achieving their aim, but as she ducks out of the way the two men almost kiss, to which they show their distaste by pulling faces and poking their tongues out at each other. During the performance, the audience is shouting, cheering and clapping for their respective captain. There is an air of excitement and people are laughing and joking. This half of the show ends and during the following interval, the meal is served. There is not long to eat and the platters bearing the food are quickly cleared away. As the audience is waiting for the second half of the show to start, people are singing and having mock fights with their swords. As the performance is about to begin, a safety announcement is made warning people to stay off the stage because the acts are dangerous. This heightens expectations and the sense of danger.

Part two is largely given over to the 'French' pirates. Jacques Laffite appears and shouts of 'you French Bastard' come from the audience. Some people leave their seats to shout at him, calling out 'you French Bastard' and pointing at him with outstretched arms and fingers. As the 'French' and 'English' fight, the audience continues to cheer on their designated captains. The English have been routed and the French are now going to party. This section of the play consists of various acrobatic feats set against music, ranging in style from popular to classical. The bodies of the performers are necessarily fit and agile for the type of skilled performance being delivered. They become increasingly covered in sweat and their bodies glisten, which serves to heighten awareness of their bodies. Every time Jacques Laffite appears, the audience shouts 'you French Bastard'. Even when, at the end of the show, Laffite appears to receive the audience's appreciation, people continue to shout at him: 'you French Bastard'.

The English re-emerge for a final battle in which they defeat the French. At one point, a female 'French' pirate is about to be killed, but one of the male English pirates intervenes saying 'put her below deck there's washing-up to be done. It's women's work', to which the audience cheers. The captured Jacques Laffite is made to walk the plank, and as he goes down behind the ship, two inflatable sharks are thrown in the air and there is a burping noise. In Family Pirates, the audience is asked 'shall we kill him?' and the call back is 'yes', then he walks the plank, the shark burps and 'he is dead' is announced to more cheers. The crown from the treasure chest is lifted into the air and everyone cheers again. At this point, we are encouraged by the tour operator reps to stand up and sing along to the songs that are being played and to wave our arms in time with the music.

The main show is followed by another audience participation game involving eight contestants playing a sort of musical chairs. Each contestant must retrieve items from the audience during which time the chairs are reduced in number. They have to collect first a pair of boxer shorts, second a white bra, third a topless girl to sit on the player's knee, and lastly a £20 note. They return to the stage after each item is collected and are then told what to get next. There is an emphasis on speed as the contestants are in competition for a seat. In Family Pirates, the items that have to be retrieved by the adult participants are: a pair of sunglasses, shoe laces, a postage stamp and a man's leather belt. As each contestant goes to the audience to retrieve the desired item, there is shouting and screaming in support of the player.

In Adult Pirates, on one occasion, in order to get a pair of boxer shorts, one contestant grabs a man, pulls his trousers down and rips off his boxer shorts. The contestant is helped by those in his party. On another occasion, a pair of trousers with the boxer shorts inside is flung across the room. When it comes to getting a topless girl, the compere keeps saying 'get your tits out for the boys'. Once on stage, one contestant bounces the breasts of his girl up and down as she sits astride him. Each of the women now on stage is supposed to stand up and show her breasts off – to cheers from the audience. One woman does not want to go topless. She is followed onto the stage by another girl who sits on her lap. The compere tries to encourage the first woman to expose herself, 'come on get your tits out for the boys'. When she still refuses, he comments, 'don't worry lads it wouldn't be worth it'. He asks another woman, who has not been sunbathing topless, 'I tell you what love don't you ever think of getting them out on the beach?' As each girl does her twirl, the audience is cheering. After the exhibition of bare breasts, the compere advises, 'you notice we didn't take any chairs away then, that's because we're sexist'.

In a different show, the items for retrieval include two condoms, a £20 note, an Irish lottery ticket and a topless girl. In another show, it is two condoms, a white bra, boxer shorts and a topless girl. In one performance, the girls come on stage clothed and are lined up. Each girl is then asked to reveal her breasts, under the mantra 'get your tits out for the boys'. One young woman with a large bust is requested to show her breasts three times and to come to the front of the stage to do so. Another of the women does the splits, and is then asked 'can you do it with your tits out?' She is asked to repeat the feat twice. The breast is a highly significant symbol, which I will explore in more detail later. However, one observation at this juncture is that in the context of Pirates it is firmly linked with women as the objects of the male gaze for the purpose of titillation. This analysis is given because of the context of the action in which there is an admission of sexism, women are cast in the role of the domestic, and heterosexual relationships are promoted.

In the final game, the audience is divided in two and everybody is standing. The different teams in the audience have to shout for their captain. Then, each half of the audience is given a song to sing. Each team has to take it in turns to sing their song, but periodically are asked to sing other songs before reverting to the team song. The team regarded as the loudest wins.

In Family Pirates, one game is played with children as the contestants. The winning prize includes a pirate's baseball cap, 'a manicure set for mum' and a pirate's towel. In relation to the towel, the compere advises, 'put that on the sunbed and no Germans will bother you, but you'll have to get up early'. A contestant in one of the Adult Pirates games won a similar prize that included a condom. The reference to condoms and giving them out as prizes also serves to highlight Magaluf as 'Shagaluf'. On one occasion, contestants are told that they have to put their hotel keys on the floor and 'shag' the owner of the keys they pick up.

During this show, another 'game' is also played with a member of the audience, in this case one woman participant. There is a large wooden board against which Sir Francis Drake demonstrates axe throwing. The woman is taken to the board where she stands against it with her arms stretched out and she is blindfolded. She is told that on the count of three, an axe will be thrown. At three, Drake walks up to the board and bangs an axe into it. Each time this happens the blindfold is lifted so that the woman can see where the axe fell. Captain Darling, who is compering, comments, 'I bet you wish you'd shaved your armpits'. The woman is then asked to stand with her legs apart, and as she complies, Darling says, 'open wider this is Magaluf' and everyone cheers. Then he claims, 'your legs are crying'. For taking part, the woman is given a bottle of champagne. As she goes to collect it, Darling says, 'by the way the toilets are over there'.

In both versions of the show, the entertainment ends with the tour operator reps going onto the stage to receive thanks from the tourists (chivvied along by the compere) for all their hard work. Tina Turner's song *The Best* is played. In the adults' show, the tourists are also invited onto the stage to dance. When this ends after about 10 minutes, they are advised that a coach is waiting outside to take those interested to a nightclub in Palma.

By the time the show ends, many of the tourists are extremely inebriated. For example, one girl falls between two rows of tables and has to be helped from the building. One lad, who looks very ill, is sick into one of the sangria jugs. His friends, who had made him drink a whole jug of sangria, are hitting him on the head with their swords. He is unsuccessfully trying to push them off until a third party intervenes and he is carried from the premises. Outside, people are mock fighting with their swords. After one show, there is a skirmish in the car park and another man is arguing with one of the security guards, inviting him to fight. Similar incidents indicate that the tourists have taken up the violence and fighting represented in the show and have set out to perform it for themselves.

An analysis of Pirates Adventure should begin with some facts. Firstly, Sir Francis Drake, Blackbeard, Sir Henry Morgan, Barbarossa and Jacques Laffite were real people. Drake's fame is derived from his association with the defeat of the Spanish Armada. He is also associated with folklore that hails from Devon, where his drum is kept in Buckland Abbey. Some stories link him with the devil and a mythology has grown around him that he will rise from his deathbed in the event of England being invaded (Simpson & Roud, 2000). The stories fix Drake with the likes of Robin Hood as representative of particular British characteristics associated with patriotism, freedom and honour. Both Drake and Sir Henry Morgan were involved in skirmishes with the Spanish. Blackbeard fought against the French, but was also known for battles with the British. The history of Barbarossa is as one of the Barbary pirates operating from the coast of North Africa. His main conflicts were with the French, who suppressed piracy in the area. Jacques Laffite's real name was Jean Laffite and he operated off the south coast of New Orleans at the beginning of the 19th century, during which time he engaged in conflict with the British. The point in presenting the background of the various pirates is that although they are presented in playful pastiche (in reality, they were separated by several years and geographical distance, and would not have met), they all share a background of bloody and violent conflict that occurred predominately between the British and Spanish. So, although Pirates Adventure is presented as a fight against the French (and again in the real life of Jean Laffite this did happen), it also speaks of or refers to conflicts between Spain and Britain. Both the hostilities with France and Spain are referred to in the names of some of the establishments already discussed.

The show of pirates compounds notions of ownership and possession by force, of winning and glory that speaks to an idea of a national identity because many of the pirates operated under the eye, or as representatives, of the English establishment. As such, the pirates occupied an in-between place and thus can serve as reminders of the liminal nature of some of the tourists' experiences. The undercurrent of violence that runs through Magaluf and underpins the notions of pirates (which also speak of romance, fantasy and legend) is also evident in some of the show's promotional material, which reads: 'They attack you with fun, torture you with laughter and capture your heart!' (1998). Regardless of the context of fun, the tourists are not seduced, relaxed and set free. In actuality, pirates did attack and they did torture those they held captive. Among the latter activities were, for example, being forced to drink, being compelled to eat the heart of another victim and other general physical abuse. These acts of humiliation correspond with that exhibited in the games played with the tourists as part of the show. From the start, the tourists are brutalised in the abusive and violent language used to open the performance. In addition, the idea of being forced to drink is acted out elsewhere in the resorts. In one bar (Cheeks in Palmanova), again in the guise of fun, punters are offered the option of having beer squirted into their mouths from water pistols. Although, undoubtedly they can exercise choice here, the connection with a gun still links it to violence. The link between the consumption of alcohol and force is also made by one expatriate, Brenda. When discussing the drunken behaviour in Magaluf, she comments, 'they are given cheap booze by the bars even though they [the bar staff] know it will make them ill'. The bars are 'forcing it down them'.

The figure of Captain Scarlet is played by a woman, and her badge or coat of arms is a red rose. No pirate called Captain Scarlet is listed in accounts of piracy, although there were two notorious female pirates, Anne Bonny and Mary Read.[6] It is curious, therefore, as to why the character in the show has not been cast from history as is the case with the majority of the male pirates. As the content and language of some of the show suggests, the role of women is presented as conformist. Undoubtedly, there is a desire to present the audience with a name that they will recognise and the lack of fame associated with the real female pirates is a disadvantage in this respect. It also appears that the desire to maintain a conventional role for women, e.g. washing the dishes, is maintained by not acknowledging the ability of women to behave in the same bloody and violent manner as their male counterparts. History is glossed over and the woman pirate is presented as femininity itself. This is signified in the rose and the attempts to kiss her by two of her male counterparts, who reject outright the homosexual innuendo of when they almost kiss.

There are two possible sources of the name Scarlet – that she is named after a male puppet from a children's television programme or reference is being made to Carr's (1953) film *Captain Scarlett*, based on a story by Howard Dimsdale (1953). In the film, a swashbuckling Captain Scarlett returns to France a war hero, following the Napoleonic Wars. The character and related story is akin to that of Robin Hood – a dispossessed nobleman, fighting an unjust tyrannical figure (Napoleon) and opposing unfair laws. In fighting on the edge of society, he occupies the same liminal position as the other pirates already discussed.

Captain Darling is also not based on a real pirate. His namesake appears in a popular British television programme, *Blackadder*. As in the programme, the calling of this character Darling by another male is used to raise laughs. It also heightens awareness of masculinity and is suggestive of the absurdity (and distaste) accorded to homosexual relationships by normative understandings of sexuality.

The reactions of the tourists to Pirates appear to be one of genuine enjoyment, in which people marvel at the acrobatic skill and strength of the performers, who are encouraged by cheers and clapping. When some feats are achieved, members of the audience raise their swords in the air. There is a celebratory feeling to the show in which the body is being worshipped. Here are fit, muscular bodies on display and the feats achieved demand a high level of control. The audience is being encouraged in the opposite direction, towards a lack of control by drinking to excess and in the frenzied dislike of Laffite. However, there is also tension because there are behavioural rules and there is containment within the physical space of the pirates building, until it spills out after the show.

Without question, the sexual role of women is highlighted, particularly in the semi-naked form. There is also attention to male bodies, but in a less overt way. Although not displayed in the same manner as the women, the references to condoms and boxer shorts also draws attention to men as sexual beings. Some women are aware of the inequalities in the show. One describes the topless female spectacle as 'a bit sad' and another comments, 'it's not fair the women go topless but the men don't take their clothes off'. In one show when three of the male pirates begin to strip, some women clap and cheer, wanting to see the men naked.

Some tourists note the Britishness of the Pirates show and, in turn, Magaluf. My outing to Family Pirates is with a family from the Midlands. They are atypical of the tourists encountered in Magaluf, in that they are middle class. The father is an architect and the mother – Karen – a court official. They are on holiday with their two sons aged 18 and 14. The holiday in Magaluf is not something they would normally do and his work friends had met their proposed trip with 'stunned silence' and her colleagues had 'laughed in disbelief'.

Karen says, 'we're disappointed that the resort is so anglicised especially in terms of the food and language [but] it is wonderfully tacky'. In addition, their hotel 'is not as tatty as we first thought it would be'. The father asks me if any Germans or French visit the show. At the time, I am unable to answer but comment that I find the 'picking on' the French interesting and wonder why the Germans are less targeted, wondering if it is because of a connection with the ancestry of the British Royal Family. The father offers the following explanation: 'It's not to do with the Royal Family but the French and English are very much alike and we both feel each other as threats. The French are more individua-listic and eccentric like the English whereas the Germans are more homogenised'. When one of the waitresses comes to clear the table of plates and cutlery, he comments to her, 'it's like a little England here isn't it?' She replies, 'yeah well it's designed for the English so everyone has to be able to speak English'.

Karen says that she likes the show, but that 'it's very vulgar'. As she says this, she puts her hand to her mouth and gestures with her head towards the people on her right. She and her youngest son also think the show is 'very slick' and 'organised into a conveyor belt system'. The family has all joined in with the 'spirit' of the occasion, buying swords that they use in mock fights, with accompanying 'arrrgghh' sounds, during the interval. The younger son gets a stick-on tattoo and the older one buys a tee-shirt and gets his face painted. When the elder son realises that his younger brother has not opted for face painting, he says, 'I feel stupid, a fool, someone might recognise me', to which his father replies, 'no-one will recognise you... if you can't do it on holiday where can you do it?' Earlier he told me, 'it's [the holiday] escapism, it doesn't matter where you are it doesn't have to be Mallorca'.

Some of the names of the tourist facilities in Magaluf give rise to a space that has been encoded with ideas of militarism, masculinity and deference to authority. The site of Pirates Adventure is a space in its own right and its physical locality on the edge of Magaluf (Map 3.1) in part represents the nature of the operation of real pirates as outside the law. The enacting of the Pirates Adventure performance, both in its adult and family versions, serves to live out, in both a physical and imagined sense, conflicts between the British and some European neighbours. Although the emphasis is on the French, references are also made to the Germans. The factual history of some of the characters makes direct reference to conflicts with the Spanish. Pirates is, therefore, predicated on ideas of national identity and ethnicity (which are also in the games and side entertainment) based on an aggressive heterosexual character in which women and men fall into normative roles. These ideas are prevalent elsewhere in Magaluf and Palmanova in the games that are played by tourists as part of hotel entertainment and on bar crawls. The violent nature that underlies some of the names of facilities discussed and Pirates Adventure itself, is also acted out by the tourists in their mock fights and the actual violence that sometimes erupts after the show. It is also evident elsewhere in the resorts.

Other elements that Pirates highlights relate to control and mediation. For the majority of the tourists visiting the show, the trip has been organised by a tour operator, who, in some cases, escorts the tourists to and from the venue. Tour operator reps also accompany the tourists inside the building, staying with them throughout the performance, getting the refills of jugs of alcohol and encouraging people to join in the team games. At the end of the performance, the reps are presented by a member of the Pirates' team to be thanked. Contrary to these attempts to constrain is the behaviour of some of the tourists who become out of control. The tension between efforts to constrain and the lack of control is heightened in that the pirates' performances require strong command of the physical body as well as intense concentration. Control and possession are inter-linked. They both imply each other, to exert control over someone is to assert possession of them as it implies a lack of independence. To possess or own a piece of territory indicates authority over the inhabitants. This does not preclude resistance or revolution, but even this implies a struggle for command, self-direction and a different or re-possession. The importance of possession as it is played out in other areas of Palmanova and Magaluf is the subject of the next section.

## Possession[7]

This section examines the way in which tourists act out ideas of possession. Ownership of place implies a right of occupancy is accompanied or associated with ideas of licence to behave as one wishes or with some form of authority. This, of course, may be disputed and resisted. For example, Bender (1993b) discusses the contested landscape of Stonehenge and shows that emotional attachments to place are not necessarily linked to legal ownership. Notions of ownership link into other concepts regarding identity, in the connected thoughts of belonging that link people with a particular place. In his analysis of the way in which the Israeli landscape is used as a metaphor, Selwyn (1995) explores constructions of identity and ownership that instils a need to defend the land from those perceived to be outsiders. Thus, proprietorship and senses of kinship link with beliefs concerning ethnicity, which are also evident in Palmanova and Magaluf in the naming of some of the establishments in ways that are specific to particular regions or countries within the UK.

Before proceeding, I wish to acknowledge Hann's (1998) caution of oversimplifying the use and understanding of the words 'possession', 'ownership' and 'property'. Nevertheless, the first two words do appear as synonyms, and it is in this, perhaps more generally understood meaning of the words, that they are used here. Similarly, Hann (1998: 4) concedes that '[i]n contemporary ordinary language usage, property commonly refers to the "thing" over which a person claims more or less exclusive rights of ownership'. It is with this sort of usage that the current work is concerned, while keeping in mind that property directs us 'to a vast field of cultural as well as social relations, to the symbolic as well as the material contexts within which such things are recognised and personal as well as collective identities made' (Hann, 1998: 5).

Hann traces some of the theoretical debates concerned with understanding property and makes some observations that are pertinent to the current discussion. Firstly, the importance of the ideal of private property has grown over the last 200 years, particularly with the emergence of 'democratic' states. Private property became associated with the conditions necessary for a 'healthy society', and was seen as a fundamental human right and a pre-condition for full citizenship.[8] This applies to the 'liberal paradigm', which is characterised by 'free individuals', 'competitive markets', 'pluralistic civil societies' and 'the rule of law'. Many of the ideas were spread globally by European societies involved in empire building. This was intimately linked with conquest and the ownership of land. In consequence, Western property relations were imposed on existing social structures, which were quite often completely ignored (Hann, 1998).

Secondly, in the UK, the Conservative governments of Margaret Thatcher (1979–1990) brought about the privatisation of industry, the promotion of share holding and increased private home ownership. Part of Thatcher's success was related to the opportunity she afforded people to make 'easy money' in the selling of publicly owned companies. Another aspect of this success was the right-to-buy scheme. Appealing to the sentiment of the 'Englishman's Castle' and the associated idea of freedom, Thatcher's governments eroded the affordable publicly owned housing sector. In so doing, a sense of competitive individualism was imposed, while at the same time undermining public institutions that served to bind society together, both literally and metaphorically. For Dumont (1970, 1977), this rise in the individual is one of the distinguishing factors between modern and 'traditional' societies.

The importance of having competitive possessive individuals is that they are crucial for the development of a free-market economy in which there is less and less reliance on the state for the provision of anything. As Hann (1998) notes, the problems that the UK faces in terms of welfare provision are, in part, due to the rise of the individual and ideas of private ownership in which there is increasing reluctance to share the 'catch' as it were with those unable to hunt. Speaking to a couple from Hull, the man expresses discontent with the local council. He tells me that Hull has a surplus of empty council housing that is being made available to people from other councils and there is concern that the houses will be filled by 'people from those boroughs with a bad reputation – Tower Hamlets – that council with a bad reputation. It doesn't really bother us because we own, but we don't see why we should accept those who might cause problems from elsewhere'. In this case, the identities of the individuals are very localised and the threat from outside is from another part of the UK. The main points to note here are the fear of the unknown and particularly of an unknown that has no recourse to the possession of its own property and the unwillingness to share the resources with those unable to buy their own.

Another point made by Hann is that ownership of property will instil a sense of identity as the owner relates to objects within her/his environment. As the theoretical and academic usage of property is linked to the 'rights' over it rather than ownership of the thing, Hann (1998:4, emphasis in the original) comments, '[p]roperty *relations* are consequently better seen as social relations between people', and as such, they give an insight into how people see themselves and their relationships with others.

In addition, property cannot be separated from the social, cultural and political contexts within which it is embedded. The attempts to 'own' or 'possess' Palmanova and Magaluf in the ways suggested speak of a collective attitude to territorial acquisition. The British Empire was built on the forceful possession of land. Coupled with the idea of working the land, a sense of belonging also comes about. So, representations of a rural idyll have resonance because 'many patterns of ownership demonstrate important continuities which provide effective stabilizing anchors in even the most rapidly changing "post-modern" societies' (Hann, 1998: 31).

Property ownership, then, signals continuity within a framework of a national identity seen to be threatened by outside forces, in the form of immigrants and the European Union. At the same time, it also marks another tension in the world of the tourists in the need, on the one hand, for a sense of national identity against, on the other, the message and practice of free-market individualism.

Feelings pertaining to threats to national identity related to ownership or occupancy of space were often articulated by tourists. One retired lady told me that when she first got married, she lived in a basement flat in St Johns Wood and paid one pound a week in rent. From there, she and her husband had moved to Hayes where 'we had a beautiful detached house. Then blocks of flats were built up around but we didn't move because of our son's schooling.... We used to go to Southall shopping, it used to be lovely' [then] 'all the Asians took it over and they told us "you don't come here anymore, it's not your town." They burnt a pub down (which used to be lovely) because they didn't like the English'. Her husband then comments, 'oh you'd be surprised what goes on' and she says, 'I said to him "can't we go and live in Spain. I feel more at home here than I do in England"'.

Another couple, Bert and May, are from the Midlands. They are interested to know about house prices in London, and what wages are like. They tell me that they paid £13,000 when they bought their council house and that it is now (1998) worth £37,000. They go on to talk about council tax, saying 'we don't get anything, whereas the Pakistanis – the Muslims – get what they want'. Bert advises, 'Indians are cleaner than Pakis. The women [i.e. Pakistani women] are only brought here for breeding'. The conversation then turns to the street vendors in the resorts, often referred to as 'Gypsies' or 'Moroccans'. The origin of the vendors is mainly North African, but some come from Senegal and Ghana. As we are talking, one man passes our table. May laughs as she sees him approach from behind Bert. As the man passes, she gestures her head towards Bert and the man turns to look at him. When he sees Bert, he pulls a face and continues on. Bert and May laugh, referring to the man as 'nig-nog'. Bert then comments, 'I don't like these people, they try to rip you off, they're rapists'. He goes on to explain that when the sellers come up to him 'they say 4000 [pesetas] I say 1000. When they eventually say ok to 1000 I say "fuck off." You said 4000 I said 1000 you said "no" now you say "1000" I say "fuck off"'. Bert and May's antipathy, violent (sexual) language and outward hostility towards the Pakistanis in their home area and the street vendors in Palmanova is racist. However, it is also connected to some of the issues raised by Hann. Firstly, Pakistanis are seen as 'free loaders' coming to the UK and being given things (property) without any investment in the form of local taxes. Secondly, the street vendors are known to operate outside the law. So, not only does the colour of their skin and their trading practices (which can be aggressive) offend Bert and May, but also they subvert one of the principles in the liberal paradigm, which contributed to Bert and May's ownership of their own home, that of the rule of law.

The dislike of Asians expressed by some of the tourists is also connected to rights. In the case of Southall, the British couple felt they were being told they had no right to go there and in Bert and May's case the rights or needs of the 'Muslims' are being placed before their own. This gives a sense of being dominated by another 'outside' group of people. Another couple of tourists describe their area of the country (the Midlands) as 'infested with them', in reference to people of Indian ethnicity. The following discussion examines the way in which threats from the 'outside' are lived in Palmanova and Magaluf.

## Don't Mention the Germans

The sense of 'Britishness' is highlighted in the attention sometimes drawn to the presence of other nationalities, but particularly the Germans in other resorts. For example, the selling of tickets to a water theme park attraction by one tour company representative was couched in the following terms: There are two water parks, one just outside Magaluf and the other on the other side of the Bay of Palma in Arenal. Basically, the attractions are the same but the one at Arenal will be full of Germans. This, the rep goes on to say, 'gives you an indication of the sort of people you'll find there. If you don't mind being surrounded by Germans that's ok'. At a different time, the complexity of the journey to Arenal as well as the presence of Germans is used to deter people from visiting the attraction. In a separate incident, two tourists were re-visiting a hotel bar to see the head barman, who they remembered from a previous trip to Palmanova. The male tourist advises, 'we went to Arenal a couple of years ago but didn't like it, didn't like it'. The barman asks 'full of Germans?' to which the reply is, 'just didn't like the place'. Although the tourist did not make a direct reference to Germans, that the question was asked is indicative of an understanding of the imagined relationship between the two nationalities.

Speaking to one tourist staying in Palmanova, he complains that the sunbeds around his hotel pool get reserved from as early as eight o'clock in the morning, 'it's not just the Germans, the British are just as bad'. This sentiment is echoed by a female tourist staying in the same hotel. She comments, 'some people put their towels there [on sunbeds] at 6 am. They're worse than the Germans'. Comments made in Pirates have already hinted at the tensions between the Germans and British over sunbed occupancy. It is also about competition, of being first and coming first implies being the best. In another sunbed story, which did not involve the Germans, another tourist relates how she had overheard two women arguing about the sunbeds by the pool in the same hotel. One had reserved a sunbed with her towel and 'the other woman said she didn't want to stay in a hotel where the likes of her [the first woman] stayed'.

The apparent antagonism felt towards the Germans by some British tourists was exemplified in one particular hotel and self-catering apartment complex, which lies to the east of Palmanova in Son Caliu. The Hotel Son Caliu is a four-star Best Western hotel with a German manager and a mainly German clientele. Only one British tour operator uses the complex and few British tourists stay there. A common cause of complaint arises when people arrive to stay in apartments and are unable to go straight to them, instead having to spend a night in one of the hotel bedrooms. The explanation for this given to tourists is rumoured to be that 'the apartment has an electrical fault'.

On one occasion, two families have not been able to go straight to their accommodation. One of the women complains, 'I feel we are being treated like second class citizens because there aren't many of us here'. Another tourist comes to complain that he and his wife are unhappy with their apartment. He also complains that the complex is dominated by Germans and 'you've got to have someone to talk to. Last night I tried going round all the tables to talk to people but didn't get anywhere.... The hotel is lovely but there aren't enough English people'. He makes enquiries about moving to a different hotel. The following day, he is still talking about moving accommodation but, he confides (the rep is out of earshot), 'we like the Son Caliu area and probably won't move, but you have to give the rep something to do'. He goes on to say, 'last night I walked into Palmanova and went to the Stadium Bar which was full of British'.

Whenever the issue of the hotel being dominated by Germans is raised with the tour operator rep, he always replies, 'the brochure states that the hotel is exclusive to Unijet'. Things in the hotel come to a head when two groups of British tourists are evicted. According to management, they had been given more than one warning that their behaviour is disturbing other guests. The last straw is when others threaten to leave the complex, so the British are thrown out. The rep makes attempts to resolve the situation but the manager is adamant. The evicted tourists are found alternative accommodation. The rep blames the whole situation on the manager, 'it's all down to one man... he only cares about his precious Germans'.

The idea of German domination has a political reference to the home world of the tourists, as many Eurosceptics fear that closer links with the European Union will herald the way for both German and French takeovers. The idea of Germans 'taking over' 'British' territory mirrors the fears expressed by some about the 'take over' of areas of the home world, as the example of Southall discussed earlier demonstrates.

The preference by the British for the British is noted by the German owner of a café in Palmanova. Situated next door to a British-owned bar, in 1998 the German-owned café has been established for three years. The owner complains, 'each year it gets worse, we work hard and get little reward for it... Sometimes people start to come into our place, then they hear English spoken next door and go there instead'. The attitude of the tourists in seeking out Britishness 'is also a problem for the Spanish bars. People look for "British owned", they bring home with them'.

What all this illustrates is that constructions of British identity are bound up with notions of fear, dislike and lack of knowledge of outsiders. The British are perceived in some cases as being treated in an inferior manner and the unwillingness or inability of the Germans to communicate with their fellow British tourists acts to exclude the latter from, in one example, a particular hotel in-group. Thus, there is a desire for a community built around the symbols of Britishness. Along with this is a sense of appropriate or fair behaviour, which early morning claims to the territory of the hotel sunbed is seen to go against. It is with this theme and that of possession that discussion continues in the next section.

## Tourists Behaving Badly

'If I go into someone else's hotel I sit at the back, but they don't ... he was climbing over the chairs to get to the front'. This statement was made by a retired man from South Wales on holiday in Palmanova with his wife and granddaughter. He says that he finds the other people staying in the hotel cliquey and that their 'sticking together' is particularly noticeable during the evening cabaret at which time the hotel is also visited by outsiders who do not know how to behave. In addition, 'at meal times we are seated with other young children ... some of them are very badly behaved'. As a result of the 'bad' behaviour of the other tourists, he and his family visit the café-bars in close proximity to the hotel for their evening entertainment. What this example illustrates is that there is a sense of the hotel being 'our place' and that this understanding of ownership should be respected by outsiders.

The sense of 'ownership' has emerged through the financial transaction of the holiday purchase that entitles the buyer to have occupancy of a hotel room and the use of its facilities for a set period of time. Miguel, who serves in a drinks and ice-cream kiosk on the promenade in Palmanova, expresses his dislike of British tourists. He claims that 'they are monkeys. They don't behave in the same way at home ... They smash the place up. In these apartments [he points to apartments behind the kiosk] we charged 300,000 pesetas to one guy who wrecked the place, the windows, beds everything. Because they have paid for an apartment they think they own it'. The idea that tourists believe they can please themselves is also noted by Martin who is working for the summer in the café Loro Verde. He advises, 'tourism is horrible...in Magaluf [where he had worked during a previous summer] you get to see the other side of people. Because they're in a foreign country they think they can do what they want'.

The hotel referred to by the man from South Wales is the Santa Lucia in Palmanova. It attracts a number of repeat visitors, who during the summer of 1998 expressed concerns that they would not be able to get a booking for the following year. The anxiety is based on the idea that because the hotel is due to be refurbished it will become more popular. A rumour is circulating that half the hotel has already been pre-booked for the next year. Bert and May, for example, have only ever been on holiday to Mallorca and they are repeat visitors to the Santa Lucia. Along with Lucy, another long-time visitor to the island and repeatedly to the Santa Lucia, they are worried that they will not be able to book into the hotel the following year. All of them have started to look at alternative hotels in Palmanova. Bert comments, 'they should give people who come to the hotel on a regular basis the first option of booking for next year ... they must be able to tell from their records ... it's not fair that those who have come in June have had the advantage of two months more to book the hotel'.

The kind of inside information indicated by Lucy, Bert and May, not just in relation to their knowledge of the hotel but their familiarity with other facilities and the staff of both, is at odds with the ideas of fleeting relationships and the quick pull associated with 'Shagaluf'. Indeed, some tourists do form long lasting and very personal relationships with local people. For example, during their stay, one family visits the home of a waiter and his family in Palma whom they had become good friends with over a number of years. In other examples, tourists marry into local families and go to live in Mallorca.

The sense of belonging that has come about from the feeling of ownership has, in the examples of Lucy, Bert and May, established a form of loyalty and intimacy that is tied to a particular place. With that location is the idea of familiarity and an expectation that the relationship should be deeper than a superficial financial transaction. For Bert, it seems that his continued loyalty to the same hotel should be recognised and rewarded, as he fears exclusion the next year. For some of these tourists, they are not simply buying a product, but rather buying into all of the feelings and associations that go with their experience of Palmanova over a period of several years. Part of this will also be linked to a knowledge of what is being bought, as another tourist comments, 'when you come to Spain you know what you are getting'.

That a particular place holds associations for tourists that go beyond a financial transaction is also illustrated in an example from Hotel Son Caliu. A couple are returning for the second year to stay in the apartments and are disappointed that they have not been allocated the same apartment. The man says, 'it's not the same holiday if you can't have the same apartment'. Urry (1995: 131–132) comments that the purchase of the hotel room is 'often incidental' to tourists' experiences, but the desire expressed by this tourist contradicts that assertion. Notions of familiarity are linked to knowing one's place, both in a literal and metaphorical sense, to which the next section turns.

## A Sense of Belonging

The previous section used the theme of possession, extracted from the ideas of militarism associated with the naming of some café-bars and other tourist facilities in Magaluf, to explore the nature of tourists' experiences. This was done in terms of national identity, the latent and actual aggression of some tourist activities and feelings of belonging. In the case of the latter, which I will demonstrate is linked to creation of identities, the feeling is associated with familiarity as well as a sense of ownership. Although the idea of ownership is linked to domination and control or the freedom to be out of control, it is more than a financial transaction and connects with loyalty, friendliness and having a good time. These ideas are also linked to having an understanding of where one fits in. The man from South Wales felt discomfort in his hotel because he was not part of the cliquey in-group, and the people from outside were misbehaving because they were not in their own place. The proceeding discussion will explore other ways in which people feel their place, or rather, feel out of place or disorientated and the ways in which some of these ideas are constructed.

One scenario in which tension arises from who has the right to occupy certain spaces, and leads to feelings of discomfort, is that between tourists on all-inclusive packages and those who are not. This transpires, in some cases, when an overbooking has occurred at the hotel where the all-inclusive tourists should be staying. When this happens in one hotel in Magaluf – The Honolulu – the tourists are sent to a hotel in Cala Vinyes located to the south west of Magaluf. This hotel is a four-star hotel, one star higher than The Honolulu. The source of tension arises because the existing tourists in the four-star hotel see other tourists enjoying the same facilities for less money and receiving 'free' drinks. According to one tour operator rep, this results in a large number of complaints from the four-star guests.

The all-inclusive market is often blamed for low commission earning by the reps, and contributing to the demise of small, local businesses because all the tourists' needs are perceived to be catered for in the hotel, having been paid for in advance. There is also a perception that where all-inclusive tourists are accommodated with half or full-board tourists, there is animosity between the two groups. Indeed, one informant advises, 'they hate each other'.

In the case of one hotel, the demarcation between the two groups is spatial. The bar in one of the lounge areas has separate queuing points for the different types of tourist, and drinks and some food items in the dining area are sign posted as 'all-inclusive'. The division between the two types of tourists is further highlighted in that, on arrival at the hotel, the all-inclusive tourists are given plastic bracelets to wear (somewhat reminiscent of those worn by hospital patients). Although the majority of people wear these around their wrists, others attach them to necklaces or watch straps for easy removal. The all-inclusive tourists are also often associated with having particular characteristics as their reference as 'scum' and descriptions of their bodily appearance by one rep indicates.

Despite ideas attached to all-inclusive tourists – they do not venture from the hotel and are disliked by non-all-inclusives – in practice this is not the case. As one woman says 'people say you're restricted, but we've been out ... we have a couple of drinks in the hotel and then come out for a walk'. Similarly, a period of observation in a hotel that catered for both types of tourists did not detect any particular antagonism. Although the queues for the bar are separate, the seating arrangements for the hotel entertainment are not and people, regardless of their 'status', intermingle in much the same way as in any other hotel.

If there is antagonism, it is more likely to be from both sets of tourists towards the tour operators. One all-inclusive tourist expresses dissatisfaction because she feels that the holiday does not cater for teenagers: 'you pay all that money and then have to go outside for entertainment'. In another example, two women have paid £750 each for their all-inclusive holiday in Magaluf, but the hotel is overbooked and so they are moved to another hotel only to be moved again, all within a period of 12 hours. They end up in the four-star Cala Vinyes, which they describe as 'in the middle of nowhere' (which it is, compared to The Honolulu in the centre of Magaluf and Palmanova – Map 9), and there is the 'need to get taxis everywhere'. In addition 'we haven't felt comfortable because it is very posh. The bar staff were a bit funny with us at first but are all right now'. They are at the end of their holiday and glad to be going home because the holiday has been a 'disaster'.

For these two women their vacation has been in the wrong place geographically being in the middle of nowhere compared to the centre of somewhere; and, also in that their own sense of self and identity has been undermined as they do not feel they belong in a four-star hotel. The references to the hotel being 'posh' indicate that the women do not feel that they are in their *habitus* (Bourdieu, 1979). It is not only the case that one is born into a particular *habitus*, but that also during one's life course the *habitus* can be confirmed, rejected or altered. One way of confirming particular *habitii*, is through the construction of differences that occur in space. The next section explores this issue by an examination of a visit to Andratx market.

## Andratx Market

The tours of the rest of the island offered by tour operators and the independent travel agents in the resorts include visits to markets, among which is the general market that takes place every Wednesday in the inland town of Andratx, to the west of Palmanova and Magaluf. The visit to the market is a morning excursion and includes a trip to Port d'Andratx approximately 3.5 km from the town. The port is a predominately German resort, although this is not highlighted as a reason not to go there. It is also used to moor yachts and part of the purpose for visiting the port is to view these vessels. In one sales pitch for the excursion, the fact that Peter Stringfellow[9] has a yacht moored in the harbour is highlighted, along with the possibility that he might also be glimpsed. The possibility of seeing a celebrity adds a dimension of glamour to the visit.

My trip is organised by an independent travel agent. We are taken to the market by coach. On arrival, the coach parks next to two others and there is a short walk over a small bridge to the market. The market is spread out over several streets full of stalls selling, among other items: linen and lace, leather goods, kitchen equipment, watches, African crafts, jewellery, carpets and food. The pathways between the stalls are narrow and crowded (Figure 3.8). At times, the crowd shuffles along, periodically stopping because there is no room to pass. As the number of people

**Figure 3.8** Andratx Market

seems to increase, the shuffling and stopping continue. In parts, music is playing and there are many cries of 'looky looky' by the stall holders.

My impression is that the main streets of the market all look the same and I am concerned that I will lose my bearings, particularly as I have no-one to whom I can refer. When I do ask for directions to the coach park, I am given the wrong ones. This is because there are two coach parks and the incorrect directions refer to parking spaces for the tour operators' coaches, which are next to the market. I am also constantly aware of the time and find it difficult to use the two hours allocated for the visit. Other people are also checking their watches and asking each other the time. In the market, it is very hot and airless and people are sweating. I return to the coach 20 minutes early and expect to find it empty, but others are already there or on their way.

The next stage of the excursion is the visit to the port. As we arrive, another passenger comments, 'this looks like a nice place', her partner rejoins, 'it's not as nice as Palma', to which the reply is, 'well that's bigger with the bigger boats'. The coach stops at the northern end of the town. We have just under an hour in the port with a pick-up time of 1 pm. I have never seen the Port of Andratx this crowded. Having alighted from the coach, most people head straight for the sea wall and beach. Some take photographs of the harbour. The tourists follow the curve of the bay, walking in a southward direction along the seafront. The cafes are crowded and many people buy cans of drink to consume as they walk.

I discuss the outing to the market and port with Vicky, a tourist staying in the Son Maties Hotel, Palmanova. She found the market 'a bit too enclosed' (echoing the words of another tourist who had found it, like me, 'claustrophobic'). Vicky did not buy anything, principally because she thought the items too expensive. In connection with the port she comments, 'the port is beautiful. I've got my eye on one of the apartments overlooking the harbour for sale. There were some nice yachts in the harbour. Our room overlooks the sea... there are some nice yachts outside. I'd like that kind of holiday, a few days here and decide you've had enough and go somewhere else' and with reference to one particular yacht 'I've seen people diving into the sea off the back'.

What the excursion to the port and market indicates is, firstly, that by being shown yachts in a place that is more expensive than Palmanova and Magaluf, the tourists are being shown their place in the world and their class identity is being reinforced. Yachts are items that the people on the trip are unlikely to be able to afford; they can only be objects of desire. The presence of the yachts in both Andtrax and in the bay at Palmanova fuel a fantasy of what life could be like, in Vicky's case associated with a freedom to move at will.

The fantasies associated with yachts and their reality as a commodity are in direct contrast to the experience and goods of the market. People have two hours in the market, twice as long as at the port. The space of the market is enclosed and claustrophobic and the tourists are being brought into contact with 'bargains' (people are told they can haggle when the trip is being sold, which serves to reinforce this idea). There is pressure to buy. This is not just in the practice of some of the vendors, which at times is aggressive, and the time limit set by the tour company, although clearly this can be circumvented; but also in the way in which the space is constructed as enclosed and difficult to move around. This is compared to the open seas, sea breezes and freedom to move on represented by yachts, which are described as luxury items.

The yachts act as cultural markers. To dream of having one means that a desire to obtain such an object has been instilled and individuals are given something to aim for which they might achieve by continuing the work effort. When speaking to the man from South Wales who felt out of place in his hotel, he complained about the large number of beggars at home. 'There are a lot of beggars in Bournemouth. I don't understand it ... they could at least wash dishes. You've got to make something of yourself'. The reference to 'making something of yourself', fits into the ideal of the self-made 'man' prominent in free-market capitalism.

Not only is identity confirmed or displayed in the spatial differences between Palmanova and Magaluf, but also in the different spatial practices between the market and the port. The former is constructed around active consumption, the latter more passive. The enclosure of the market acts to keep people in their place quite literally. The feelings that some of the tourists experienced in the market are also found in Magaluf. In a similar way to that of the tourists who felt out of place in a hotel in Cala Vinyes rather than their expected all-inclusive hotel in Magaluf, the visit to the port can potentially undermine ontological security. By contrast, Palmanova and Magaluf do not pose such threats as they are seen to offer a familiar, comfortable and, therefore, secure environment.

In connection to the spatial distribution of the coaches used to take tourists to and from the market, those for the tour operators are parked in a car park that is next door to the market. Tourists on an independent trip are faced with a walk, albeit a short one, which is longer than the walk for the tour operators' tourists. This illustrates the dominance of the tour operators who are able to bring their clients virtually into the market. However, slipping out of their control and consuming the excursion independently is punishable with increased physical exertion. In addition, one's place outside the 'fold' of the tour operator is marked by the outside location of the independent buses, the need to cross the bridge to the space of the market by foot, which the tour operator bus drives over.

## Summary

This chapter began with a consideration of some of the place names in Magaluf. It starts with those that have a military connection or overtones and suggests what their presence in Magaluf indicates about the construction of British identity in this context. The discussion of Pirates Adventure examines the ways in which some of these ideas are acted out both in the performance of a play directed at the British and in the way that the audience then deals with these ideas. The appeal is to an identity based on violent behaviour that is conformist in terms of the roles attributed to women and in terms of male–female relationships. It shows a dislike of the other, which is exercised in the aggressive attention aimed at Jacques Laffite. The show also conveys notions about territorial possession and connects with a romanticised historical image of conflict and land ownership between Britain and some of her European neighbours. At the same time, pirates occupy liminal spaces in that they operate on the edge of society. This mirrors the idea of tourists being in a liminal state (Graburn, 1989). In addition, the pirates embody the ideals of patriotism and freedom associated with the British national character. Pirates Adventure also carries latent ideas of humiliation and subjugation that can be coupled with attempts to control and possess. The tourists are, on the one hand, being reminded of the characteristics of freedom fighters and the need to resist outside domination, but then need to be reminded of their place as customers of tour operators who are brought on to be thanked at the end of the show. The subjugation and humiliation serves to remind the tourists of their vulnerability and need to be within the fold of commercial enterprises.

Ideas relating to possession or ownership were then explored. Consideration of the terms and their relationship to property allows concepts of identity and fear of the other to be further examined in the focus on the relationship between the British and the Germans. Property ownership is used to consider codes of behaviour, in that the temporary possession of the hotel room is seen by some tourists as giving them rights above others. 'Misbehaviour' is interpreted as disrespectful of those rights and continued possession (that is, loyalty to a particular hotel) should be rewarded with an extension of rights.

The question of loyalty also illustrates that holidays present opportunities for more than the fleeting casual relationships portrayed in ideas such as 'Shagaluf'. In addition, the desire to return to the same hotel, and in one case the same apartment room, year after year indicates that the purchase of these items is not, as Urry (1995: 131–132) suggests, 'incidental', but rather integral to the holiday experience. The feeling of familiarity also brings with it a sense of belonging, which is also linked to knowledge and 'knowing one's place'. The notion of *habitus* is brought to the distinctions made between all-inclusive holiday makers and half or full-board customers. *Habitus* is further explored in relation to the visit to Andratx market and port. Here, the contrasting experiences of the two spaces serve, in the case of the market, to show the tourists their controlled, uniform, bargain-hunter identity compared to the possibility of the freedom to roam on the open seas if only they were rich enough to afford a yacht. The role of the tour operator is never far away as their close mediation of this experience for a large number of tourists indicates.

The chapter demonstrates that tourists' experiences evoke the idea of going forth to dominate the other. This links to a nostalgic understanding of Britain's role in the world during the time of Empire building. In essence, there is a feeling of a return to greatness, which, at the same time, allows for feelings of belonging and unity in the face of a common enemy. Identity can thus be reaffirmed as the other becomes a point around which the collective can congregate to repel. As such, boundaries between the in-group and the out-group are re-established and upheld.

The point of *re-establishing* boundaries connects to the notion, as does looking to the past, that there is a sense of loss felt in the home world of the tourists or a feeling of threat from the other in the form of immigrants and the European Union. In Pirates Adventure, the British become the winners, they wrest back control from the other and re-create order. The British are in charge and women know their rightful place as serving men, whether it be washing the dishes or making available their bodies for men's gratification.

All of this takes place within a commercial setting. Feelings of a 'winning Britain' are bought into – it is a commodity that the tourists buy from tour operators. The feeling of belonging to a collective, in the form of the nation, is purchased. Tourists are reminded time and again of their roles as consumers. For example, at Andratx market they are taken to an environment in which the goods on offer are generally within their spending power. Then they are taken to the port where the luxury yachts are displayed. The desire to want to consume more is instilled as the tourists are brought into comparison with those who have greater accessibility to more expensive objects of consumption. The contrast is that the buying of 'everyday' products does not give the freedom or satisfaction that consumerism is oft claimed to provide. If the tourists had more, they could experience the autonomy of the open seas. The need to remain compliant in the capitalist system is inculcated.

## Notes

1. 'Space' is conceptually challenging in that what is meant by the word is not straightforward. Indeed, Urry (1995: 66) contends that 'there is no simple space' and Shields (1999: 154) notes, 'Space has been understood in vastly different ways dating back to medieval scholasticism'. Another problem is that many of the issues relating to space are discussed under the terms 'landscape' and 'place' in the academic literature. As Corsín Jiménez's (2003: 138) observes, '[a]nthropologists grounded their discussions on space, and they did so through the idioms of place and landscape'. Given this scenario, space, landscape and place will be used interchangeably in the text of this book.
2. Although this probably more accurately refers to the English, but the way in which history is represented the military folklore is all encompassing.
3. During one evening's entertainment in this hotel, four couples were in competition with each other. Only one set was married and happened to be the only childless couple.
4. Vindaloo was a popular song, a sort of anthem for the English during the 1998 World Cup competition, and could often be heard in Magaluf and Palmanova.
5. Although the song related to the presence of the English football team in the World Cup, it was also sung by other nationalities in the resorts, including the Scottish.
6. On WWW at http://despina.advanced.org/16438/fact/general.htm, 1999.
7. I am not referring to possession or ownership in the true legalistic meaning, i.e. that the tourists have deeds to property, but rather in how they *feel* about where they are and the 'rights' they think are attached to their experience. As part of the holiday package, they rent accommodation that forms part of their experience and thus they have paid for that experience. If they have no ownership of their experiences, surely they do not have responsibility for them and is it possible to only rent experiences?
8. A contrary position can be found in the work of Marx (1845: 51–53, in Jordan, 1971: 143), who suggested that 'freedom' for the proletariat would arise from the abolition of 'what makes it the proletariat, i.e., private property'.
9. Famous in the UK for his establishment and ownership of nightclubs. His appearance in British television programmes and his connections with attractive young women have made him a celebratory associated with a glamorous lifestyle.

**Appendix**

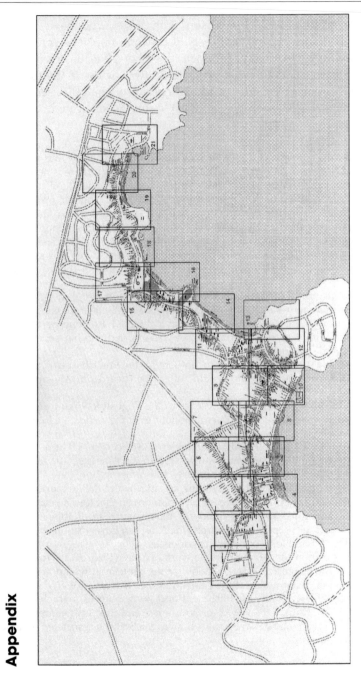

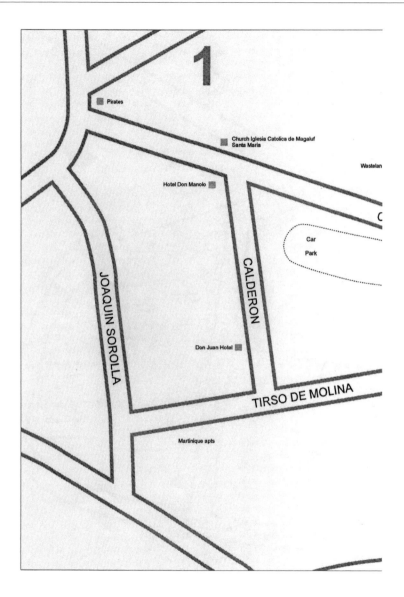

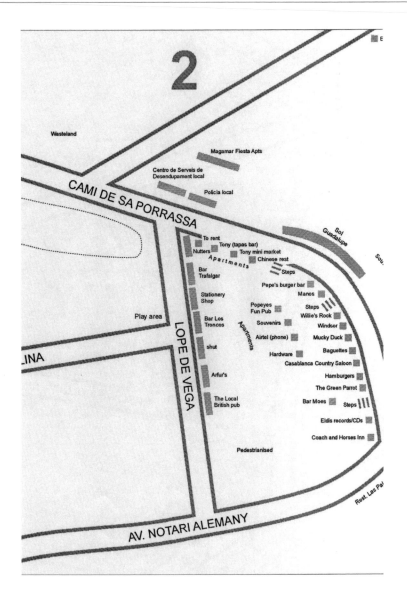

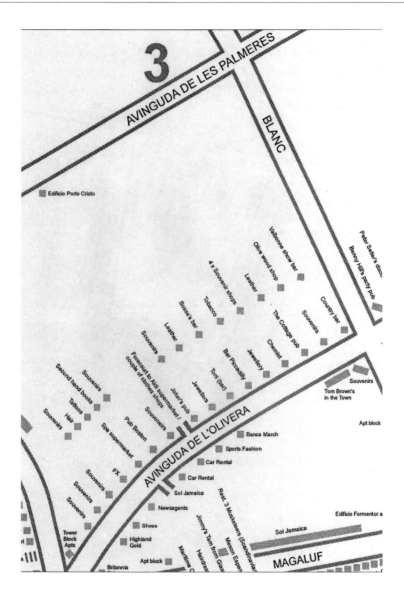

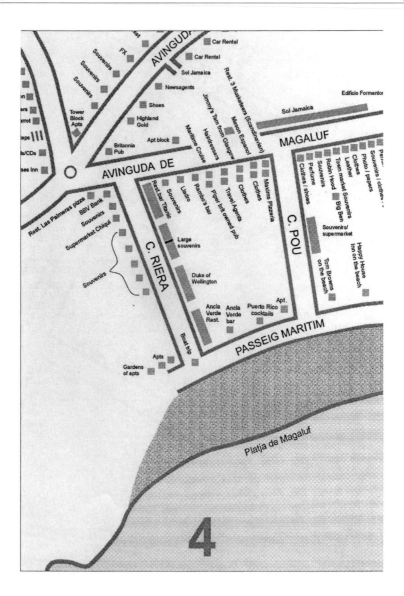

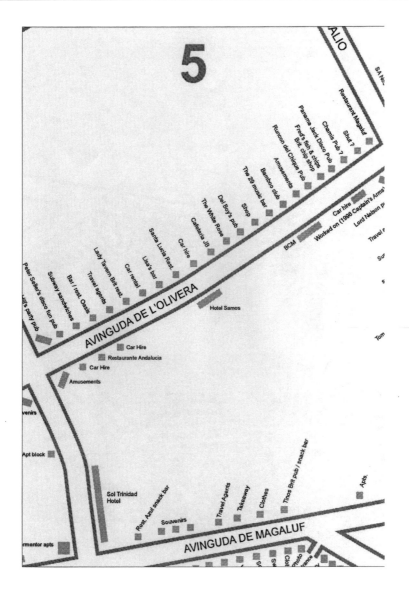

5

ALIO

SA No

Restaurant Magaluf
Stud ?
Chamis Pub ?
Panama Jack Disco Pub
Fred's fish & chips
Brit. chip shop
Runcon del Chique Pub
Amusements
Bamboo club
The 29 music bar
Shop
Del Boy's pub
The White Rose
Cafeteria JB
Car hire
Santa Lucia Rest.
Lisa's bar
Car rental
Lady Tavern Brit rest.
Travel agents
Bar / rest. Oasis
Subway sandwiches
Peter Safari's disco fun pub
Bill's party pub

Car hire
Worked on (1998 Captain's Arms'
Lord Nelson p
BCM
Travel r
Sur
s

AVINGUDA DE L'OLIVERA

Hotel Samos

Car Hire
Restaurante Andalucia
Car Hire
Amusements

venirs

Apt block

Sol Trinidad
Hotel

Tom

Rest. Azul snack bar
Souvenirs
Travel Agents
Takeaway
Clothes
Tinos Brit pub / snack bar

Apts.

mentor apts

AVINGUDA DE MAGALUF

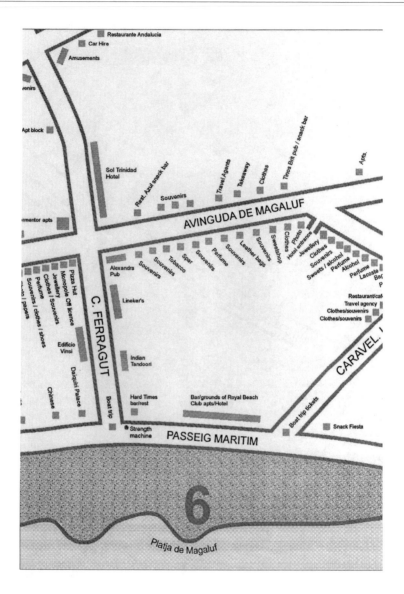

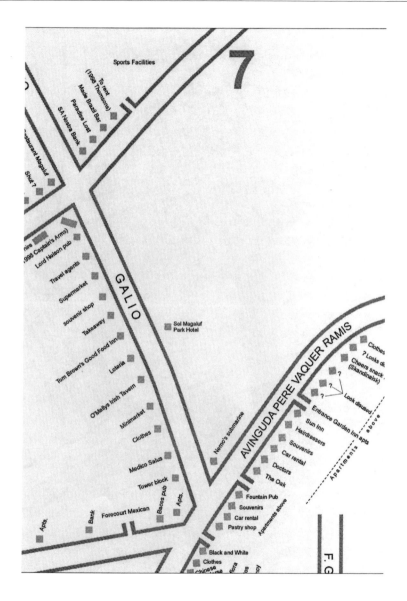

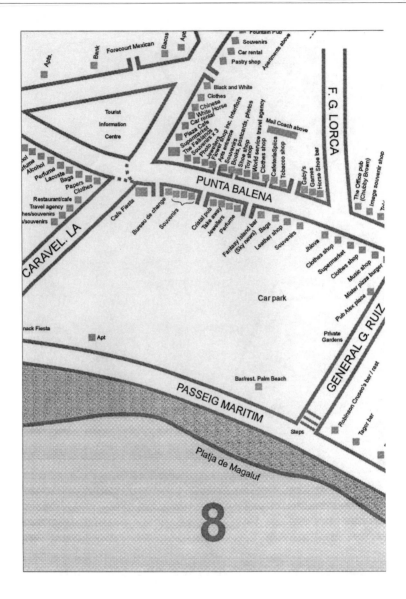

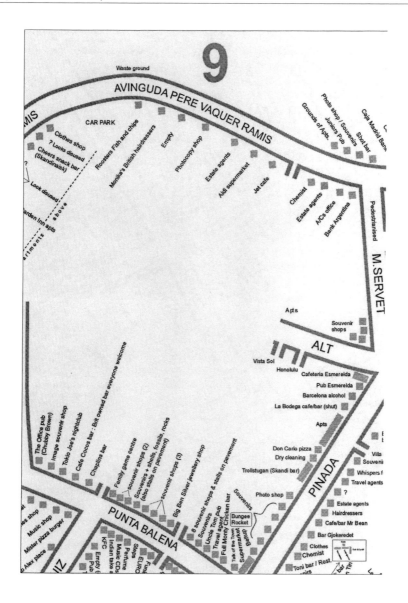

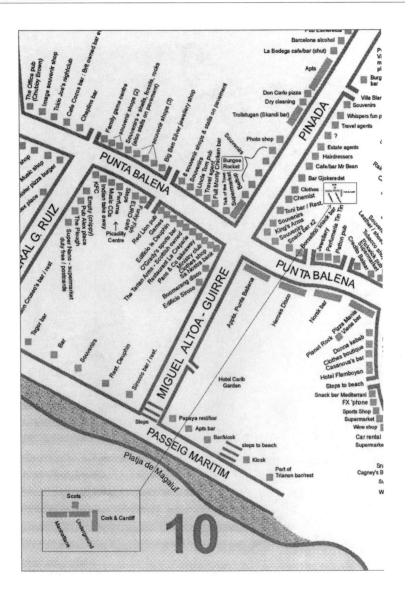

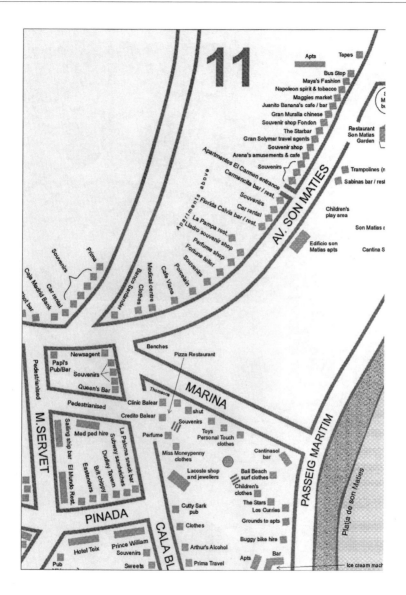

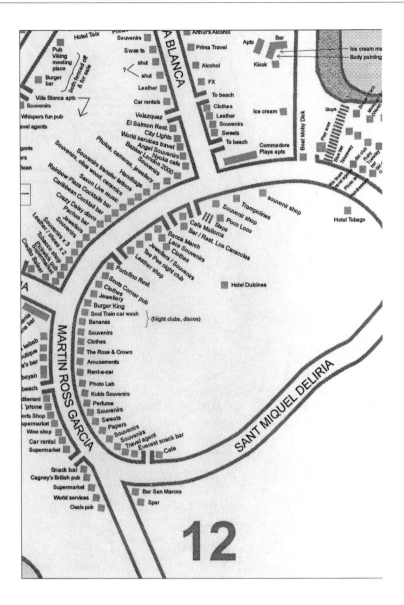

Hotel Teix
Prima
Souvenirs
Sweets
Pub
Viking
meeting
place
shut
Burger
bar
? shut
Leather
Villa Blanca apts
Souvenirs
Whispers fun pub
Car rentals
avel agents
Velazquez
El Salmon Rest.
gents
City Lights
World services travel
rs
Photos, cameras, etc
Bazaar London 2000
Bean
Souvenirs, olive wood, ceramics
Angel Souvenirs
Nyoka cafe
Souvenirs transfer tattoos
Handbags
Rainbow Plaza Cocktails bar
Saxon Live music
Caribbean Cocktail bar
Crazy Daisy disco
Pachas bar
Jewellers
Souvenirs x3
Leather / shoes x 2
Tobacco shop
Chiswick Pub
Supermarket
Credito Balear
A

MARTIN ROSS GARCIA

ria
ina bar
kebab
outique
a's bar
boyan
beach
diterrani
'phone
orts Shop
upermarket
Wine shop
Car rental
Supermarket
Snack bar
Cagney's British pub
Supermarket
World services
Oasis pub

Portofino Rest
Scots Corner pub
Clothes
Jewellery
Burger King
Soul Train car wash
Bananas
Souvenirs
Clothes
The Rose & Crown
Amusements
Rent-a-car
Photo Lab
Kukis Souvenirs
Perfume
Souvenirs
Sweets
Papers
Souvenirs
Souvenirs
Travel agent
Everest snack bar
Cafe

} (Night clubs, discos)

Bar San Marcos
Spar

A BLANCA

Arthur's Alcohol
Prima Travel
Apts
Bar
Alcohol
Kiosk
FX
To beach
Clothes
Leather
Ice cream
Souvenirs
Sweets
To beach
Commadore
Playa apts

Trampolines
Souvenir shop
Souvenir shop
Poco Loco
Cafe Mallorca
Steps
Bar / Rest. Los Caracoles
Banca March
Lace Souvenirs
Clothes
Jewellers / Souvenirs
Tee Pee night club
Leather shop

souvenir shop

Boat Moby Dick
Steps

Hotel Tobago

Hotel Dulcinea

SANT MIQUEL DELIRIA

Ice cream me
Body painting

12

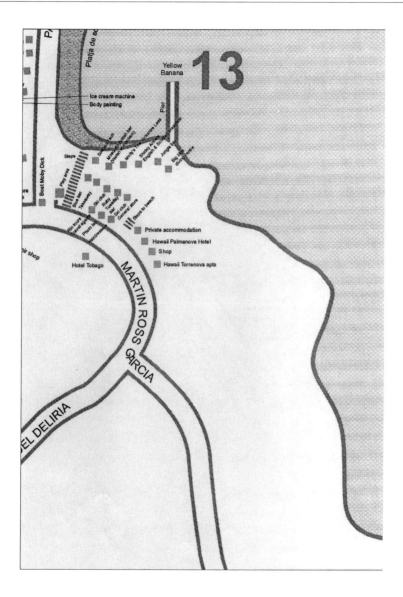

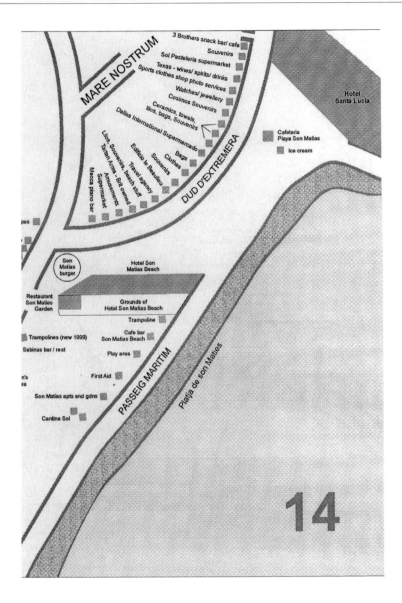

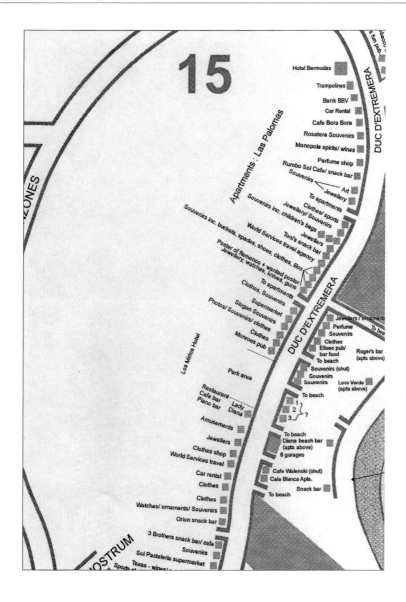

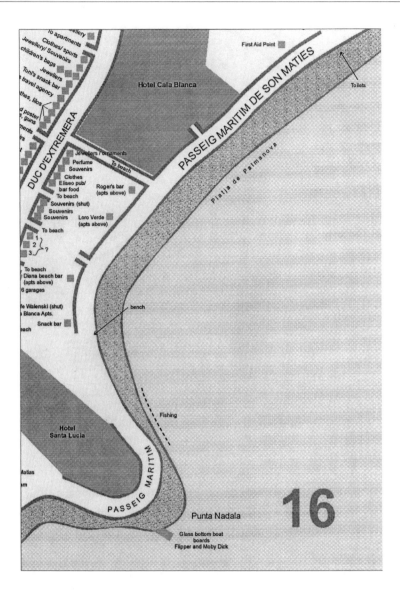

To apartments
Clothes
Jewellery/ sports
Jewellery/ Souvenirs
children's bags
Jewellers
Toni's snack bar
travel agency
thes, lilos
d poster
e, guns
ments
rs

First Aid Point

Hotel Cala Blanca

PASSEIG MARITIM DE SON MATIES

Toilets

DUC D'EXTREMERA

Platja de Palmanova

Jewellers / ornaments
Perfume
Souvenirs
Clothes
Eliseo pub/       Roger's bar
bar food          (apts above)
To beach

To beach

Souvenirs (shut)
Souvenirs
Souvenirs         Loro Verde
                  (apts above)
To beach

1
2      ?
3

To beach
Diana beach bar
(apts above)
6 garages

bench

e Walenski (shut)
Blanca Apts.
        Snack bar
each

Fishing

Hotel
Santa Lucia

PASSEIG MARITIM

Aatias
m

Punta Nadala

**16**

Glass bottom boat
boards
Flipper and Moby Dick

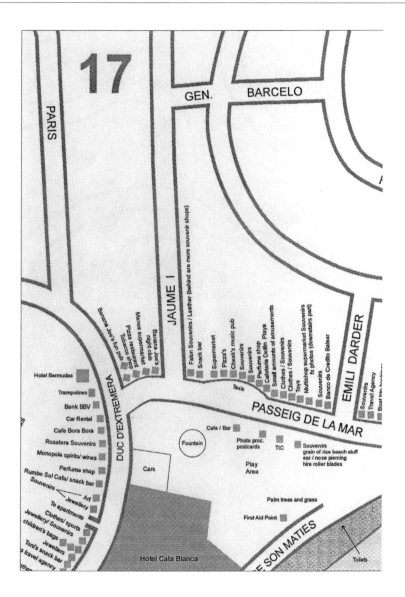

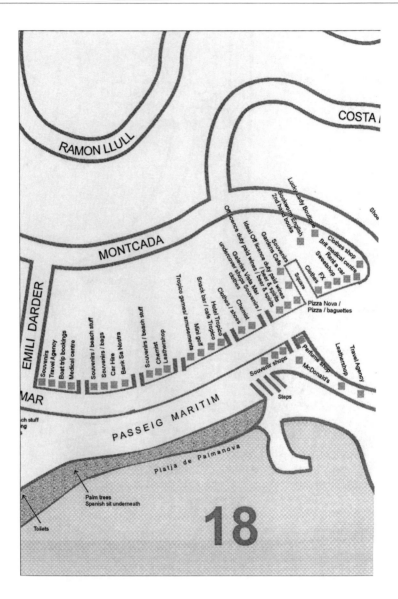

RAMON LLULL

COSTA

MONTCADA

EMILI DARDER

MAR

ch stuff
ng

Souvenirs
Travel Agency
Boat trip bookings
Medical centre

Souvenirs / beach stuff
Souvenirs / bags
Car Hire
Bank Sa Nostra

Souvenirs / beach stuff
Chemist
Leathershop

Mini golf

Tropico games/ amusements

Snack bar / cafe Tropico

Hotel Tropico

Clothes / shoes

Chemist

Galerias Vista Mar
undercover shops Souvenirs/
clothes

Ideal Off licence duty paid wines / beer & spirits

Off licence duty paid wines / beer & spirits

Gardens Cafe

Souvenirs

Bookworm/English
2nd hand books

Lucky Lady Boutique

Clothes shop

Brit medical centre
Rent a car
Sweatshop

Clothes

Shoe

FX

Square

Pizza Nova /
Pizza / baguettes

Souvenir shops

Steps

Perfume shop

McDonald's

Leathershop

Travel Agency

PASSEIG MARITIM

Platja de Palmanova

Palm trees
Spanish sit underneath

Toilets

18

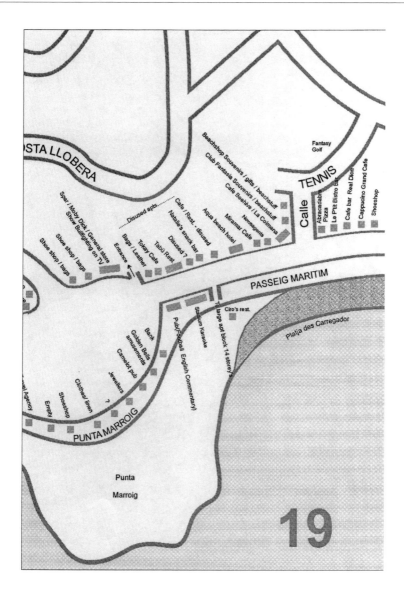

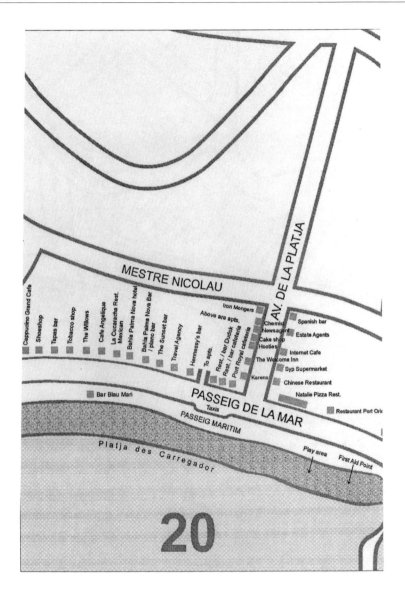

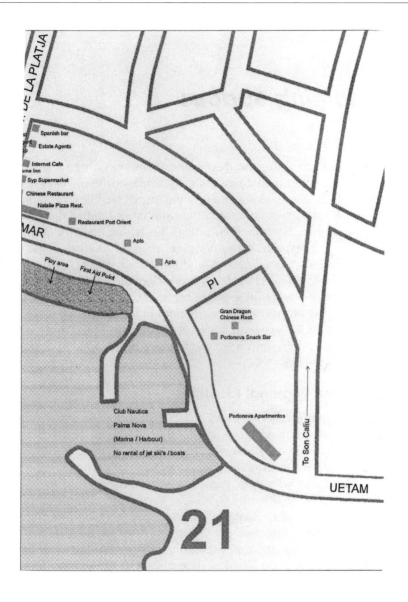

DE LA PLATJA

Spanish bar

Estate Agents

Internet Cafe
ome Inn

Syp Supermarket

Chinese Restaurant

Natalie Pizza Rest.

Restaurant Port Orient

MAR

Apts

Play area   First Aid Point

Apts

PI

Gran Dragon
Chinese Rest.

Portonova Snack Bar

Club Nautica

Palma Nova

(Marina / Harbour)

No rental of jet ski's / boats

Portonova Apartmentos

To Son Caliu

UETAM

21

# Chapter 4
# *Consuming Spaces*

## Introduction

This chapter continues the discussion of the encoding of space. By again working within the framework of symbolic analysis, I examine the meanings attached to names given to some tourist facilities. I explore the way in which identity is manifest in the national and regional naming of café-bars and how these are then articulated by the tourists. A similar method is used to explore the associations attached to ideas of the rural under the category 'Cosy England' and its relationship to constructions of national identity. This chapter also considers the differences between the two resorts and what these might represent in terms of identity and behaviour. Lastly, I focus on the beach, both in terms of what it signifies and in relation to the experiential facets of tourism. The chapter begins with a focus on national and regional identities represented in the names of the resort café-bars.

## National and Regional Identities

The names in this class are listed in Table 3.1. The names act like those in the section on military names in that they are a way of labelling the spaces of Magaluf and Palmanova. The majority of the café-bar names discussed in the encoding of the landscape says something about identity. The reason why these names have been categorised specifically under ethnic/regional identity is because they relate directly to places, e.g. 'Molly's the Yorkshire Lass' and 'Scots Corner'. Names like 'Big Ben', with a model of the tower on the top of the café (Figure 4.1), and 'The Underground', with signs that are easily recognisable as modelled on those that appear on the London tube network, act as signifiers of a specific place – London. In the case of the 'City Lights', the reference to a place does not become clear until entering the small bar and seeing the mural sky-line of London painted on the bar walls. The overall message is the provision of the familiar, names that are easily recognisable and include places in the UK that some people may have a real attachment to. The Dudley Tavern is owned, and often patronised, by people from that

**Figure 4.1** Big Ben, Magaluf

town or its region. The bar, like many other establishments, has a sign proclaiming the nationality of its owners (Figures 4.2 and 4.3). Also, like many other facilities, it states that there is 'cooking like mum's'. The combination of a statement of national identity and the idea of mother gives the nation a female identity. This is borne out in the name of a pub in Magaluf called Britannia.

Britannia is the Latin name for Britain. The personification of the land mass was first used by the Romans on coinage in which Britannia was depicted as a female figure. The image continues to be used on some Bank of England notes and coinage in the present day. The symbol of Britannia with sword and shield at once places her with the militaristic symbols already discussed. At the same time, in her seated position, she is a passive figure and while she undoubtedly connotes patriotism and conquest (as in 'Britannia Rule the Waves'), her role as a mother figure also casts her as a defender and protector.

**Figure 4.2** Cafe signs declaring British ownership

**Figure 4.3** Prince William mini

'British Owned' frequently appears on signs in the two resorts. Some are even more specific, for example, one facility in Magaluf called 'Jimmy's' also states 'Tam from Glasgow'. Another example is a shop selling items crafted from olive wood, which states that it is 'Geordie Owned' and 'We also Speak English'. This proclamation, like Molly's the Yorkshire Lass, speaks directly of a specific place. The reference to also speaking English goes further in that it highlights a regional identity distinct from other areas of the UK. This 'regionalism' is expressed elsewhere not only in the names of facilities, e.g. Eastenders, Windsor and The Geordie Pride, but also in the activities of some of the tourists and their thoughts about their place in the UK.

The Geordie Pride is in Magaluf. It is, like many of the bars, small. Inside, there is Newcastle football regalia pinned to the walls and ceilings. In 2009, there was a display of trophies behind which was a picture of a pig asleep in a hammock. Outside, the televisions are housed in boxes decorated in the Newcastle football strip. This shrine-like quality is found in other bars, e.g. The Cork and Cardiff,[1] resplendent with its symbols of Wales and Ireland (Figure 4.4).

One of the most obvious ways in which these identities are lived and embodied is in the wearing of football shirts that show allegiance to a particular team. This is expressed on a national level (particularly during the 1998 World Cup), but also on a local level with the shirts of teams including Manchester United, Arsenal and Newcastle being worn mainly

**Figure 4.4** Outside the Cork & Cardiff

by adult males. The Newcastle strip is one of the most popular. The representation of a country or town by the success of a football team gives a sense of identity to the supporters as 'the best' and links to ideas of heroism. The support of a team is no guarantee that the person derives from the city it represents, but in the contexts of Magaluf and Palmanova it is a fair indication of the origin of the wearers.

The sense of fidelity to regional identity is not just expressed through items of clothing. Many 'warm-up' sessions in entertainment venues and hotels attempt to use identification with place as a way to engage the audience: asking people to cheer or shout for their town or region is a common tactic. In addition, one of the most frequently used opening gambits of PRs[2] is to ask 'where ya from?' On learning this, some will attempt to adjust their accents to sound, e.g. more Geordie or Scouse. Another tactic is to identify with the potential customer by reference to, for example, a city or well-known attraction of the region.

The sense of loyalty to one's 'home' town or region is not just about stating it in the wearing of a football shirt or cheering for a place name, but also in the creation of an other. In the discussion about property and possession, a conversation with a couple from Hull was noted in which they expressed dislike of the idea of people from London (with a 'bad' reputation) being housed in empty council housing in *their* city. The divide that they created was also manifest in their perception of the way of life in London being different from their own. The idea of difference based on region, but particularly that of the so-called north-south divide, is articulated by other tourists in the resorts. For example, Jill from Yorkshire says, 'in London everyone is rushing around, Yorkshire is more laid back'. These understandings of what a place is become practised in the lived experience of people. As Shields (1991: 245) notes, 'the mythology of the British North has been appropriated and re-worked in indigenous narratives, which have made this mythical "North" into their own regional identity'.

The names discussed are statements of identity. Not only do the names in this category state a national identity, but some also make reference to regional identities within the UK. This occurs in the form of direct connections to the countries of the UK, e.g. Scots Corner, Cork and Cardiff[3] and SospanFach (Welsh for 'little saucepan'), while others point to a more localised identity – The Geordie Pride, Dudley Tavern and Eastenders. The differences between the areas of the nation state that the names refer to are acknowledged by some tourists who use the imagined geography of the homeland to construct their identities in marking oppositions that are thought to inform the identity of the other. Carter *et al.* have noted:

> The construction of Englishness as an identity has involved not only a celebration of the geographical integrity of the nation-state, but also an assertion of its opposition to other communities and identities through narratives of empire and exotic others. (Carter *et al.*, 1993: viii)

In relation to the names with a military background and the exercise of empire acted out in Pirates Adventure, Carter *et al.*'s observation is pertinent. However, the complexity of Englishness (and Britishness) as an identity must also recognise the differences present within it as exemplified by the regional identities marked in the names of some of the facilities and lived in the actions and attitudes of some of the tourists. Indeed, Daniels (1991: 96) argues that 'the region' is 'an important ingredient in the making – and unmaking – of national identity'. However, he goes on to note that 'landscape has played a key role in articulating English identity', and that the associated image, constructed mainly in the last century, is one of a 'vernacular, agrarian, home-counties countryside' (Daniels, 1991: 98). This link to the rural lays the foundation for the next section.

## Cosy England

The purpose of grouping these names together is that they conjure up images of rural England in a past time. The names in this classification make reference to *The Countryside Ideal* (Bunce, 1994) and an association with nature which 'especially when set in the cosy landscapes of lowland England, served to define much of the essence of the countryside ideal, and indeed of the national character as a whole' (Bunce, 1994: 47).

Again, it is not possible to examine every name in detail. However some general observations can be made. Many of the names are linked to a time before mechanisation – Coach and Horses Inn, The Plough and Mail Coach. The use of the word Inn is similar to the use of Tavern in being a reference to past times. The idea of welcome (Andrews, 2000) speaks of a Gemeinschaft community that all of the names conjure up, associated as they are with the rural world in which close, emotional ties were supposed to have existed.

One female tourist in her twenties claims, 'the thing about holiday is that everyone is really nice, happy, friendly, everyone wants to know where you're from'. Another tourist comments to an expatriate waitress, 'everyone's so friendly here saying hello, you don't get that at home'. The waitress agrees saying, 'the trouble is no-one there's got time anymore'.[4] Craig, a male tourist, also expresses dissatisfaction with England but for different reasons. During one conversation with him and his wife Jill, the topic of tourists' motivations is discussed. Jill's immediate response is 'people come for the weather'. However, Craig states 'it's because of British bureaucracy'. He goes on to say that 'we're supposed to be a member of the EEC but we're not governed by the same rules . . . we can't drink all day'. He compares the price of a bottle of whisky in the UK to one in Spain and goes on to do the same with petrol and cigarettes and claims that the government 'is screwing the taxpayers' and 'if we're a member of Europe the prices should be equivalent all the way through'. He concludes, 'if live in Britain like that, will move, sell house and move to Spain' and 'if Great Britain . . . not great Britain . . . bureaucratic want to move, we live in an oppressive society'.[5] The view of the home world as less liberal than the experience found in Mallorca is echoed by a younger male tourist. When discussing nightclubs, I ask 'why is it different from going to a nightclub in the UK?' His reply is, 'you couldn't go to a nightclub in t-shirt and shorts, they are too strict in England, here there are no restrictions'. However, one aspect to emerge from this is the idea that aspects of Britishness can be recreated in Magaluf and Palmanova, which make people feel British but, at the same time, places them outside or on the edge (as in Pirates Adventure) of British society per se.

The appeal to heritage is made by the use of the word 'tradition' as in the 'Traditional Fish and Chips' sold at the British Chippy, and the stating of the date of establishment of some facilities. For example, the sign for 'Arthurs Alcohol' carries the information that it was established in 1984, and Pickwicks declares itself the oldest pub in Magaluf. Further, the idea of history also provides a form of assurance and comfort in what is essentially an alien environment. Many of the names already discussed and others on the list convey familiarity, taken as they are from popular culture and therefore stand in contrast to the unknown other, e.g. Car Wash, Ministry, The Office, Talk of the Town, Uncle Tom Pub, Hard Times, Karen's, Fred's Fish and Chips. All contribute to encoding the spaces of Palmanova and Magaluf with words that the British are likely to be well acquainted. Attendant with familiarity is the amicable 'chumminess' of the Gemeinschaft community.

Some of the familiar names of facilities are appealing because they pertain to a sense of 'fun'. Among these names are Benny Hills Party Pub, Peter Sellers[6] Disco Fun Pub and Del Boys Pub. These are all well-known British comedy figures. The sense of fun is added to by the broadcasting, in both resorts, of *Only Fools and Horses* in which Del Boy is the central character, Billy Connolly's stand-up routines, *Mr Bean* and Roy Chubby Brown. Chubby Brown is shown on television screens in the bar called The Office.

Other café-bar names that link to this idea of the ludic are Crazy Daisy's Disco, Poco Loco (a little mad), Nutters, Cheeks Fun Pub and Banana Joes Fun Pub. The point is that the appearance of these names code the spaces of Magaluf and Palmanova, giving meaning and fixing them as places of fun. At the same time, fun becomes a commodity, something that is bought into, as the advert for med-ped (mopeds) hire proclaims 'we rent fun' (Figure 4.5). Fun, therefore, is something that is

**Figure 4.5** Sign stating 'We rent fun'

purchased. It is not spontaneous, but is hired in the form of a motorised bike and mediated in the form of the 'fun pub' where the in-house DJs orchestrate 'party games' for the tourists.

A key theme to emerge from the category of Cosy England is the underlying notion of nostalgia, itself based on a notion of a 'rural idyll' (Wright, 1985). Such ideas link with those discussed at the beginning of the book about the trope of travel and the urge to find a paradisical or utopian existence. Such a landscape needs protecting. As Rose (1993) notes of some of the call to arms in World War II, an appeal was made based on the need to defend the sanctity of the rural landscape. She also observes that this rural landscape is one that has been masculinised and, drawing on work by Pollard (no date), on ethnic exclusivity.

The majority of the names discussed so far appear in Magaluf. The presence of the names there and not in Palmanova gives an indication of the physical differences between the two resorts, although the experiential aspects are found in both. Nevertheless, there is a difference between the two places, which is discussed in the next section.

## Differences Between Palmanova and Magaluf

Although Palmanova and Magaluf are intimately linked resorts in that they run into one another and they both accommodate overwhelmingly British tourists, there are differences between the two places. These differences are manifest in both their physical natures and the tourists that inhabit them. This section will explore some of these differences, allowing, at the same time, the ideas of boundaries, enclosure and disorientation to be explored.

In the first place, both Palmanova and Magaluf are distinctly bounded areas. The base map (p. 80) shows that the sea forms a natural barrier to the south-east and that the road network forms a barrier to the north, running from east to west. The effect is the creation of a zone that is enclosed and separate from the rest of the island. The idea of enclosure is accentuated by the way in which differences between the resorts and other parts of Mallorca are painted. This occurs, for example, in the portrayal of other resorts as German dominated, difficult to access or out of reach. The reality is that the areas are connected to the rest of the island through the movements of people, legislation, road and communication networks.

The discussion of the excursion to Andratx market highlighted feelings of claustrophobia experienced by some tourists. The sense of being in a confined space is also evident in some tourists' visits to

Magaluf and is a chief marker of understandings of its difference from Palmanova. The main drag of Magaluf, Punta Balena, is built up on both sides of the road. There is no view of the sea and many of the facilities appear in layers and as densely packed together. By contrast, Palmanova is more open with a sea vista possible from the main road.

The relationship between the two resorts in terms of the practice and creation of identity comes about in several ways. Firstly, the particularly British character of Magaluf although not entirely absent from Palmanova, is less pronounced. Secondly, the tourists in Palmanova represent a more cosmopolitan background in that, although mainly British, other nationalities are easily distinguishable. This also reflects the relationship between hotels and tour operators. For example, both the Santa Lucia and Son Maties (in Palmanova) have an entirely British clientele because their dealings are exclusively with British-based tour operators. During the course of a welcome meeting in one of the hotels, the tour operator representative (rep) advises: 'this is an English hotel, everyone has come from England and everyone speaks English so it's safe to talk to people'. On another occasion, I am advised by the same rep that 'this is a very friendly hotel, everyone is English [pause] oh we had some Americans, so we do get other nationalities'. The rep's words were trying to provide reassurance that the hotel was not populated with an unknown other that the tourists would not be able to communicate with. Language, in all its forms (words and symbols), is a way of structuring experience. An unfamiliar language would go some way to prohibiting that ability. On the other hand, the lack of an unfamiliar language also inhibits experimentation, improvisation and difference. However, not all tourists appreciate the single nationality approach. One man, staying in the Santa Lucia, advises that although he likes the hotel, 'I was a bit dubious because it's all English and I prefer a little bit of a mix of other nationalities'.

The Cala Blanca, also in Palmanova, takes tourists from a range of countries and has only one British tour operator working in the hotel. The international element of the Cala Blanca is reflected in the hotel entertainment, which is conducted in French, German, Dutch, and Danish, as well as English. During the summer months, the evening entertainment in the Cala Blanca is outdoors. In the Son Maties and Santa Lucia, however, it is always indoors, which reinforces the sense of control over and definition of boundaries around the tourists.

There are also differences in the way that the hotels mark their boundaries. The Cala Blanca denotes the end of its territory with a low wall, making it is possible for people from the outside to see over. It has open access to the beach. Although other hotels in the Sol group have different types of boundary markers, e.g. the Guadalupe in Magaluf has a high concrete wall, it is worth noting that in Palmanova the three main hotels are different. The ones dominated by UK operators have greater boundary controls. Both the Santa Lucia and Son Maties have a glass wall. The latter also has a secured metal gate. All of the boundaries allow people to see in and out, and, like all fences, are designed to keep people in as well as out.

Boundaries can also take the form of both spoken and written language. During the 1998 World Cup, England's games were broadcast from many bars in Magaluf. The Red Lion is one such bar. It becomes very crowded during the first game. As the audience is waiting for the game to begin, some are singing Vindaloo and the in-house DJ is attempting to engage with the fans. Two people walk by and as they do, one starts to video the scene. On seeing him, the DJ holds up a sign saying 'Fuck off', at which the man ceases recording. Similar boundaries are also erected by the simple declaration of 'British Owned'.

The greatest exertion of control in a spatial sense is in Magaluf with its feeling of claustrophobia and the actual physical enclosure of the space. The contrasts between Palmanova and Magaluf are used to construct differences in terms of identity by some tourists. Tourists in Magaluf are sometimes described as 'animalistic' or as 'animals' because of their association with violence. Complaints about the behaviour of some of the tourists are not restricted to those staying in Palmanova. One woman, staying in Magaluf, explains as she watches the England match in The Red Lion, that it is something she and her family would not normally do; 'but we've come for the atmosphere'. She goes on to say that 'Magaluf at night is terrible. I think the language is shocking. They [the other tourists] are a different class of people'. She explains that the holiday is for her daughter in celebration of her degree and 'normally she [the daughter] wouldn't have anything to do with such people, she wouldn't normally entertain them, she would want someone educated like herself'. In this respect, the woman is constructing her class identity or *habitus* in opposition to the other tourists around her, based on their activities in a particular place. What people do means that space and place are experientially constructed, involving all the senses. One of the main forms of distinction between the two resorts comes through the auditory senses related to noise, which forms part of the next section.

## Experiential Constructions of Space and Place

For many of the tourists, one of the defining aspects of Magaluf is the noise. What noise is, is open to interpretation, meaning different things to different people. However, it appears to be generally accepted as '*any annoying or unwanted sound*' (Rodda, 1967: 2, italics in original). Noise is one of the experiential aspects that contribute to marking space and give it an identity as a place. Schafer (1985), drawing on the work of the anthropologist Edmund Carpenter (1960), points out how the sound of the church bell or the voice of the muezzin calling the faithful to prayer defines the contours of parish or local community. The ordering of physical and geographical space through the primacy and range of acoustic space can thus be applied with equal validity to the 'sounds-capes' of Magaluf and Palmanova.

The lack of sleep attributed to noise is often given as a reason for being glad to go home or for thinking of revisiting at a different, quieter time of year. However, the most notable comments about noise are those made in relation to the differences between Magaluf and Palmanova. The proprietor of one set of holiday apartments in Palmanova explains that he tells the young tourists: 'You can make noise in Magaluf but you must be quiet when you get back to the flats'. One young couple explain their decision to stay in Palmanova, 'we can be quiet but if we want to we can go to Magaluf'.

Two tourists, who live in Devon, compare the noise that spills over from Magaluf into Palmanova when tourists are returning to their accommodation in the early hours of the morning. The woman says, 'from three to sixish they all come along making noise. I know they've got to have a good time'. Her husband explains, about their home, 'at night you wouldn't hear a pin drop we've come here for the noise'. By contrast, two women complain about the lack of noise in their hotel in Palmanova, 'you feel like you have to whisper, come 12 o'clock everything is finished. They've got an entertainer who sings Scottish songs but ... we're going to Son Amar[7] tonight'. For some tourists, then, too much noise is a problem and for others, too much quiet is a problem.

Noise combines with feelings of enclosure found in Magaluf. The presence of noise can be oppressive as, given its 'unwanted' nature, it impinges on the senses. Expressions like 'I can't hear myself think' are indicative of how unwanted sounds are disruptive. In this respect, the presence of noise acts to oppress activities and senses. The couple from Devon who contrasted the lack of noise at home with the noise of the resorts comment of Magaluf, 'we went up there and just thought we want to get out. It's noisy and enclosed somehow'. Another tourist from South Wales says, 'Magaluf has got dirty now. You go to the end here and then into Magaluf and it's stuffy and noisy'. It is not the case that such feelings are only experienced by older tourists staying in Palmanova. One male, in his twenties, staying in Magaluf explains, 'we're used to having everything in one strip, but here there are lots of back streets. It takes a bit of time to find your way around. We went for a walk and ended up walking in a circle, back to the hotel ... there is a feeling of enclosure around Punta Balena which makes it feel hotter, there is a lack of air circulating'. Not only is he referring to the confinement of the space of Magaluf; but, also, in getting lost and to feelings of disorientation.

The idea of enclosure is linked to control. For some tourists, their lived experience of Magaluf is a place that is airless. By corollary, in metaphorical terms, it becomes a place in which it is difficult to breathe and from this it becomes difficult to think or exercise self-control. This is all bound up with the way in which the landscape is inscribed. As already discussed, the tour operator reps have a role to play in this construction by their attempts to mediate tourists' experiences. The naming of facilities can also have a similar part to play and in this respect there is one shop in Magaluf that stands out, it is called 'Belt-Up'.

Situated in Magaluf (see Map 10), 'Belt-Up' sells leather goods and belt buckles. In the shop window there is a sign that conveys the message to 'feel free to come in and wreck the joint' (Figures 4.6 and 4.7). Once inside the shop, the smell of leather is unavoidable, and every wall

**Figure 4.6** Belt-up

**Figure 4.7** Sign in Belt up shop window

display is full to capacity. The buckles for sale carry messages that refer to ideas of the open road, and make direct statements of nationalism, e.g. 'Welsh a breed apart' or 'English by the Grace of God'. The wording appears along with national flags and other symbols of national identity, e.g. bulldogs. There is an aggressive air to these buckles in their overt display of nationalism and sense of exclusivity. Their display next to buckles that pertain to the 'Wild West' links to ideas of freedom and territorial acquisition. The aggression is the violence inherent in the invitation to 'wreck the joint'.[8]

The name 'Belt-Up' is clearly a pun connected to the shop's merchandise. At the same time, belt-up has other connotations. For example, it means to shut up, keep control and prohibit. It is violent, to belt someone is to hurt them, exert power and force submission, which can be degrading and humiliating; although, for some, this is also a pleasurable experience. The term is also connected with safety as in putting a seat belt on and, as such, is an expression of care. Magaluf is an environment in which, both metaphorically and literally, the tourists are encouraged 'to let it all hang out'. Large beer guts spill out over the tops of shorts and women are encouraged to 'get their tits out for the boys'. On the one hand, tourists are encouraged to drink and engage in casual relationships; but, then, on the other, they are being advised to keep control. Control the beer gut by holding it in place with a belt and keep the noise down by belting up. Even within the concept of having rented fun in the form of a med-ped, there are few options other than to go round in circles following the road network's one-way system. The shop

'Belt-up' represents the tension between freedom and control that is found elsewhere in the resorts. It further connotes the aggression and violence that underpins some elements of control as well as providing representations for the expression of national identity by the tourists.

The control referred to in the organised excursions by the tour operators acts in both a metaphorical and a literal sense. One male tourist, on holiday with his family, had been on a trip to the east coast attraction of the Caves of Drach. He comments that he would like to return to Mallorca the next year, hire a bike or car and explore the island more. In relation to the Caves of Drach, he advises, 'I would have liked to drive myself and be outside the confines of the coach, not be restricted by it'. He goes on to say that he would like to explore the rest of the island on a motorbike. He says that he has been biking since he was eight, 'it's in your blood, the freedom of it ... When life gets me down me and my son go off on the bike'. The coach trip represented a restricted experience for this man, which would have been heightened by the visit to the enclosed attraction of underground caves (which other tourists describe as 'claustrophobic', 'stuffy and unable to breath in'). The bike represents freedom of movement and self-autonomy. This man's thoughts and feelings link well to the image of the 'easy-rider' frontiersman promise of some of the buckles in 'Belt-Up'.

Another aspect of control is to prevent unwanted loss. A feature of the bar crawls organised by tour operators is that between venues the tourists must be escorted along the road. In the first place, it is a requirement of the local authorities and, secondly, because the commission-earning reps fear losing the tourists to bars not on the itinerary. This links back to ideas of possession. In the scenario here, the 'owners' are the tour operators and their reps who attempt to exert ownership over the tourists.

Smell also constitutes an element of experience. It has an important social role in the construction of taste and is a contributing factor in developing a sense of place and space (Urry, 1999: 34). In Magaluf, one smell that is noticeable is that of vomit. A tour operator rep comments, 'the holiday is about getting drunk and being sick, you can sometimes really smell the vomit'. A female tourist staying in Son Caliu also mentions smell, but in a different way, advising that 'this is a nice area until you go walking up the road to that bit of waste land, there's that smell, the drains. Makes you appreciate England then'. The location of the unpleasant smell with wasteland is significant in that not only is it the presence of a bad smell that is contrasted with England, which contributes towards the creation of a spatial other, but that bad smells are connected with by-products and the periphery (Urry, 1999: 41), and therefore the creation of an other. The tourist then appreciates Britain in relation to being in an environment that is literally and metaphorically outside of the self in terms of odour and place.

## 'Is Mallorca an Island?'

The subject of disorientation has been touched on in its connection with knowledge and feeling comfortable. For example, the tourists who felt out of place in the four-star hotel that they found themselves in, as opposed to the all-inclusive hotel that they were supposed to be in, were to some extent disorientated. The confusion, feelings and, in some cases, actuality of being lost come about for some tourists because they have no knowledge of where they are. By way of example, Douglas is on holiday with his partner and their daughter. The two females are on the beach, but Douglas sits by a drinks kiosk on the promenade. On one occasion, he ventures to enquire of me and the barman about Mallorca, 'like it's a little island on its own isn't it?' On receiving an affirmative answer, and in light of his having taken a boat trip to one of the markets in Palma, he then enquires 'is Palma on the mainland?'

Other tourists would ask for directions to Magaluf when they are staying in the resort and, on one occasion, two tourists who have ventured out of Magaluf to Palmanova looking for Banana Joes Fun Pub request directions for the bar. On receipt of instructions, they then enquire how to return to Magaluf. The feeling of being lost can be disconcerting as the experience of Andratx market indicated. In many respects, not to know one's place, but to be free floating and unfixed is the epitome of freedom. That this is unnerving gives an understanding of why some tourists want to know exactly where they are. For example, during one welcome meeting, a tourist requests to be shown his position on the island on a map. This is from a man who claims to know Mallorca very well, having visited the island several times. At another meeting, a tourist staying in Son Caliu wants to know 'exactly' how far from Palmanova he is. At yet another welcome meeting, a man asks how long and wide Mallorca is. Enquiring about one's geographical position is a way of fixing the self in a place.

In the preceding discussion, I examined the ways in which Palmanova and Magaluf are intimately related but also very different. Much of this difference occurs because of the activities undertaken in the places and the attitudes and dispositions towards them by the tourists. The consideration of noise and smell demonstrates ways in which a sense of place can be experientially constructed. Noise in Magaluf is often connected to the feeling of enclosure about the place in contrast to the openness of Palmanova. The link between enclosure and control is explored in the form of the shop called 'Belt-Up'. The Britishness of Magaluf, coupled with the enclosure and control that can be read into the resort, suggests, firstly, something about the nature of British consumption practices in that they need to be mediated and constrained. For all of the exhibition of conquering other lands in Pirates Adventure, for example, the British show a need to be 'led by the nose' (Dann & Jacobsen, 2002). The outlet of resistance is in the invitations to behave in a violent manner and in the actuality of being sick (Andrews, 2000).

Part of the need for mediation derives from the fact that many tourists have lost their sense of place, leading to feelings of disorientation and, by corollary, insecurity, which can be overcome in the comfort of the guiding tour operator rep and the familiarly named British pub. The idea of the holiday as a time for freedom and the ability to do as one wishes is a contrivance that is propagated through the media of tourist programmes and brochures. People are being told to have fun, so when they do they are acceding to the requests of the people who chivvy them along into participating in the fun activities. So, renting fun and being told 'having fun, that's what it's all about', as one entertainer puts it, means that, in the words of MacCannell (1992: 231), 'the moment of complete abandonment of self-control is also necessarily the moment of complete accession to state control'.

One of the major differences between Palmanova and Magaluf is that the sense of Britishness is much more marked in the latter. Most of the place names discussed in the preceding sections are found in Magaluf. What all the place names and the allusions to tradition and heritage do is refer to a culture outside the space in which the references are situated. That is, the names and their associations along with many of the activities and food and drink available do not refer to Mallorcan or Spanish culture. In short, Magaluf and to a lesser extent Palmanova are heterotopias (Foucault, 1986) because of their reference not to the culture in which they are situated, but to Britain. A similar observation is made by Philips (1999: 92) in relation to theme parks, which may have 'a recognisable geographical location, but ... [make] no reference to the local landscape or culture'.

References to spaces outside Mallorca are continued in the names of some hotels, e.g. The Honolulu, The Tobago, Hotel Bermudas,[9] Hawaii, Barbados and Jamaica to name a few.[10] The names represent tropical, exotic paradises imbued with ideas of the fantasy island in which 'want' and 'need' are not issues, but rather all desires can be satisfied. To add to the discussion and further appreciate the way in which Magaluf and Palmanova are contrived spaces, Cohen's (1982: 25) observations seem pertinent: 'the tourist industry plays upon and exploits the hidden desires of modern man, by tantalizing his imagination with the prospect of the realization of his paradisiac dreams'. These names also articulate a further tension in the tourist experience of the resorts. Fuelled by the creation of place myths for an exotic paradise that the names of the hotels conjure up, along with ideas of freedom and escapism, the tourists arrive at their destination to be confronted with representations and reminders of the home world. It is true that many tourists are attracted to Magaluf and Palmanova because of their familiarity. However, the heterotopic nature of the resorts coupled with the attempts to control and mediate the tourists' experiences contradicts notions of abandon and liberty. In effect, the tourists are held in place, metaphorically 'strapped in'. An area also associated with freedom is the beach, which forms the subject of the next section.

## The Beach

In both Palmanova and Magaluf, the beaches are bounded by walls along which the promenade runs. There is development on the land side of the promenade consisting mainly of café-bars, which is more dense in Magaluf than in Palmanova. The idea of boundaries, along with codes of conduct concerning exposure of the body, links to the notion of control. This section will discuss these issues in relation to the beach.

The beach can be interpreted as a distinctly different area from the hotel pool. Often represented as a site of freedom and held in opposition to ideas of the built environment, the two different spaces can be used to demarcate categories of social being: the family member by the pool and the 'member of a social mass' on the beach (Selwyn, 1993: 124). This structuralist interpretation upholds a boundary between the two areas. However, a post-structuralist interpretation would conflate boundaries (Selwyn, 1993: 126–128). The beaches of Magaluf and Palmanova do have physical boundaries, therefore it is necessary to appraise whether the social practices of the beach uphold the literal boundaries or erase them.

A structural analysis is a way of encoding the beach, a Lefebvrian representation of space. Such understandings of the space of the beach inform the 'spatial assumptions' that Shields argues are associated with the area. 'Mention "beach" and people immediately tend to think ... of a particular *kind* of place, peopled by individuals acting in a specific manner and engaging in predictable routines' (Shields, 1991: 60, emphasis in original). He goes on to argue that beaches are liminal zones in which dominant discourses can be subverted. In this respect, it becomes a space of representation. In relation to Magaluf and Palmanova, the exposure of the body that the beach allows subverts the codes of dress associated with the built environment. Away from the beach, this inversion is not acceptable or it becomes a spectacle of titillation in the likes of Pirates Adventure, and 'spontaneous' displays of nudity in the nightclubs. This section continues with an exploration of the extent to which the beach can be argued to be a liminal zone and the extent to which ideas of control, possession and boundary maintenance spill over the beach wall.

The beaches of Palmanova and Magaluf are well organised. In Palmanova, there are three beaches: from east to west they are Platja des Carregador, Platja de Palmanova and Platja de Son Maties. The first beach has three sunbed sections, the second has four sections and the third beach has three. The sections vary in the number of rows; some have three rows others six or seven. All the sunbeds are laid out in pairs, and each pair has a parasol. The situation is similar in Magaluf, which has one long stretch of beach with eight sunbed sections. The majority of the use of the beach takes place during the day in the summer season when they are colourful places as tourists bring different coloured lilos, parasols and towels to the beach (Figure 4.8). At the end of the season (31 October), all sunbeds and parasols are removed.

The beach can be a place of much noise and activity as well as quiet and tranquillity. This differentiation is largely based on a seasonal demarcation. The use is also temporal. In the high season the greatest use is during daylight hours. The beach is not exempt from use during the night as it is often the site for sexual liaisons and 'rowdy' behaviour, such as throwing a drunken friend into the water, or messing around with the sunbeds.

Work is only allowed to take place on the beach if it is licensed by the local authority. The beach is therefore worked in terms of the control and maintenance of the sunbeds and the endeavours to keep it clean. In the summers of 1998 and 1999, another group of people – the Gypsies and Moroccans – attempt to work the beach. They walk the beaches carrying buckets of soft drinks and trays of fruit. The products are sold at grossly inflated prices and often form the basis of disputes between buyer and seller. The illicit nature of the vendors means that they are targets for the local police, who confiscate and destroy their goods and serve notice of fines on the vendors. Another group of workers is the 'sand artists', who create sculptures from sand (Figure 4.9) and invite people to show their

**Figure 4.8** The beach at western end of Platja de Son Maties

**Figure 4.9** Sand Sculpture, Palmanova

appreciation in a monetary way. The beach is also used in the selling of rides on an inflatable banana and as the starting point for paragliding. People usually go to the beach as a family or with a group of friends. Occasionally, there are people sunbathing by themselves. Activities include sunbathing, reading, playing ball, playing with frisbees, playing ping-pong and playing with buckets and spades. People periodically lie down, sit up, chat, go to the sea, come back and go off for food and drink and return.

The notion of the beach as a different place is often indicated in the way in which it is discussed. For example, two tourists speak about the temperature. One claims that 'it's about 200 degrees ... out there', by which he means the beach. Not only has he identified a difference in space in terms of how it feels – hotter than the built environment – but by using 'out there', he is denoting a separate place in concrete geographical terms.

The idea of the beach as an area in which 'unlicensed behaviour' becomes acceptable (Shields, 1991) is countered in the tension signified in the legal provision of sunbeds and parasols and the illegal activities of the fruit and drink sellers. The beaches in Magaluf and Palmanova are areas in which activity is controlled. In the first place, along with signs that welcome tourists to the beach and those indicating the price for the hire of beach furniture, are those that mark the sunbed areas and, on Magaluf beach, prohibit the playing of football (Figures 4.10 and 4.11). It is not possible to move the sunbeds out of the zone. Tickets for sunbed and parasol hire are bought at their point of use. During one afternoon, a woman visits the beach and drags a sunbed from out of the designated sunbed area. The vendor removes the sunbed back to its original position. The very layout of the sunbeds imposes a control on the use of the beach. One way to avoid this is for the tourists to bring with them their own seating (lilos, towels) and parasols, and many do (Figure 4.12).

The element of control is also signified by the use of a barrier out to sea in the form of buoys (Figure 4.13). The effect is to prohibit people from floating on lilos or swimming too far out to sea. The idea of floating is concomitant with relaxation and freedom. It is also connected with being unfixed and with a sense of placelessness. What actually happens is that the tourists are fixed in place and held in by the barriers. Undoubtedly, there are practical safety measures for the use of the barrier, to stop people getting out of their depth, or to keep them away from boat movements. However, regardless of these reasons, the barriers act to keep people within a confined area. This continues the theme of spatial restrictions discussed in relation to the land and the controls that the tour

**Figure 4.10** Magaluf Beach sign

operators attempt to exert. On the whole, the tour operators have not found a way of organising the tourists on the beach.[11]

As already discussed, there is a strong connection between the idea of control and that of possession. This is often exercised in the use of sunbeds around the hotel pool and many of the arguments already made in connection with this issue are also manifest on the beach. Possession of a sunbed and parasol in the designated areas, and more importantly the shade the latter provides, is only possible through the purchase of a ticket

**Figure 4.11** Sun-bed zone

**Figure 4.12** Tourists arrive at the Beach, Palmanova

**Figure 4.13** Floating to the lilo barrier

or tickets, which give the buyer exclusive use. Once some beach furniture has been 'bought', ownership is often indicated by the laying of towels on the sunbeds. In one instance, a woman has claimed her position early in the morning. At about midday on Platja des Carregador, she approaches two sunbeds and a parasol. As she does, she calls across to a group, without shade, outside the zone, 'it's the early bird that catches the worm'. It transpires that she visited the beach at 8 am and claimed two sunbeds with beach towels, which she and her son were now, four hours later, going to use. After buying her tickets, the woman continues to be loud as she fusses around organising her child. She seems to enjoy her triumphant entry to the beach, a winner in the contest for shade. Her denial of someone else's use of shade for four hours and her subsequent gloating over others taints her actions with an unpleasantness that is concomitant with the aggression necessary to appropriate another's land.

Towels used to mark territory come in different sizes, colours and patterns. One pattern is the Union Jack flag, an obvious expression of national identity. During the 1998 World Cup, Union Jack towels were being sold with holes cut in their centres and the buyers wore them like ponchos. The appearance of the Union Jack is ubiquitous in Magaluf and Palmanova. It appears in shop signs, on bodies and draped over balconies (as do flags for England, Scotland and Wales). As a towel, covering one's body with a Union Jack is a way of immersion in one's national identity. At the same time, towels are associated with warmth, comfort, luxury, softness and protection. Covering oneself in a towel in the way described in the two resorts not only proclaims an identity, which one can hide in, but also speaks of comfort and nurturing that further connects the idea of nation to the parent, particularly the mother. On the beach, towels have a practical purpose. In addition, to lie on a towel, which is also a totem of identity, removes the user from the land and soil of the other and allows them to lie on a piece of home.

The appearance of national flags on balconies is a way of displaying the identity of the room's occupants. Balconies are ambiguous spaces, often appearing to hang in the air. They are neither of the house or not of the house. In this respect, there is a tension between the outside and inside. The idea of the balcony as an in-between space makes it one that needs to be brought into a sense of a whole. In Magaluf and Palmanova, balconies lack identity and can be brought into the control of the British (English, Scottish or Welsh). The marking of balconies as a possession of a room's occupant(s) is by flying a flag that proclaims a particular identity.

The triumphal entry to the beach of the woman who 'caught the worm' was also an act of display, which itself is an action associated with the beach, in particular with reference to displaying parts of the body not usually on view. The beach is an arena that allows the body to spill out, it is loosened from the stricture of clothing (apart from genitalia) and put away again when the beach is left. The beach is also an area in which activities, normally considered to be private, are acted out in public. For example, rubbing someone else when applying suncream. It is also acceptable to rub a stranger and rub someone of the same sex. Washing is another element of the usually private that is conducted out in the open. This occurs when tourists make use of the on-beach shower facilities when they leave the beach (Figure 4.14). The beach is also the site of the most private and intimate of acts, that of sex. Although this happens at night, making it less visible under the cover of darkness (not that the possibility of discovery can be excluded), that the beach is the place to go is because of the association of it as 'bare, carefree and relaxed' (Shields, 1991: 60). In addition, the practice of an act that is usually conducted privately in an open public space is a way of undermining normative attitudes towards sexual encounters.

It is very tempting to understand the beach in the ways that suggest it is a space marked out as different from others and a zone in which 'conventional wisdom' is overthrown. A problem arises, however,

**Figure 4.14** Tourists leaving the beach, Palmanova

because some of the activity is replicated in the built environment. For example, women go topless, men's beer guts spill out from the tops of their shorts, tourists (on occasions) conduct sex in public and the plastic bucket associated with children playing on the beach is used to serve cocktails. From this, the conclusion would seem to be that it is the resorts as a *whole* that are the liminal spaces in which a carnivalesque disorder reigns. The idea of seeking difference as a tourist motivation in whatever guise – activities, weather or culture – can be interpreted as an attempt to overturn the established order on a macro social scale or micro individual level. However, Magaluf and Palmanova are constructed on sameness, on being British, fun is licensed and approved, a sense of identity and place is heightened and emphasised. Tourists kick and vomit against this, only to find that this, too, is conformist, normative behaviour as they continue to construct the spaces of Palmanova and Magaluf in their own likeness.

## Summary

This chapter began in a similar vein to Chapter 3 in that it considers the meanings attached to the names of some of the café-bars in the two resorts, in particular with reference to regional identities and a rural idyll. These ideas are not just presented in representations of space, but are lived-out in some of the opinions expressed by the tourists. The scenario of regional identities and 'cosy' ideals demonstrates the intimate connection between understandings of identity and specific place.

The idea of difference between places is played out in the variations between Palmanova and Magaluf. Not only are they used by some tourists as markers of distinction, the differences are practiced in understandings of how they should or could behave – party in Magaluf, sleep in Palmanova. The physical construction of the resorts is used to explore notions of freedom and control – the openness of Palmanova compared to the confines of Magaluf. In the case of the latter, this is where the greatest mediation of tourists' experiences is located. The shop 'Belt-Up' encapsulates the tension of freedom and constraint offered by the capitalist system. The belt buckles represent ideas of free movement and yet Belt-Up reminds people to stay in their place, to conform and keep safe within the commercial environment.

Lastly, this chapter discusses the distinctive physical space of the beach. Beaches can be understood as different and there is a sense of difference as the beach is referred to as 'out there'. However, as the sunbed zones and signs prohibiting football indicate, they are also sites of control. Beaches are argued to represent ideas of freedom and to be sites of disruption to the established order (Shields, 1991), but similar behaviours in the built environment weakens the notion that the beach is an entirely liminal zone of the carnivalesque. Beaches also link to discussions of possession and the ability to take hold of an object or space by laying claim to it through marking it with some form of symbol of identity.

This chapter has again highlighted the sense of a need to belong, to have part of one's identity established or affirmed through the collective. The idea of the collective that is on offer, and therefore presented for purchase, firmly relates to the concept of the nation. It is an under-standing of the nation that can be regressive. In Chapter 3, the tourists ventured forth, they went out to assert their identities by conquering others' lands. This chapter demonstrates that there is a disposition to look more directly to the home world. Although this romanticises the idea of the nation, in terms of a countryside ideal for example, the look to region and individual UK countries also demonstrates the tension inherent in such a construct. By de-scaling the collective in this way, the importance of boundary maintenance is brought even nearer to home. People demonstrate their understanding of their sense of self in terms of a particular locale. That there are perceived to be threats to and differences between that and the outside further confirms the view that the tourists' sense of self is precarious and feels threatened by outside influences.

At the same time, that the idea of difference is disliked or shunned suggests that this group of tourists do not seek the other. Rather, they go on holiday for their sense of self to be confirmed. There is thus a desire to maintain control and be in possession. In short, to be powerful, a tact demonstrated by the woman on the beach who made an early reservation for her sunbed. Her ability to mark her territory and get her shade affords her some sort of freedom, it makes her a winner. What it demonstrates is that even the beach, often presented as the epitome of freedom, is subject to manipulation and control by the market. She had to get up early to stake her claim. If she had true power then there would have been no need to do so, she could expect to get a sunbed whatever time she arrived on the beach. This demonstrates that the market itself is limited and bounded. The freedom of choice, an illusion.

What is also evident from this chapter is that the way in which people relate to and experience space occurs through their bodies. How places smell, how they feel and the activities practiced bring the body into focus. The body is the subject of the next two chapters.

## Notes

1. By 2009, this establishment had changed ownership and had a new name, The Bollocks Bar. The displays outside the bar also changed accordingly.
2. The name 'PRs' refers to those people who are employed by individual bars to tout for custom on the streets.
3. Cork is obviously not part of the UK.
4. Many expatriates expressed similar feelings of community, referring to Mallorca as 'our place' and 'there's a real sense of community here everyone looks out for each other'. However, there was a tension in this as one expatriate bar owner said that, 'we've been ripped off more by the Brits than the Spanish'. Others complained about Spanish bureaucracy and many still referred to the UK as 'home'. Indeed, one woman commented, 'I've got a lovely home. I couldn't imagine packing that all up and bringing it here'.
5. What he is trying to say becomes disjointed because his partner keeps interrupting him to tell him to keep his voice down. He is also, at this stage, more inebriated.
6. Both Benny Hill and Peter Sellers are dead, which adds to the idea of looking to the past.
7. A cabaret-style night-time entertainment venue.
8. In 2009, this notice was no longer there.
9. The plural spelling is correct as it appears on the tourist map of the resorts 1998/1999.

10. These names also refer to places that have been subjected to white Western colonisation, and thus they also become linked to the theme of possession and territorial acquisition discussed in Chapter 3.
11. One tour operator's children's club did organise children's activities on the beach, and one entertainer from the Cala Blanca was observed organising tourists in beach games.

## Chapter 5
# The Tourist Body

## Introduction

The purpose of this chapter is to address the issue of the body in tourism in Magaluf and Palmanova. It describes and analyses the way in which tourists use their bodies, and the way their bodies are used, to understand, reinforce and construct their identities. The body is central to the experience of tourists in Magaluf and Palmanova – how they feel, how they appear and how the body functions.

I will begin with the body as object. This concentrates on the appearance of the body, the way that the self is presented, and the symbolic significance of that presentation. It is also linked to the idea of the gaze (Urry, 1990, 2002), in which the sites are mainly the bodies of other people. That is, tourists spend time watching each other and using this information to form judgements and pass comment on those they watch, in order to reflect on their own sense of identity. At the same time, the tourists are under the ever-watchful gaze of the mediators of their experience.

## The Symbolic Body

At the basis of an understanding of the symbolic body is the idea that it is socially and culturally constructed (Durkheim, 1915; Ellen, 1977; Ebin, 1979; Synnott, 1993). As such, it is a vehicle of expression. For example, tanning the body is an indicator of having been on holiday, and, in one example, a sign of social status. The clothes worn, and how, when and where they are worn can also all be interpreted. As Barthes (1972) discusses in connection with striptease, the way in which the bodies of the women are adorned establishes them as objects of male desire.

Skin, too, can be read. The suntan, as already suggested, can be understood as a sign of having had a holiday and of social status. As work undertaken by Carter (1997: 145) with Glaswegian tourists suggests, the suntan is viewed as a sign of health and 'is of crucial importance as a symbolic souvenir to be shown to others on return'. He also argues that it is a central component in the visual consumption of others.

Other ways of changing the skin are through the inscription of symbols. Body decoration, either permanent or temporarily, is a way of showing allegiance to a social group (Ebin, 1979). The bodies of some of the tourists are encoded with symbols – animals, names, flags, rhymes – all of which can be read, in the semiological tradition, for meaning. The skin itself can also be interpreted as though it were a layer of clothing adorning the skeletal frame of the body (Perniola, 1989).

In terms of Magaluf and Palmanova, how much of the body is revealed, when and where, and what its shape is, are all open to reading for their symbolic significance. The abundance of tattoos that proclaim a British identity can easily be read. The appearance of fat bodies and beer bellies can also be analysed. The latter, for example, can be indicative of drinking a lot, being able to hold a lot of alcohol and, with that, associations of masculinity, holding one's own, and strength. The unabashed display of such a body indicates a belligerence, a 'couldn't care less' attitude and two fingers up to the authorities who attempt to limit alcohol intake and promote good health care. Such ideas are also concomitant with lack of freedom and threats to being British. For example, the so-called English sausage is the subject of change through European legislation (2003), which will reduce the fat content of the food. The health education authority has run campaigns to reduce fat in the British diet, thereby reducing the overall 'fatness' of the nation.

Moving on, but still within the structuralist tradition, Douglas (1966) makes the observation that the body can stand for society itself. In the examples of Palmanova and Magaluf, the body can be interpreted as standing for a wider social system. One example is the gendered body. In bar crawls, the difference between male and female is highlighted and exaggerated by the assigning of gender-specific names – Wilma for women, Fred for men – and a change in toilets. That is, women are expected to use the men's toilets and the men are expected to use the women's. This draws attention to the body because it highlights the different practices of dealing with a commonly held bodily function. Failure to stick to the rules results in punishment, a public admonishment and penalty. As Douglas (1966: 15) attests, '[i]t is only by exaggerating the difference between … male and female … that a semblance of order is created'. She also notes that transgression of the systems set up to establish order results in punishment. The order referred to is of conventional male–female roles, and positions in society. Similarly, in other games and conversations, the identification of women as 'heels' and 'skirts', and men as 'trousers', picks up on particular codes of dress and turns them into a way of ordering the social world. 'Wearing the trousers', for example, is indicative of power.

A further promotion of male–female difference is in another use of synecdoche, again in a game played, with reference to the terms 'right and left'. In the game, women are asked to stand to the right 'because women are always right', so the joke goes. The significance of 'right' has been examined by Hertz's (1973) classic study of right and left in *The Hands*.

Another method for thinking about the way that the body can reflect or symbolise society as a whole, in the way that Douglas (1966) suggests, is through the use of the body. An example is found in Arnold's (1977) assessment of the introduction of poses into Peruvian brothels, which establishes a different set of relations with the women and reinforces the idea of prostitutes as being outside the home. The poses allow the men and women to relate to, or understand, each other in different ways. In Magaluf and Palmanova, the body is displayed in a number of different ways – on the beach, dancing and game playing. Many of the games are concerned with heightening the awareness of the differences between men and women. Some games include a competitive element, and an emphasis on consumption activities. Competitive consumption is a feature of advanced capitalist societies. In addition, many games incorporate a sexual component. For example, simulating and demonstrating knowledge of sex, i.e. demonstrating various sexual positions using a balloon to represent either a penis or a pair of breasts. The whole point is to emphasise the normative sexualised aspects of relationships; 'because these days you never know' as one hotel entertainer reminds her audience. The words in this quote are indicative of many aspects of experience in which there is uncertainty associated with threats to the status quo (e.g. the 'influx' of immigrants; greater acknowledgement and acceptance of homosexuality). At the same time, the sexual games are part of a competition, they can be judged and there is a winner. The performance can be given a score, whether as part of the game or with more serious connotations. Indeed, one informant recounts a story of a female tourist who spent the afternoon with several males in their apartment having sex with all of them. After his encounter, each male emerges onto the apartment balcony to hold up a card with a number, taken to be indicative of 'the score',[1] for how good the experience has been.

Another example of the grading of sexual performance is found in the availability of 'rings of light'. These small plastic tubes are filled with a liquid that glows in the dark. Three colours are available: yellow indicates 'young, free and up for it', blue indicates enjoyment or willingness to participate in 'kinky sex' and red denotes that the wearer is 'a first-class shag'. The rings are popular, the purchase of which is encouraged by commission-earning reps during bar crawls. The practice of display through the rings of light and scoring of sexual activity link to both ideas of the presentation of self in everyday life described by Goffman (1959) as well as inviting the gaze of others.

As Foucault (1976, 1977) demonstrates, an important aspect of an objectification of the body is its connection to power relations and methods of control. This mainly concerns the shift from medieval systems of chastisement inflicting punishment onto the physical body, to a focus on the use of the gaze as a means of control and discipline. The gaze then is a technique, a practice of power because the subjective self becomes subjugated to objectified regimes. The gaze is a way of objectifying power and the system becomes so embedded in society that it becomes internalised as a mechanism of self-control by the individual. By being the object of the all-seeing gaze, the subject moves towards self-regulation in the knowledge that she/he is being watched. In terms of Magaluf and Palmanova, that people watch each other and form judgements is evident from many of the comments that the tourists make. The tourists are also subject to the gaze of the tour operator reps and bar and hotel staff. With reference to hotel staff, a group of male waiter informants advise that 'we like watching the young female tourists, it's like watching a fashion parade'. On the way home following an evening shift, the waiters make a detour along Punta Balena with the specific purpose of looking at the young female tourists.

The magnification of the system of control to which the gaze alludes is also evident in the games played in the resort. In all of these games, people are displayed, they become the object of attention and they are the entertainment. In the bar crawls, the setting of rules invites surveillance to monitor for their transgression, inviting the participating tourists to be policed. Relationships are normalised and transgression of the rules (as the person is not then part of the group) is a public penalty – a petty humiliation – in which the perpetrator of the crime is the focus of the watchful eye of her/his fellow tourists. Many of the games played in the form of hotel entertainment are about comparison, judging and assessing the individuals taking part. In addition, it is not uncommon to find individuals in the audience of a nightclub (Pirates and discos), bar or hotel singled out for attention. An individual, usually ridiculed, is the object of everyone else's gaze. For example, during one evening at the Palmanova-based fun pub Banana Joes, one punter, a middle-aged man on holiday with his wife and two children, becomes an object of attention. He is short, plump, balding and wears glasses. He is often the butt of the DJ's jokes. One joke is about the man and his wife, 'we could hear you humping last night' quips the DJ. The man tells me that 'people have joked about me all my life, about my body and hair, but I just laugh'. Although he appears to be able to deal with the mockery he receives, the taunting demonstrates that in the world of the white heterosexual male, there is a bodily ideal against which he can be measured, and shown to be 'deviant'.

The practices on the bar crawls and in the fun pubs set standards – this is how to have sex, these are normative sexual relations (Fred and Wilma), you are consumers, you are competitors. As Foucault (1977: 269) observes, 'the mechanisms of power are addressed to the body, to life, to what causes it to proliferate, to what reinforces the species, its stamina, its ability to dominate, or its capacity for being used'. In Magaluf and Palmanova, the standards are demonstrated by tourists participating in the games played in hotels, bars and on bar crawls and in their general performance practices. In addition, jokes about disabled people also serve as a comparison, drawing attention to difference and serving to exclude. Not to play the game, not to join in, is probably the biggest transgression that can be made. Searle-Chatterjee (1993: 182) makes a similar observation about the role of Christmas in constructing social relations in contemporary Britain: '[p]eople must be jolly, be part of the group, and engage in group rituals'.

Foucault's ideas are insightful in helping us to understand the role that the representation and presentation of the body has in the construction of social relations. In the next section, the discussion continues by considering the representation of the body in terms of its state of dress and as a site of representation in relation to body decoration.

## The Body Adorned

As previously discussed, Urry (1990) suggests that the underlying motive in tourism is to gaze at sites of difference. These sites are objects, features of natural and built environments. However, in Magaluf and Palmanova, there are none of these more 'conventional' attractions to look at. Instead, as Carter (1997: 144) notes, 'an important part of ... visual consumption involves the body itself becoming an object of the gaze'.

Much of what appears to preoccupy tourists' gazing is what others look like and what they are doing. Speaking to an elderly man from Newcastle about sunbathing, he comments, 'we see a woman everyday who sits out by the pool'. He then offers the following observation: 'you see some right sights here'. I ask him if he is referring to the young tourists, he replies, 'no the older ones, the way they dress'. Another tourist from South Wales also shares her, and her husband's, enjoyment of 'people watching'. She says, 'We often sit on our room balcony and watch people walking by on the promenade. One morning at 8 o'clock there was a young man staggering, drunk along the beach, he fell in the sea. It took three attempts to stand him up right. We've also seen people sleeping on the sunbeds at night'. The woman feels that this behaviour is inappropriate and suggests a way to combat it, 'I'd have two burly policemen there charging for sunbeds [because] we have to pay for them during the day. That'd learn them'. In addition, 'we see young girls walking up and down at night... it's dangerous'. Another female tourist also comments: 'the way some of the teenage girls dress... I feel frightened for them'. What the latter comment refers to is the scant nature of evening wear by some of the younger girls, very short skirts and skimpy tops. What both comments about the young women suggest is that the girls are vulnerable and exposed, objects of a male gaze. With specific reference to the beach, Black (2001: 110) contends, '[b]eaches are places for looking, and particularly in terms of looking at bodies, it is the female body which is on display'. The comment made about the sunbeds, although made with humour, is indicative of a desire to control, police and punish transgressive behaviour. As such that some tourists are not paying for the use of sunbeds means that they must be brought into the system of fee paying under the watchful eye of two establishment figures.

Watching and judging is not only concerned with institutional systems of power. Looking at others is a self-reflexive activity and a way of understanding the nature of the self and demarcating differences from the other. An example of this is found in Vicky's attitude to some of her fellow tourists. Many of my conversations with Vicky appear to revolve around material objects, which she sees as a representation of her status, wealth and difference from other people. She is on holiday with her husband and two children and advises: 'we do not usually holiday in this part of the island, we prefer Alcudia, it's more expensive'. She explains, 'I was one of the first people in my area to have cable television installed and to own a mobile phone, they were expensive. Of course the cost of things has come down now'. The lower cost of the consumer items means that they are accessible to more people, thereby affording Vicky less of an opportunity to use them as objects of distinction (Bourdieu, 1979). With regard to her holiday, she advises: 'the more you go round the bay that way [points to the East side of Palmanova] the more expensive the accommodation becomes. We're sort of in the middle. I don't want to appear snobby but the hotel is in fact quite expensive. I don't know how some of these people can afford it'. Vicky is making her assumptions about the purchasing power of the other guests based largely on their appearance and behaviour. During Vicky's occupancy of the hotel, another family, or friendship group, consisting of three or four couples and their children is also staying in the hotel. One evening, several children are running around and there is another asleep in a buggy in the bar. Vicky advises, with reference to the running children, 'I don't like to see this happening'. Moving on to the sleeping child, she states, 'buggies don't provide support for children ... they'll end up deformed', and with reference to the larger group, she advises: 'it's probably one of theirs'.

One evening, we discuss tattoos and body piercing. Vicky explains, 'it's ok to have a pierced belly button if the person has a flat stomach, but she has layers and rolls of fat over her navel'. She is referring to a woman from the group with the 'unruly' children, and points her out to me, commenting, 'the lady in the turquoise dress and I use the term lady loosely'. On another occasion, the same woman is wearing a pair of short white shorts and an off-the-shoulder white top. Having made her comments about the hotel being expensive, Vicky nods towards the woman and says, 'she's Nell Gwynne tonight'.

All of these comments point to a liking of control. The tourist group that Vicky appears to dislike allows both their children and bodies to spill out in an uncontrollable way. They are all 'loose' and lacking a moral framework. Nell Gwynne, famous as the mistress of Charles II, is outside the rubric of respectability afforded to the 'official' relationship of husband and wife. There is a warning, the inability to control will end up in punishment. Buggies, which are not as firm as prams, cannot provide the same sort of support to the body, hence the child user will 'end up deformed'. The lady in the turquoise dress has no support for her flabby stomach or control, in Vicky's eyes, of her morals. Social status is important to Vicky (she is a magistrate in the UK) and she communicates this through material objects. These objects are achieved through a degree of wealth that is connected to 'correct' behaviour involving control and restraint. In the hotel, Vicky is confronted by people who she judges to have less material wealth than her, yet can act in a free and unfettered way.

On another occasion, Vicky points out one of the male tourists staying in the same hotel. He has below collar-length grey hair, which, during the day, he wears tied back in a pony tail. He is also heavily tattooed. Vicky advises me: 'he's a grandfather'. She is expressing surprise as his appearance is incongruous with the respectability she associates with being a grandfather. His hair, although controlled during the day in the pony tail, is allowed to fall freely during the evening. Like the ripples of the skin of the 'Nell Gwynne' woman, his hair is free and overflowing. This is another example of forming judgements about people based on how they look. In this case, even the skin is adorned with decoration. There is no concern expressed by Vicky about what the tattoos might mean, it is rather that he has tattoos at all, and in such number, which forms the basis of her opinion. Gell (1993: 19) contends that in the West, tattooing has been understood as a characteristic of sub-cultures representing a class of being that is opposite to 'the dominant canons of taste'. The issue referred to is the alteration of the tourist's skin to express ideas to himself and others.

The lack of containment that the Nell Gwynne figure and tattooed grandfather represent is indicative of a broader framework concerning boundaries. In Chapter 3, I referred to 'tourists behaving badly'; that is, those tourists who were perceived by others to be breaking some sort of unwritten rule about behaviour. In one case, this referred to the boundaries around hotels and who had rights over them, making, for some tourists, the hotel a distinct space. I also noted that the beach is understood as a separate space from the built parts of the resorts as it is often referred to as 'out there'. In spatial terms then the resorts are split between hotels, beach, nightlife and quiet. Another way in which boundaries are articulated is through the use of dress codes.

## The Clothed Tourist

This section considers when and where it is appropriate for tourists to reveal their bodies. It deals with what clothes are worn, when and by whom. It considers how the boundaries between nature and culture are manifest in rules of dress, and the tensions between concealment and revelation. Part of being on holiday (in the climate offered by Mallorca) is to wear fewer clothes. People arrive dressed for the (cool) British weather, and leave in that way. As he waits to start his journey home, Trevor tells me, 'this is the first time I've worn socks for two weeks'.

In Chapter 1, I outlined the way in which tourism has been discussed as being akin to a sacred journey (Graburn, 1989) and described the preparatory lengths for a holiday undertaken by one tourist, as reported by her husband. Not only is this indicative of a ritual associated with the holiday, which marks it out as a special event, but that they also have special holiday clothes indicates that what is worn on holiday is significant for the tourists concerned. This argument is given further credence by Donald, one of three male friends on holiday together. He explains, 'we went shopping together for clothes the weekend before the holiday ... we spent about £500 each'. Having established the importance of clothes for some tourists, I want to explore the codes governing what is worn and when and, by corollary, the meanings attached to the codes and the acceptability of transgressing them.

During the summer of 1999, the *Majorca Daily Bulletin* ran a series of articles about tourists' dress codes. It was reported that the French Government was to introduce measures to ensure that people are 'appropriately' dressed in the country's northern tourist resorts. The paper asks, 'would such measures be welcome in Majorca [sic] where the government is publicly striving to establish a new brand of tourists – "quality" instead of "quantity"?' (Bungay, 1999: 9). The investigation in the paper is aimed at young male tourists. The opinions of bar workers and tourists were solicited and pictures of bare-chested male youths appeared in the report. Many felt that it was inappropriate to be bare-chested in a café-bar or in the centre of Palma. However, opinions were divided and others felt that any attempt to get men to cover up in Magaluf, for instance, would deter tourists from visiting the resort. By contrast, approximately two weeks earlier, one of the paper's columnists reported his delight at having seen some women cavorting topless in the centre of Palma (Lasch, 1999).

What the different accounts demonstrate are varying attitudes towards exposure of the body. The idea of appropriate dress suggests that permissible exposure of the body is embedded in a moral and ethical framework. Given the availability of bare breasts and the opportunities to stare at them on the beaches of Mallorca, Lasch's excitement at seeing bare breasts in Palma might be attributed to the particular context in which these breasts were revealed. What both stories of naked female *and* male breasts suggest is that there are boundaries within which exposure of the body is acceptable. These boundaries are spatial, temporal and further defined by gender and age.

In Palmanova and Magaluf, an example of the spatial boundary that determines what clothes are worn is that defined by the demarcation between the beach and the 'built' parts of the resorts. The code of dress for the beach generally conforms to the following rules. Males wear shorts (often part of a football kit) and have bare chests. Women often bathe topless, but when they do not they wear two-piece bikinis, or one-piece bathing costumes. The colours of these are as many as there are people, except for the football shorts, which are predominately black or white. The majority of people enter the beach carrying something, e.g. parasols, lilos, bags and towels.

Dress codes change away from the beach. While it remains, in most cases, acceptable for males to maintain the same level of exposure wherever they are, the same does not apply to women. Once off the beach, it is no longer acceptable for women to be topless, or simply to wear their bikinis or swimsuits. There is no written code, but women rarely leave the beach without some form of additional covering. A bikini top is generally acceptable for the upper part of the body, but invariably the lower half of the bikini bottom is further covered by the wearing of shorts, a sarong or towel. Although it is the case that in the majority of circumstances men wear football shorts, on the occasions when swimming trunks are worn, they rarely leave the beach uncovered. For example, one afternoon, sunbathing on Magaluf beach a man goes to buy ice-cream for his family. Putting his shorts on before he leaves, he says, 'I'd better put my shorts on just in case'.

Attitudes to spatially based codes of dress can be seen in the comments made by Lucy. She advises, 'topless bathing, it's ok on the beach, but not elsewhere. The sight of women in the shops and cafés only in bikinis is not nice'. She also says that it is always the large women who go topless; Lucy herself is short and slim. She relates her views to her own experience of a previous holiday in Italy. During the holiday, she had gone on an excursion wearing shorts. 'I noticed local men staring at the female tourists, and I saw local women didn't dress in the same way. I felt uncomfortable. I bought a skirt to cover up'. The lack of clothing that Lucy perceived in the women off beach in Palmanova and Magaluf would suggest a feeling of discomfort with exposed flesh. Paul, who is in his late twenties, is one of the male tour operator representatives (reps) and has similar reservations about the state of dress that women should adopt. He reports, 'I saw two girls walking along the promenade in Magaluf, both were topless'. He does not approve and concludes, 'they've got no morals'.

From the discussion concerning tourist dress codes in the local press and the attitudes of Lucy and Paul, it is possible to suggest that the moral codes associated with dress revolve around ideas of decency. The dilemma or anxiety brought about by violation of such codes brings us into the boundary between nature and culture. Wilson (1995) argues that clothes are the most immediate way we enter culture, as along with hairstyles, they are cultural manifestations and statements that draw gender distinctions.[2]

A similar point is made by Perniola (1989: 237), who claims that humans, when dressed, are seen as different from animals, and '[c]lothing gives human beings their anthropological, social and religious identity, in a word – their being'. Given this position, nakedness becomes an indicator of a 'negative' state, one of 'loss, privation and dispossession'. To be naked, or semi-dressed, challenges the boundary drawn around nature, and the distinction between being human or any other type of animal. Not to be dressed, or to be inappropriately uncovered, challenges conventions. For women to be topless on the beach (or by the pool) is acceptable because the beach is often seen as a different place from the built environment, pertaining to nature rather than culture.

In addition, the nature of much beach activity, that of lying down, is suggestive of a way of being in the world. The relaxed nature of sunbathing and its association with the unconstrained nature of the holiday finds exposure acceptable. To be in the in-between state of dress or undress, a liminal mode of bodily exposure is expressed in the way in which the tourists sit down while on the beach to robe or de-robe. Once standing, notions of being upright or upstanding in society come into play, and, with that, are codes of dress that enforce those ideas.

Notions pertaining to appropriate states of dress are echoed in other areas of the resorts. For instance, it is the case that hotels have rules about acceptable standards of dress in their dining rooms. In one hotel, a written notice stands outside the dining room making the following request: 'We wish to ask our distinguished clients to please dress correctly for dinner in the restaurant. Thank you'. In another hotel, the rule is verbally communicated at the tour operator welcome meeting. At breakfast the standard is relaxed, but for the evening meal, men must wear long trousers. No prescript appears to apply to women. Wearing long trousers is not required in the hotel bar, and men therefore have the option to change back into shorts, although few appear to do so. In another hotel, people are requested, by written notice, to come 'appropriately dressed' to the dining room. In this case, there is no restriction on shorts, the main concern being that people do not enter the dining area directly from the pool. The codes of dress for the dining room suggest a number of things. Firstly, the dining room, the associated formality and the cultural transformation of food from the raw to the cooked (Lévi-Strauss, 1964) brings us back to the oppositions of nature and culture and the boundaries that are seen to demarcate the two. The wearing of clothes, the covering of the body firmly places the wearer in the cultural domain; as does eating a meal in the formalised setting of the dining room.

That nakedness is taboo, for some, has been discussed by Bataille (1987 [1957]) in his work on eroticism. He claims that the difference between animal and human sexuality is that the latter is surrounded by taboo, and that eroticism comes about as the result of transgression of these taboos. I am not trying to suggest that states of undress described by Lucy and Paul are erotic, although they might well be, but rather the statements about morality are an indication of the way in which the 'body revealed' is thought about. According to Bataille, the sight of flesh is contrary to Christian values, which are seen, by him, to be opposed to ideas of freedom.

Here, the discussion leads back to Vicky and her judgement of the woman with rolls of fat being Nell Gwynne. The woman's ripples of skin represent an unchecked body, a lack of morals and freedom that is threatening. Inherent in this is a tension between a desire for freedom (expressed in the interest in yachts by Vicky) and the actuality of living that ideal, as it is symbolised in the body of the Nell Gwynne figure.

The codes of dress that have been discussed so far not only dictate what should be observed and where, but also when. This gives dress codes a temporal nature as particular ways of dress are associated with particular times of the day, most notably around the time of the evening meal. The evening meal itself is a significant marker as it contributes to the structure of the day. It is after this period or the preparation for this period that activities change. It marks the end of the use of hotel pools, and coincides with the end of the predominant use of the beach.

The change in dress that concurs with the evening meal can be observed throughout both resorts and is carried through the evening and night. Although football shirts are still worn, long trousers have replaced the shorts. In place of football shirts, men wear long-sleeved shirts, worn loosely over long trousers and unbuttoned at the neck. Very rarely, despite the heat, are male tourists encountered in the evening wearing shorts. Being able to wear loose shirts is indicative of not being at work, as one man advises, 'if I tuck my shirt in... that's what I have to do for work'.

For female tourists, the general code of dress that comes into play is dressing-up, which often requires much preparation (Black, 2001). During my fieldwork, the predominant fashion for the younger tourists is a short dress or skirt worn in the case of the latter with little t-shirt tops characterised by low necklines and 'bootlace' straps. Faces are adorned with make-up, and glitter often applied to the hair and the upper chest. Although the clothes covered they also revealed, often snugly fitting the contours of the body revealing cleavage and layers of skin beneath the clothes. The tightness of fit and the minimalist aspect of the clothing do have a practical purpose. Many of the younger tourists go out to dance and the type of dancing engaged in requires ease of movement and generates heat. Longer clothes restrict movement causing excessive sweating.

Older women also wear make-up and 'dress-up', but reveal less, often wearing long dresses or skirts with blouses. The prevailing fashion at the time is to wear clothes made from fabric carrying a big cat print pattern, derived from big cats. Many of the accessories – handbags, shoes or sandals – are yellow gold in colour. The absence of older women from nightclubs and their presence in the more sedentary environment of the hotel bar allows more restrictive dressing as well as reflecting that age group's fashion. The gold and glitter worn by some of the female tourists in the resorts act as signifiers and tell the onlooker not only about the person adorned, but also the nature of the occasion. Rich colours and sparkling objects are associated with wealth and luxury; but, also, they are vibrant and playful.

For older men during the summer, daytime wear tends to be of two types: a short-sleeved shirt and long trousers worn with socks and sandals or shorts with a short-sleeved shirt that is left unbuttoned. Often, a floppy, cotton hat is also worn. When shorts are worn, they often sit below a large exposed beer gut or fat stomach (this can also apply to younger men). In one case, a man's shorts were hanging so low that his wife told him to pull them up. The effect of shorts sitting just under stomachs, worn with an unbuttoned shirt, is to frame the protruding belly, giving it more emphasis as it pokes out from the material demarcating its boundaries. The belly is not contained or hidden, it is allowed to flop out and be exposed. As one woman comments, 'I've never seen so many beer bellies'. She then looks at her husband's stomach, and her own and pats both.

What is striking about all the modes of dress, for young and old, female or male, is the uniformity of what is worn. The apparent regularity in the way that people dress is somewhat contradictory to ideas associated with individuality and freedom concomitant with free-market capitalism. What is also interesting is that while the holiday is seen to be premised on a search for an other (Urry, 1990), the homogeneity of what is worn is not about creating an other. McDowell's (1995) appraisal of the body in the workplace noted how, particularly in the case of male workers in the City of London, there was a remarkable similarity in the way that they appeared. She also recorded that the body is one of the main sites of discipline in the workplace, and that the extension of this discipline into self-discipline comes about in the way that people dress. Conformity to a norm is expected and largely heeded. An alternative perspective suggests a feeling of belonging, being with like-minded people and being a member of a social group. At the same time, following the crowd shows a lack of originality and independence, the latter purportedly a British national characteristic.

With regard to feelings of belonging, the football kit is a case in point. The wearing of a football kit, itself a sort of uniform, is also about identity and belonging. The purpose of the kit is to mark players out as belonging to the same team; they can be identified as, for example, supporters of Arsenal or Liverpool. The wearing of kit by the public identifies them with a particular team and also links the wearer to others wearing gear from the same club. The kit becomes a marker. In Palmanova and Magaluf, Newcastle's outfit is among the most common, which is indicative of where a large number of the tourists originate from. The England strip is also popular. One male tourist from Birmingham advises, 'I really regret not bringing my football shirt. I've not seen anyone else wearing one for Wolverhampton. It'd be something different'. On another occasion, a male tourist wearing a football shirt is walking down Punta Balena. He is being followed by another lad who is giving him a wanker sign behind his back, and calling out the name of the player emblazoned on the shirt. Football shirts, especially those related to a 'home' team, contribute to the structure of society because society is made up of smaller cultural groups who have in common a relationship with a place or thing, which, in this case, is symbolised by a form of bodily adornment. Football clubs also act to differentiate the café-bar market, which demonstrates the role that football has in the symbolic world of identity construction. Furthermore, it also shows how that identity can be broken down from the level of nationality to a region or town or city.

Clothes are one way of adorning the body, of sending a message about the wearer. They are governed by codes of acceptable times of dress and undress and what and where particular items can be worn. They can thus be used as a way of understanding boundaries around types of behaviour, and in particular spaces. Perniola (1989) highlights the way in which skin has also been treated as though it is a layer of clothing. Skin is the subject of the next section.

## Skin

This section is concerned primarily with the appearance of skin, how it is decorated and the transformative process it undergoes in acquiring a tan. Skin is being discussed in this way because it is being treated like a layer of clothing. Skin is more than a functional organ acting as protector, sensor and regulator, it and its appearance are, as Synnott contends (1993), also social and cultural entities. Perniola (1989) notes that in 15th-century anatomical drawings, skin appears as a garment, a theme found in fine art from at least the Baroque period to the present day.

Tattoos are important because body decoration is a code of communication, which is culturally defined and acts as a signalling system. In the same way that clothes are argued to give people their status as human beings (Wilson, 1995), so do other forms of bodily decoration, including tattooing and scarring (Ebin, 1979). Tourists' bodies often bear tattoos. The majority of these are permanent, but it is also possible to buy transfers that give the impression of a tattoo. Opportunities also exist in the resorts to have permanent tattoos made. During the 1998 World Cup England games, many tourists decorated their bodies by painting England flags on their faces and arms. Although not permanent fixtures, painted images and transfers nevertheless symbolise identity. In this respect, having a Union Jack or England flag (sometimes accompanied with a bulldog) becomes an outward expression of nationality. With the bulldog, more is being articulated, as the animal connotes national characteristics, e.g. strength and resilience. In the case of a permanent tattoo, the expression of identity is interwoven with the skin, becoming part of the person.

Where on a body tattoos appear and the size of the tattoo varies between people as do the actual decorations, which include: a single rose, tigers' heads, a panther, country names (England, Scotland, etc.), Yogi Bear, a naked woman, the words 'mum and dad', hearts accompanied by a female name, daggers, dogs, the name of the wearers' children – in one case, as the owner of the tattoo confessed, incorrectly spelt – swirly patterns, and in one instance, although probably not unique, a rhyme, which reads 'the sweetest woman I ever kissed was another man's wife my mother'. The rhyme attempts to be daring, but in reality it links the wearer to a conformist role. It hints at adultery but brings the reader back to conventional, standardised roles by reference to the mother, and refers the reader to the wearer as child. At the same time, it both honours and dishonours the mother. In the case of the former it elevates the mother – she *is* the sweetest woman – but at the same time she is dishonoured because she is linked to a possible sexual taboo. As Vicky indicated, the presence of a tattoo is suggestive of someone's status in society. Given Vicky's apparent concern to promote her own position as moneyed and therefore 'superior' to her fellow tourists, it seems reasonable to suggest that she associates tattoos with a lack of respectability or 'niceness.'

That the presence of tattoos is an indicator of 'inferiority' is also evident in the attitude of Kevin, a male tour operator rep in his early twenties. He works in a hotel that caters for half-board and all-inclusive tourists. He advises that 'all the tourists staying in the hotel are "pond life". They should sell stick-on tattoos at the entrance. They're [tattoos] obligatory for that hotel, especially the all-inclusives'. Kevin's conclusion is that 'tourists wearing tattoos are scum'. Tattoos act to transform the skin of the wearer as they are a permanent alteration of the skin. The next section also examines another transformative process, that of sun tanning.

## Sun Tanning

Part of the popularity of the resorts of Palmanova and Magaluf, and indeed Mallorca and the Mediterranean, is the climate. An aspect of this appeal is that the climate allows the opportunity to sunbathe and acquire a tan. Several tourists comment on discovery of my long stay in the summer of 1998, that it will give me the opportunity to get a good tan and that I will probably end up looking like one of the locals. One group of young male tourists from Oxford tell me that the main activity of their holiday is 'getting drunk and sunburnt mostly'. When I venture that they can undertake such activities in Oxford, the spokesman of the group replies, 'You can't get sunburnt though'. The reality is that it is possible to get sunburnt in Oxford and many other parts of the UK. This suggests therefore that the process of acquiring a tan has significance beyond getting tanned or burnt.

At one time, a tanned face and body was associated with outdoor, manual labour. The present day popularity of the suntan and its attendant significance in terms of social status has been attributed to Hollywood and the rise of the cinema, particularly the appearance of a dark-faced and fit-bodied Douglas Fairbanks, in the 1920s (Featherstone, 1991). Thus, sunbathing, which had begun as a medical treatment of tuberculosis in 1890s Germany, also took on the mantel of a cosmetic device. This was followed by recognition of the beach as being a place to gain the tan, and so it became an indicator of having had a holiday (Featherstone, 1991), and also of wealth, as holidaying abroad was not open to the masses. It was not until the 1960s that the availability of holidays for most people in climates that would guarantee a tan came into being. By the 1990s, medical evidence highlighted the dangers of acquiring a tan. Doctors' surgeries carry health-warning pamphlets, and the Health Education Authority conducted a poster campaign in 1998, drawing attention to the harmful effects of the sun. Some of the posters and postcards issued depicted tourists frying themselves along with sausage, egg and bacon, being served on a plate as part of a grill, and being barbecued on a spit. However, the popularity of the tan remains, and the majority of tourists in the two resorts engage in some kind of sunbathing activity. Sunbathing, then, is similar to other leisure or pleasure activities that also carry risks (Carter, 1997). The significance attached to acquiring and displaying a tan means that it is both a social process and a natural bodily reaction. Having a tan is associated with body image, feelings of well being and attractiveness (Carter, 1997). Knowledge of the 'dangers' of sun tanning among informants in Magaluf and Palmanova varies. The risks associated with acquiring a tan are sometimes highlighted at welcome meetings, and in advice provided to tourists. The Direct Holidays information pack left in one hotel includes a rhyme:

> We all come away to relax in sun,
> But it's not much fun when it's overdone,
> The Best advice DIRECTLY from me;
> Is take it slow and carefully,
> Remember for the first few days,
> Always protect yourself from the rays,
> Don't think of this as being a bind,
> For that golden tan is yours to find.
>
> © Thomas Cook

The message is, doubtless, intended to be useful. However, it also indicates the way in which tour operators attempt to involve themselves in the activities of tourists. In addition, Direct Holidays cannot help but remind its customers of who they should be grateful to for the holiday and advice.

Despite such warnings, Bill and Trevor, two, male, middle-aged tourists, state, when commenting on my opportunity to get a tan, 'it doesn't do you any harm'. However, another retired couple from South Wales caution against sunbathing, based on the fact that someone they knew died from skin cancer. However, both have tans and, despite their warnings, associate a tan with actual as well as visual well being. Indeed, she comments, 'you do feel healthier', and he responds, 'yes you do look healthier'. Another tourist from Newcastle cautions, 'you have to be careful, some of them out there [on the beach] are baking'. The idea of baking goes beyond the surface appearance of the body, suggesting that the whole body, including the insides, is being cooked.

The longevity of some people's sunbathing practices is commented on by other tourists. Vicky tells me that after a trip to Andtrax market, she and her daughter had done a couple of hours sunbathing, but had ended up going for a walk because: 'I can't just lie there like some of them, and anyway when I get back to the UK I'll end up covering it up when I go to court in case anyone thinks I have lots of money'. Another tourist from South Wales travelling with her husband and two friends, tells me that normally she enjoys sunbathing but for some reason during her current holiday she had been unable to settle, and had found the beach uncomfortable. She then remarks that she has seen a younger woman sunbathing all and every day, and concludes, 'she's a lovely colour, but I don't know how she does it all day long'.

Although initial responses to my lengthy stay are to comment on my 'luck', many tourists feel that it is too long to have to experience a hot, dry climate. The husband of the female tourist from South Wales says, 'I wouldn't like to stay here for 6 months, not in this heat. I'd like to be able to feel the wind and rain on my face'. What this statement leads into (and which has already been hinted at in the comments about suntans making one feel healthier) is not only a connection between the presence of sunshine and warmth, but the physical feelings associated with being in a warmer climate, indicating a sensory connection with place. So, being in the sun is not just about getting brown and how that affects appearance, it also has an experiential aspect; how the tourists are made to feel is as important as how they are made to look.

Not all tourists enjoy the heat and sun, as one middle-aged woman from Liverpool explains of her husband, 'he doesn't like being in the sun he prefers to sit in the shade'. In addition, while the acquisition of a tan and the ability to feel warm are reasons given for a holiday, that some tourists suggest that too long in the sun would make one look like a local, or there would be the desire to feel other extremes of weather, suggests that one could become too closely associated with the space of the other or is in danger of being transformed into that other.

However, feelings of warmth are important. This attitude is borne out by a man in his 50s from Torquay, who initially complains about the weather: 'it's too warm for me. My wife [who he describes as a "cold bird"] likes the warmth'.[3] He goes on to say that the warmth 'feels nice, makes you feel good. As an arthritis sufferer it makes me feel less stiff'. He contrasts this to what he terms as the rain and grey of the UK, which 'puts you in a sombre mood somehow'. The reference to someone as a cold bird is open to interpretation. If someone is described as cold it is generally meant, metaphorically, that they lack feeling. Literally, this woman may feel the cold or feel cold to the touch. The association of warmth with feeling better, or good, suggests a lack of warmth (loving and emotion) elsewhere. A younger tourist in her mid twenties, on holiday with her husband explains, 'the sun makes me feel happy, although I've enjoyed the air-conditioning in the hotel'. On sunbathing, she comments that 'it doesn't appeal to me, I find it boring'. Despite this, however, she still spends half of nearly every day of her holiday sunbathing on the beach. What this indicates is that the weather links to bodily sensations, and, also, or as a result, to emotions. The tan has both an experiential and symbolic dimension.

Another facet is the discomfort brought about by the sunshine and constant heat, mainly because of the inability to sleep at night. One day, Lucy tells me, 'I'm ready to go home because of the heat. Last night I couldn't sleep properly. Although there's a fan in the room because of the position of the plug socket I didn't get much benefit from it'. She says that the previous evening she, her daughter and grandson had gone to McDonald's. Her daughter had queued for the food and was 'melting' by the end because of the heat (the daughter also later came out in a rash that was diagnosed as an allergic reaction to the sun). Lucy also comments: 'I don't particularly like the beach, I've been on it mainly for Jake [her grandson]. Sunbathing on the beach would be torture to me. . . . I've seen some women who are black all over. I don't see the point in a tan because when you get home and go back to work you tend to cover up and no-one will see it'. She is also aware of the risks, saying that 'sunbathing is dangerous now and it makes the skin – particularly for women [indicates the area just above the breasts] look like leather'.

Ideas of discomfort associated with sunbathing are not uncommon. An elderly woman sunbathing by a hotel pool explains that the sunbeds are uncomfortable and that the tan should be built up slowly rather than 'some of them [who] lie out there all day frying'. She also feels that there is little point to the tan as it fades on the return home. This comment, along with those made by Lucy and Vicky about covering up at home, indicates that getting a tan is about display and the visual consumption of others (Carter, 1997). The reference by Lucy to looking like leather is indicative of the transformative process involved (and tanning is the process by which animal skins are turned into leather); and, like the references to frying and baking, implies a change from one state to another. Sunbathing, however, does not lend itself easily to a simple dichotomy of the body being uncooked nature transformed, by a social process, into cooked culture. Although acquiring a tan is a cultural activity, it is a natural process. The skin will brown, or darken, with exposure to the sun as a natural defence against the potential damage caused by burning.

A young male tourist holidaying with his girlfriend advises, 'we've mainly been sunbathing, just lying on the beach veggin' out... boring but I just wanted to completely veg out'. The idea of 'veggin' out' (being like a vegetable: inert, close to the ground, unthinking and unfeeling) suggests two links. The first is with nature, a vegetable is devoid of the attachments of culture, and secondly it is a food metaphor. The connection between cooking food and sun tanning is evident not only in the way that tourists describe the activity, but also in the images found in the resorts. A third interpretation is that being like a vegetable and the associated inertia is a way of embodying the experience of the holiday. Physically lying down and being close to the ground is concomitant with relaxing and not having to think about the demands of the quotidian world. In addition, the cooking process referred to, in some of the language used by tourists, is an example of the actual physical, embodied understanding of the holiday as a transformative process, whether this is, in the words of one tourist, to feel 'set up for the year', or other feelings of well being. The next section examines the idea of tourists being cooked in more detail.

## The Cooking Tourist

Considering the language of tourists first: a couple discuss whether they should wake up a friend who has fallen asleep sunbathing on the beach. They conclude that they should 'let him frizzle'. The retiree lying by the hotel pool describes sunbathing tourists as 'frying'. The elderly man from Newcastle uses the word 'baking'. Bill and Trevor discuss their progress in gaining tans in terms of 'sides done' and 'turning over'.

That sunbathing is articulated in cooking terms is also signalled in many of the postcards available for purchase in Palmanova and Magaluf. For example, one is a picture of the bare back of a male. In the middle of his tanned and glistening back is a well-fried egg. Another postcard consists of six pictures of a pair of female breasts. The face of the model is missing. In the first picture (reading from left to right) the breasts are white and partly concealed beneath a denim jacket. This picture is entitled 'fresh meat'. The following five pictures are entitled 'still raw', 'medium', 'well done', 'very well done' and 'tanned'. Each picture shows a progressive degree of tanned or brown skin. Apart from the connection between cooking and tanning, the images in this postcard can also be read in terms of the objectification of the female body and the presentation of women as being like food for consumption. The absence of the model's face suggests that the person is not important, she can be viewed as a pair of breasts.

Skin colouring is a mark of identity. As Carter's (1997) informants suggest, the absence of a tan at the start of their holidays marked them out as newcomers. For Vicky, the presence of a tan is a sign of wealth. Douglas (who had asked if Mallorca is an island) also links skin colour to identity. Douglas is black. He tells me, 'I like to come on holiday because I can get away from everything at home'. By 'everything', he means 'the bills which will be piled up when I get home'. He tells me, 'here [Mallorca] I can lie out in the sun and totally relax'. However, although he has done some sunbathing, on the days that I encounter him, he is always drinking by the kiosk. He says, 'I bet you can't tell if I've got a tan or not'. When I ask him why he does not spend time on the beach, he replies, 'if I get much darker I'll end up looking like an African'. As a marker of identity, skin colour is important to Douglas.

The idea of 'veggin' out', or doing nothing, is contradicted by much of the activity on the beach. Although lying in the sunbed zone can be quiet, the sunbeds are close enough to other people to hear the sound of their conversations. In addition, noise is carried from the sea, where many of the games are played, and children can be heard playing and crying. Noise also emanates from beachfront café-bars, ghetto blasters brought to the beach and the sound of people calling out to each other. In addition, there are hawkers on the beach selling fruit and cans of drink. They walk up and down the beach in among the sunbeds, calling out 'ello – cola, limon, fanta', until they get caught by the police.

When sunbathing, parts of the body are covered up, thus the exposed parts of the body become marked and stand out against the paler protected areas (and vice versa). The outlines of the clothes worn are often visible. An obvious example is strap marks on women's shoulders. Others include a square of burnt skin on the back of a teenage girl and the outline of a vest on an adult male. Some people seem to have subjected themselves to a high degree of tanning as they exhibit peeling skin and red burnt-looking skin below the peelings. Burning the skin first is sometimes seen as part of the process of acquiring a good tan. For example, Amanda is on holiday with her boyfriend. They are both in their early twenties. They visited Aquapark and Amanda got slightly burnt. When discussing their trip, and the resultant sunburn, her boyfriend tells her, 'if you stay in the shade for a couple of days you'll end up with a nice tan'.

Although sunbathing would seem to be obviously associated with the presence of the sun, by the end of the summer season and approaching Christmas the weather is less reliable, and heavy, stormy downpours of rain are not uncommon. The temperature by October is noticeably cooler than the high-season months. However, tourists are not deterred from sunbathing. While some bathe topless, others cover themselves in towels or keep T-shirts on. At this time of year, although there is often a lot of rain, as soon as the sun breaks through, the tourists go out to sunbathe, one woman doing so in her bra. With lower temperatures and a weaker sun, the possibility of acquiring a tan is lessened – even more so if one is covered up. This indicates that sunbathing is not only about the transformative process, it is also about the feelings of lying down, relaxing and being a vegetable. It is also about body and self image.

Issues of body image have been linked to the consumption practices of the capitalist system. As Featherstone attests,

> Consumer culture latches onto the prevalent self-preservationist conception of the body, which encourages the individual to adopt instrumental strategies to combat deterioration and decay (applauded too by state bureaucracies who seek to reduce health costs by educating the public against bodily neglect) and combines it with the notion that the body is a vehicle of pleasure and self-expression. Images of the body beautiful, openly sexual and associated with hedonism, leisure and display, emphasises the importance of appearance and the "look". (Featherstone, 1991: 170)

However, the irony is that tanning ages and damages the skin, working against the principles of youthful beauty. Another tension that can be identified in connection with the body and capitalist consumption is that, at the same time that people are encouraged to take care of their bodies through dieting or exercise, the opportunities exist for non-stop consumption in the form of fast food outlets and 24-hour supermarkets, all of which exist in Magaluf and Palmanova. Such a 'presentation of the self' (Goffman, 1959) opens the door for the body to be judged, adored and ridiculed. The latter refers to those bodies that are unable to fit the 'norm' or ideas relating to the body beautiful. Thus, the physically and mentally disabled are marginalised. Further 'imperfections' in the form of illness, or, for example, false teeth, become restrictive in terms of what the body can actually do.

## Summary

In this chapter, the body as object is part of the symbolic world. The appearance of the body and the way in which it is adorned can be read as signs of identity. I noted that in this objectification of the body, norms and standards are established against which the body, and therefore the person, can be judged and valued. The ethnographic detail provides examples of the way in which the tourist gaze, in this context, is not directed towards monuments or landscapes but at other tourists. This is a reflexive process that not only serves to identify the other, but, also, the self. I have examined meanings attributed to encoding the skin, through tattoos and sun tanning, within a general framework of looking and judging, practices set within an environment of control and punishment. In terms of sunbathing, the acquisition of a tan is not merely an expression of identity, but forms an embodied and experiential aspect of the holiday, which is linked to sensations of cool and warm. As such, although the weather is an oft-cited reason for a holiday, many of the tourists also express a dislike or discomfort associated with the heat. So, although the weather may form an important aspect of a holiday, it is not the only meaningful feature and citing it as such appears to be a clichéd, expected response. A consideration of how the bodies feel refocuses the emphasis on the body as subject.

The discussion of the gazing, judging tourist notes that the introduction of panoptic techniques creates a form of self-regulation – responsibility is in the hands of the individual. However, without control and mediation, the likely result is that people use sunbeds without paying for them, without participating in the system of financial exchange, and so systems of control, via the presence of the watchful eye of authority, need to be in place. This works to subvert the idea that the market and consumption practices are expressions of freedom. Indeed, the market is seen as a regulator, a way of demarcating difference through the possession of, or ability to purchase, consumer goods. The market suggests that identity can be found through buying into a lifestyle that expresses the identity of the purchaser. Not to conform to the rules of the market – use a sunbed for nothing – requires punishment. Thus, there is a need for regulation, which can be enforced through surveillance.

What this indicates is that inherent within the unregulated free market is the idea of conformity, which works against the principles of the rubric of freedom associated with consumption practices. In order to participate in even the most basic of consumption activities – eating a meal – the tourists are required to dress in a certain way, to use their bodies as a symbol of who they are and how they can be part of a system of control by hotels or café-bars. Anyone trying to circumvent these rules, or be seen to be doing so symbolically by allowing their bodies to escape over their clothes, is perceived of as a threat. In short, they are seen as outsiders taking something for nothing.

## Notes

1. To score is a colloquial expression used by some for having achieved intercourse. In this instance, the men not only scored in this respect, they also rated their experience with a number, giving it a score. Its association with football gives it a competitive edge.
2. Cross-dressing, which is evident in resorts, contradicts this simple dichotomy, but may result in the same degrees of discomfort brought about by nakedness.
3. It was quite often the case that I met women who would tell me that their husbands did not like the heat and would spend time sitting in the shade or in their air-conditioned hotel room, while they sunbathed. One woman said of her husband, 'it's a waste of money him coming'.

## Chapter 6
# *The Embodied Tourist*

## Introduction

The previous chapter examined the way in which presentations of the self are the object of the judging gaze of the other. This chapter continues in this vein by thinking about how the body can be judged as imperfect and be seen to reflect issues of dependency and reliance in a wider social context. This is followed by an examination of the performing body, which builds on, via further ethnographic detail, some issues outlined in Chapter 5. The final section of the chapter considers the body-being, that is phenomenological approaches to the body.

## The Imperfect Tourist

Watching the body perform allows it to be judged for its abilities to carry out certain tasks. It also contributes to the construction of a gendered identity in the confirmation of gendered ways of being, e.g. the association of certain types of clothes with male or female. All of the games and competitions played are couched in terms of amusement and fun, and there are some presentations of the body that invite admiration. Yet, there is also an element of the games that seeks to illustrate and punish inadequacy.

For example, during Pirates Adventure, an emphasis is placed on the body through a heightened awareness of it. The main component of the show is an acrobatic display, by both males and females, which requires a fit and 'managed' body incorporating suppleness, strength and in many cases (although by no means all, but particularly those of the women[1]) slimness. The duration of the show, even for those who are not the main acrobats, would require a degree of stamina that would, in turn, demand at least a basic level of fitness. Although a large part of the audience becomes increasingly drunk as the show progresses, there does appear to be a genuine appreciation of the skill of the gymnasts, with the bodily feats being met with cheers, applause, expressions of 'wow' and salutations. The plastic swords, purchased as part of the show memorabilia, are often raised in unison by groups of tourists when an aspect of the performance has been achieved. Similar acrobatic deeds to those found in the show are repeated elsewhere in the resorts in some of the hotel evening entertainment.

As already suggested, the ability to perform in the way that Pirates and similar entertainment routines demand, requires fit, healthy bodies. The idea of the trained and trim body is also signified in visual imagery found in the resorts. For example, some of the café-bars use icons from British football as part of their image. Football is a game that relies on the physical ability of the players. The tourists then are presented with a series of images that promote the body and draw attention to a knowledge and mastery of the body. In opposition is the idea of an imperfect body, the one that cannot meet such ideals and deviates from it.

What happens to the body during a holiday can influence the way in which it functions and the course that the holiday takes. Depending on the severity of what happens, the tourists can then be prevented from participating fully in their holiday. For example, I met two women who had injured their ankles. One had wanted to visit the Caves of Drach, but the injury prevented her from doing so because she would be unable to walk down the many stairs involved in the trip. Tracy, a younger tourist, ended up on crutches with her leg in plaster after a fall and had not been able to participate in some planned activities. She had been given medication by the hospital and told not to drink alcohol. However, she only cuts down on her intake of alcohol because she is on holiday. Her partner Mark supports her action saying, 'on holiday you've got to have a drink, got to be able to relax'. This statement sets apart the body as subject from the object of relaxation; it speaks of a mind–body dualism in which being able to relax relates to a mental state. The need to drink and feel this state is in contrast to the rigidity of the leg in plaster.

At the end of the summer season the type of tourists visiting Palmanova and Magaluf changes. There is an increase in elderly people, and it is also a popular time for parties of disabled people to come on holiday accompanied by their carers. In some cases, the nature of someone's disability can impede progress through customs or during the airport transfers, because, for example, disabled tourists may need help on and off the transfer bus. After a day at the airport when, according to one tour operator representative (rep), Paul, a large number of disabled people arrive, he states, 'they shouldn't be allowed to come on holiday'. During a phone conversation with his manager, they share a joke about one such group of people at the airport.

This hostile attitude towards the disabled and their carers is also evident in the comments of a male tourist from Wigan, although they were directed more specifically towards the carers. During a general conversation in which the disabled are being discussed, the man claims, 'It's only recently come to light in the UK that carers who take disabled people on holiday get a free holiday for themselves. It's this sort of thing that's damaged the welfare state ... There's that case of a carer going on Safari and the trip being paid for by the tax payer'.

The inability to look after oneself places the individual outside the mainstream. The fact that groups of disabled people visit mainly outside the high season speaks for itself. Similarly, the end of the main season is also a prime visiting time for elderly holidaymakers, many of whom are also physically impaired. Those working in the tourism industry often refer to the elderly by the derogatory term 'coffin dodgers'.

People described as disabled do not fit in with a particular ideal; rather they are perceived as unattractive, in the way and a burden. One evening in Banana Joes, Emily tells me that she and her cousin had got speaking to a disabled man, 'the thing is I feel he's become dependent on me expecting me to speak to him all the time. I don't like it 'cos I'm on holiday and don't want the commitment of feeling obliged to speak to someone all of the time'. Here, the idea that the disabled are dependent is clearly made and Emily would rather that this particular person could look after himself rather than being a burden to her.

However, contrary to ideas pertaining to 'perfect' bodies is the impression that for some the ideal is unimportant. Peter, a male rep, tells me that all the tourists are out to get laid, drink and have a good time. According to him the absence of the home peer group on holiday allows this to happen and that if a man is looking for a partner to have sex with, 'it doesn't matter if the girl is fat or thin. There's no family or friends to be critical'. The idea that tourists are outside their peer group and in surroundings where no-one knows them, is a common understanding of part of the holiday experience, and like references to the weather and sense of freedom is often articulated as such by tourists. For example, one member of a family group visiting Family Pirates Adventure has his face painted. He is in his late teens. He starts to complain that he feels foolish, but his father assures him that it is unimportant because he is on holiday and no-one knows him. However, opposed to this is the fact that people invariably holiday with friends and relatives, people who do know them and form part of their peer group. One would assume that regardless of teenage–parent relationships, the father and face painted-teen do indeed know each other. This suggests that it is not the absence of known persons that accounts for the behaviour of tourists, but a disruption of the *habitus* (Jackson, 1989; Andrews, 2009b), which lays open possibilities of behaviour.

The jokes about the disabled shared between Paul and his manager are not isolated incidents. Part of the entertainment provided in the resorts also involves mocking the disabled. For example, one bar in Magaluf, called 'The Office', plays video footage of Roy Chubby Brown. Chubby Brown is a British comedian who shows scant regard for 'political correctness'. Jokes are made about the disabled, profanities are liberally used, and some of the content is blatantly racist and sexist. Much of the humour is concerned with the body and what it does, especially in relation to sex. Highlighting the body and the use of the disabled as the butt of jokes, contributes to their marginalisation in society. In another example, an entertainer performing in a hotel impersonates someone with a hip replacement standing next to a radiator. The implication is that the hip melts, so he falls over. The reference is to infirmity, which is ridiculed in a sadistic manner.

This foregrounding of the 'abnormal' and abject suggests that there is a body that appears and acts in a 'normal' way. Palmanova and Magaluf emphasise a 'Britishness' in which the 'norm' in bodily terms is centred on predominately able bodied and predominately white people. The majority of British workers in the resorts are white. The absence of Black and Asian tourists is noticeable to the extent that when there is a group (in the same way that there might be a group of young white lads) they attract attention. That is, people turn to look and comment on their presence. Some of the 'humour' in the resorts uses the idea of the ethnic other. For example, one comedian tells his audience that a mistake was made when Disneyland was built in Japan in that all the rides are too big for the Japanese. Not only is this racial stereotyping, it is also about standardisation. The Japanese do not fit the bodily conventions outlined by Disney.

Another way in which body size is used to make assessments about people is made by Paul, the tour operator rep. He advises me one morning that 'later you'll meet some real scum'. He describes the 'problems' he has encountered with a recently arrived couple. They have been complaining, claiming that their child's buggy was damaged in flight, some baggage is lost and their room does not have air conditioning. According to Paul, they have refused to fill out the necessary documentation in connection with the buggy, only reported the missing bag the day after arrival and air conditioning is not advertised as a feature of the hotel. He also advises that when they complained, they were abusive and allowed their children to run around screaming. Paul describes the woman as 'fat, an inch taller than her husband and with just flat hair'.

Although Paul's attitude towards this couple is based on their behaviour, he is also using their appearance, particularly that of the woman, to cast aspersions on them. She is fat and she is taller than her husband, which does not meet with the stereotypical picture of the 'little woman'. Rather, she is unattractively fat and out of control. The reference to 'just flat hair' is indicative of the idea that fat people are not concerned with body image. Her children, too, are out of control and, like the children in the hotel described by Vicky, run around unrestrained.

The joke about the Japanese feeds into the imagination of ideas about them and confirms possible pre-existing prejudices. The differences around non-white and non-western others translates, in some cases, into obvious dislike. For example, a group of middle-aged men on a golfing holiday joke about Chinese and Black people. They particularly dislike Black people and talk about 'sending them back'. They speak jovially about one Black man that they all knew and relate how one day some of them (plus someone not present) had cornered him and tried to bleach him white. The attitudes expressed by this group of Londoners is not unlike those discussed by Bert and May who express their dislike of 'Pakis', who they see as freeloaders, and, also, by the two middle-aged men from the Midlands, who describe their home world as 'infested with them'. In the bleaching incident, the men are trying to strip the victim of part of his identity.

In a similar vein, 'deviance' from heterosexuality is also considered unacceptable. The sorts of attitudes encountered are seen in some of the evening shows in the resorts. Two performers quip 'we'd hate to be poofs' because, they argue, they would run the danger of being rejected by both men and women. Further, two male informants are in a homosexual relationship with each other. One of the men works in a hotel and the guests are not allowed to know of his sexual orientation.

The jokes about those who do not fit a perceived bodily norm, highlight their otherness. The disabled, imperfect bodily other brings the individual into contact with a potential self. As Overboe (1999: 18–19) states, '[t]heorists concerned with disability ... assert that most non-disabled people feel disabled people symbolise, among other things, imperfections, failure to control the body and everyone's vulnerability to weakness, pain and death'. Disability is a societal classification (Overboe, 1999: 27) that highlights dependency, which, according to Overboe, has become increasingly devalued and is at odds with associations of independence and liberalism (Overboe, 1999: 23). Certainly, the free market and advanced capitalism require, or have a rhetoric of, individualism and self-help. That people need carers or additional assistance in whatever guise (whether it be help on or off a bus or housing aid in the UK) works against this.[2]

If, as Overboe claims, the disabled symbolise an inability to control, the attitudes towards them are another example of the tension between ideas of freedom and constraint as exhibited by Vicky, Lucy and Paul. The holiday perceived to be the time of abandonment does not welcome those seen to be already out of control. Rather, letting go has to be within the confines of a set of sanctioned conditions, which in Paul's case refers to his role as a tour operator rep.

However, the 'humour' around disability and difference is not simply 'politically incorrect' or malicious; it can, according to Albrecht (1999: 67), be liberating and purposeful, 'disability humor [sic] is important because it points at the boundaries between cultural groups and communities and at the social glue that holds them together'. If this is the case, the social glue that holds the community of the British together in Magaluf and Palmanova, as indicated by the comments and attitudes expressed above, is one of conformity in which deviance and weakness are frowned on as a burden.

What this discussion demonstrates is that there is an idealisation of the body, a standard against which judgements about the other can be made. That there are elements of UK society who do not fit the ideal of the able white heterosexual is clear from the representation of groups, such as the disabled, as burdens or objects of ridicule, people who are outside the 'norms' and should therefore be treated differently, the most extreme being that they should be excluded from taking holidays. Some attitudes are based on monetary concerns. The elderly, often referred to as 'coffin dodgers', are seen as a group of tourists who do not spend much money. Feelings of concern for personal safety are seen as weakness and to be an other (disabled, Black or Asian) is to be in a position of dependence, and a drain on the independent. Very few people can probably attain the ideal that is set and, in some way, there is an acknowledgement of this, as Peter says, 'it doesn't matter if a girl is fat or thin' the object is to have sex, her fatness is a risk worth taking for the end result.

## 'Let me have men about me that are fat'[3]

Fatness is a social category and attitudes to fat bodies have varied historically (Mennell, 1991). The title quote for this section, taken from Shakespeare's *Julius Caesar*, continues thus:

> Sleek-headed men, and such as sleep o'nights.
> Yond Cassius has a lean and hungry look;
> He thinks too much: such men are dangerous (Act 1, Sc. 2, 192–194)

The inference is that the fat are slow and unthinking; by contrast, the thin Cassius uses his brain and poses a threat to Caesar. In this respect, Shakespeare uses the appearance of the body to symbolise something about personalities and dispositions.

Anthropologically speaking, the shape and size of the body can be analysed to gain an understanding of cultural or social phenomena. For example, Mennell (1991) explores the relationship between diet, styles of eating and body size, noting changes through time, thereby drawing attention to the importance of contextualisation when attributing meaning. For example, Mennell contends that in present times, obesity in developed countries is highest in society's poorest levels; as opposed to developing countries where it is most evident in the higher echelons. Further, he suggests that the propensity to overeat is not entirely due to the availability of food, but 'pressures to overeat are often rooted in past hunger' (Mennell, 1991: 150).

In terms of tourists visiting Palmanova and Magaluf, the evidence of fat bodies (not necessarily obese, and for men attributable to the intake of alcohol as much as food) can be taken, following Mennell, as a sign of 'social class'. The recognition by some people that they have eaten more than 'normal' is unlikely to be indicative of a 'past hunger', but rather it can be taken as a sign of indulgence and self-gratification.

According to statistics, one in five of the British population is obese, exacerbated where there is poverty and poor working conditions. Costs to the National Health Service were estimated as £4.2 billion a year in 2007.[4] The obese are like the deviant tourists, a heavy burden on society. Being overweight signifies being out of control, not being able to limit the body's intake and therefore the growth of the body. However, being fat is also associated with being warm and cuddly (Mennell, 1991). Nevertheless, mostly it is seen as a problem that must be dealt with. As Featherstone (1991: 183) notes, '[t]he calculation of the potential saving to state health services provides further grounds for castigating those who do not heed the new message as self-indulgent slobs'.

In Palmanova and Magaluf, images of the fat body are present on postcards. One postcard entitled 'Mallorca Happy Island' shows a smiling, excessively fat woman stretched out naked on a tree trunk. The implication is that happiness can be found in the natural folds and flaps of her skin and ample body. Another postcard is a view of two tourists – one male and one female – seen through binoculars. Both have large stomachs, although his is the biggest. The caption on this card reads '"You are a weight-watcher..." Isla de Mallorca'. Images of happy, smiling, fat people offering a good time fly in the face of those who attempt to contain and curb the bodies of the British.

In the resorts, fat is not hidden, rather it is displayed. An example of mocking or challenging authority (and the images of slender bodies used in marketing discourses) is exhibited by one nightclub DJ. His reference to himself as a 'big fat bastard' is indicative of a 'couldn't care less' attitude. He is not concerned that his humour might be offensive (he tells jokes about 'shagging' his 82-year-old mother) and concludes 'yes I'm offensive, I'm a big fat bastard'. Souvenir t-shirts with the caption 'You Fat Bastard' written on them are available to purchase. That he links his self-acknowledged offensiveness with his body size demonstrates that (a) being fat is a symbol of being objectionable, and (b) he has embodied this element of his personality by being fat.

According to Turner, a slim body became associated with control and morality in Britain between the 1830s and 1890s. This was manifest in the wearing of corsets by women of the 'leisure class', thus denoting them, among other connotations, as unfit for manual labour (Turner, 1996: 191). Today, Turner contends, a thin body is concerned with a narcissistic self, that is a personality concerned with self-love and seeking praise and validation from others. Thus, a slender body is needed for social acceptability, happiness, sexual prowess and success in general[5] (Featherstone, 1991). With regard to the 'narcissistic self', Turner (1996: 195) suggests that this 'personality requires validation from audiences through successful performances of the self'. 'The fat bastard', by contrast, recognises that his humour and appearance may render him unloved, but he does not care.

The contrast between the symbolic meanings of fat and thin revolves around health and self-control. The overweight are seen to be unhealthy, putting a strain on their bodies. They do not (that is they are seen not to) exercise so they are unfit, and in some cases are restricted in what they are physically able to do. Ironically, their indulgence in food and eating the 'wrong' things – fast foods and greasy foods – is encouraged by the same system of consumer culture that encourages '[i]mages of the body beautiful' (Featherstone, 1991: 170).

That weight is an issue is borne out by many tourists' claims to have put on weight during their holiday, because they have eaten more than usual. For example, Lucy advises, before her return home, 'I've been eating a lot. I don't know if I'll fit into my trousers for the journey home'. One expatriate, who regular dined on hotel food, comments that she and her husband notice that people put on weight during their holiday because of the quantities of food consumed. She also tells me that when she and her husband first came to live in Mallorca, they stayed in a hotel and, they too, gained weight because they ate so much. The food in hotels is generally presented buffet style so people can eat as much as they like. It is often the case that people pile their plates high with food and take more than one serving.

The presence of fat bodies in the resorts cannot go unnoticed. Beer guts are particularly noticeable. The gendered division of food and drink consumption outlined by Synnott (1993: 65) suggests, albeit 'stereotypically', that drinking pints of beer is symbolically and ritually masculine. The beer gut, then, is symbolic of the drinker's ability to consume beer, the size of the gut indicative of the drinker's capacity to hold their drink: the bigger the gut, the bigger the man, both literally and metaphorically. So, beer guts become signs of manliness. Rather than being held close to the frame of the body, the beer gut protrudes into the world, it is carried before the bearer, pushing through and taking up space. In the context of a holiday abroad, the beer gut reads like a declaration of presence – spreading the body out in the land of the other, proclaiming the occupancy of the other's space.

So far, this chapter has concentrated mainly on the body as object, as a symbol based on appearance. The next section is concerned with performance. Tourists perform in hotel and bar crawl games, which focus on an idealisation of body functions, thereby allowing norms and standards to be set and acted.

## The Performing Tourist

This section concentrates on the functioning body. It argues that the display of what the body does in the various games and performances is used to set standards and establish norms. The assessment of *the other* in this way links image with character. This form of judgement is an ongoing process linked to self-reflexivity. In an overt and structured way, the abilities of the body are both evaluated and praised in the organised games and competitions that form part of the evening entertainment in the resorts. What the games do is allow a quantification of the body in terms of sexual attractiveness, size of body parts and, in some games, the speed and agility of the participants.

### Musical chairs

This game is played by a group of adults as part of the evening entertainment in the Son Maties Hotel in Palmanova. It takes the form of the conventional musical chairs in that a set of chairs is laid out and the contestants must walk around them until the music stops and then take a seat. The number of chairs does not match the number of contestants and thus the person left standing is eliminated from the next round (Gomme, 1964). In this adults' version of the game, only women walk around the chairs which all have men sitting on them, who are, on instruction, bare-chested. The women are set tasks as they walk around the men and chairs: first they must touch each man on the chest as they walk by; second, they have to kiss each man on each cheek; and third, they have to touch the men's knees.

Eventually, there are only two women left, one chair and one man. The man sits with his legs spread apart, leaning against the back of the chair. As the women walk by, they have to stop and bounce on his lap three times before moving on, until finally, one of the women is eliminated. The contest is supposed to be fun and there is evident enjoyment by participants and audience. However, competition is fierce. As the number of chairs reduces, one or two of the women become quite aggressive in obtaining a free seat, with one contestant pushing another off one of the men's laps so she can sit down.

Another competition played in the Son Maties involves three male contestants. Firstly, they are each given 45 seconds to run round the audience and kiss as many people as possible. The person who collects the most kisses wins. Secondly, each man takes his turn to sit on a chair, have a cloth wrapped around his neck, lean back and open his mouth so that the entertainer can pour sangria down his throat. The man who can maintain the swallowing the longest, wins. The record held is 63 seconds. The second player does it for two minutes and the third is unable to swallow at all for laughing. The audience claps the men's achievements.

The third game is to sing a song while gurgling a drink of water. Each contestant is asked to name his favourite nursery rhyme, which each is then asked to sing in turn while gurgling. The audience laughs at the men's attempts, and the men also laugh, which hinders their accomplishment of the task. A similar competition is held on a different night for women contestants.

## Bar crawls

In the high-season summer months, bar crawls are organised by the tour operators' reps. They mainly take place in Magaluf and serve more than one purpose. Firstly, they are a means of showing tourists around the nightlife of the resort, and give them the opportunity to meet other tourists and get to know their representative. On another level, they are used to increase tour operator profits because the tourists have to pay for them, and the bars involved pay the tour operator for bringing the tourists to their bar. In some cases, the reps also earn money from commission. The bars that the tourists are taken to are sanctioned, become familiar and are therefore made safe. Also, there is a chance to encourage expenditure in the bar. However, the bar crawls are not simply these things. During the course of the evening, the tourists are 'encouraged' to participate in playing games that are designed to abet increased drinking of alcohol. At the start of one crawl, a rep begins proceedings with 'Welcome to the bar crawl from hell. Our aim is to make you as shit-faced as possible. This is the bar crawl from hell'. They also become sites for attention to the body as the games played focus on the body and its functions and highlight gender differences, reinforcing them in the process.

The orchestration of the evening and the joining in with tourists in the games by the reps serves the purpose of the tour operator remaining in control. In addition, it gives the impression that the reps and tourists are like-minded, with the idea that this will encourage the tourists to spend more money on tour operator organised events (Andrews, 2000).

The formats of all the bar crawls that I participate in are similar. The tourists meet in an appointed place, which is usually the first bar. From here they are taken to a series of four or five bars or clubs. The stay in each is usually about an hour. The numbers joining in the crawl can be as many as 200. In the examples discussed here, the crawls are run by two (on one occasion three) of the smaller tour operators working together, and the highest number I encountered was 150 people. However, as the crawl progresses, people drop out if, for example, they find a bar they particularly like. They are also vulnerable to the activities of the PRs. The reps working on the crawl will warn tourists against the PRs. If members of the group are approached the reps will intervene. The extent to which reps discourage tourist interaction with PRs is demonstrated in that, at the start of one crawl, instructions are given to adopt a certain walking position: keep the head down so as not to make eye contact with the PRs. On another crawl, during the swearing of the 'Crawl Oath', part of the promise is to avoid PRs by adopting the 'correct' walking position.[6]

One bar crawl I join differs from others in that the meeting place is the grounds of an apartment block in Palmanova, where many of the tourists are staying. This means that there is a walk to the first bar in Magaluf, shepherded by the tour operator rep, Peter. Peter organises the crocodile of people, placing some young women (referred to as 'heels') wearing high heels at the front of the line. His rationale is, 'the heels can set the pace, if the lads cannot keep up with it then they should be embarrassed'.

## Fred and Wilma

Once everyone is gathered in the first bar and had their first drink (or more), they are introduced to the oath, and told of the rules that will govern their behaviour for the duration of the crawl, and of the forfeits for breaking the rules. One of the commands is the abandoning of personal names in favour of those dictated by the reps. The appointed names do vary, e.g. *Parker* and *Lady Penelope* and *Linda* and *Jurgan*, but one of the most popular formats is *Fred* and *Wilma*. These names apply to everyone, including the reps. However, on one crawl in the summer of 1999, the reps give themselves different names. Peter is to be called 'Major Suntan (for obvious reasons)' [Peter is black], Alan is to be known as 'Major Lionel Blair (because of his haircut)' and the other Peter is to be referred to as 'Major Hangover (because that is what you'll have in the morning)'. The penalty for forgetting to call someone by their 'new' name is, usually, to down a drink in one, and it is not always the one that the tourist is currently drinking. This penalty applies to the other rules of the evening.

### Right or left?

Another edict is the hand that drinks can be held in. Instructions are given by the reps that simply state which hand people must hold their drinks in. As the evening progresses, right is swapped to left, and vice versa. The punishment for transgression of the rule is to down a drink in one.

### Ladies or gents?

Yet another dictate is which toilets the tourists can use. The rule of the evening is that people must use the opposite gender toilets. During one evening, tourists are expected to ask one of the reps for permission to use the toilet; they also have to ask a rep of the opposite sex. The decree changes throughout the evening, with a return to the use of the correct gender conveniences. This may appear as a straightforward exchange of facilities. However, it must also be remembered that not everyone in the bar, or club, is part of the organised crawl, and therefore the rules do not apply.

The price to pay for not asking permission to go to the toilet, or using the incorrect one, is again to down a drink in one. At times, the penalty is added to in that after downing the drink, the tourist has to buy another one. On another occasion, the tourists are told that the use of the incorrect toilets will incur a greater forfeit than downing a drink in one go. There is some resistance to this by some female tourists who refuse to participate in this game, they are not caught and so do not incur any penalties.

## The oath

The swearing of an oath at the beginning of the bar crawls has already been mentioned. In one oath, the tourists must repeat after the rep that they swear an oath by 'the almighty alcoholic' and they swear 'to get "transced[7]" tonight and every night of my holiday'. During the oath the tourists are again warned against interaction with PRs. In another oath, the tourists swear to get drunk, be sick, have sex on the beach and eat a kebab. That some tourists do indeed get very drunk on the bar crawls is evidenced in the example presented of one young male tourist. He is 'exhibited' to the others. He has six stitches above his left eye gained after the last crawl. Due to his inebriated state, his friends had to take him back to their apartment. The premises where they are staying is split into two blocks. They go to the wrong block, but get the room number right and somehow manage to leave him in the apartment.

## Sexual positions

One game that the tourists play is to simulate sexual positions as instructed by the reps. One of the young female tourists, Sharon, plays the game. Afterwards she says, 'I feel so ashamed'. She repeats this several times and while her friend Debbie tries to give her reassurance that she has done nothing wrong, she is clearly upset by her participation in the game.

Debbie and Sharon, both in their late teens, are on a week's holiday. Debbie started her holiday with a group of other girl friends and Sharon joined her later. Before Sharon's arrival, Debbie had not been going out because of the reluctance of her other friends to go with her. She tells me that now she is going out, she is having a good time but normally she would not begin until about 1 am – the crawls start much earlier in the evening. I meet Debbie and Sharon at the first bar on one of the crawls. Both are dressed in mini dresses, Debbie's is black and Sharon's blue. When they first arrive at the bar, Debbie in particular attracts a lot of stares from the men present. Peter tells me that she is a 'cock tease and not old enough'. Later, Debbie says, 'I know I can have sex but I don't want to, I respect my body'. Referring to the rep Alan, both she and

Sharon think 'he's attractive, but he's dirty he'll sleep with anyone'. So, although Magaluf has a reputation as *Shagaluf*, in which there is supposed to be uncontrolled sex, these tourists clearly exhibit constraint.

As part of the crawl, we visit The Underground (the home of the Fat Bastard), one of the many bars/nightclubs on Punta Balena. Because it is still 'early' (i.e. before midnight) the club is empty and the activity is centred on the bar crawl. In this establishment the tourists are advised that they must use the correct gender toilets. Like many of the bars/clubs, The Underground is basically one dark room with a bar and DJ. The tourists are given the opportunity to dance, but the DJ talks over much of the music played, with the effect of inhibiting dancing.

The tourists are gathered on the central dance floor and the DJ tries to engage them in some form of banter. He wants them to cheer when they hear the name of the place that they are from. This does not work very well so he changes tactics and asks each group of tourists, in turn, where they are from. After about an hour we leave.

The next bar is the Stop Bar and the drinks are 'free'.[8] That is, the tourists are issued with a VIP card on production of which they get 'free' drinks. In this bar, as in others (including The Underground), there is a 'strength machine'. The idea is to hit a lever and a light that runs vertically up the machine indicates the strength of the impact. In this case, the lever has lost its padding, thereby exposing the metal underneath. Despite a warning from Peter not to hit the lever, a young male tourist goes ahead and cuts his hand on it. Similar strength machines exist elsewhere in the resorts and are another example of quantifying features of the body. In the case cited here, the tourist wants to go even further by proving he does not need the cushion covering.

On one occasion, the queue into one of the bars is long and busy because the bar crawl is large. Waiting outside for all the tourists to arrive and enter the bar, a young female tourist (not on the crawl) starts talking to Peter and some of the other male reps. She is drunk and keeps lifting her dress up to show us her sunburnt bottom. She tells us, 'I get my tits out all the time, I flashed them once going through customs'. I ask her why she does it, and she replies 'I dunno, but I will'. She then tries to wrestle Peter to the ground. She is proud of her exploits and the exposure of her body appears like an act of defiance, which, along with her attempts to wrestle Peter, indicates a desire to appear to be in control and dominant. She is going to expose herself when, and where, she wants regardless of what any patriarchal figures might dictate.

On the same occasion when the tourists are waiting to go into the bar, one of the reps is shouting at them. It is not clear to me if the rep is inebriated or not, or what the purpose of what he is shouting is trying to achieve, or, indeed, if anyone, other than me, is listening to what he is saying. He is shouting out phrases, some of which are repeated and include, 'don't be shy, give it a try' and 'don't be flash, show us your gash'. Here, the demand is being made by a male that women should expose themselves.

The final bar is Boomerangs (on other nights the crawl has ended in Tokio Joes or Poco Locos, and Heroes nightclub has been included on the itinerary). By this stage, the bar crawl seems to be out of anyone's control, with the lead rep himself drunk. People are staggering around, and someone falls over. There are no attempts to organise the tourists into games or to check their behaviour. I go to use the toilet and a young woman comes out of one cubicle, obviously intoxicated, and advises me not to use it because there is vomit all over the seat. Although she is not a member of the crawl, and the sick may not be hers, like the staggering, falling tourists, it is indicative of a loss of control. Without guidance they fall over; but, it is because of guidance that they have lost control.

The foregoing ethnographic detail has highlighted the emphasis placed on the body in the two resorts. It is used to articulate ideas in society – the body is for having sex, this sex is between men and women, the body should be fit, strong and controlled as the emphasis in some games on speed and stamina suggest. The games allow comparisons between the performers, and between performers and watchers. They are a way of measuring and standardising relationships and the functions of the body.

Most of the preceding discussion has been about the body as object, how it can be read for signs of meaning. Interwoven with this, reference has been made to more experiential readings of the body – the idea of 'vegin' out, feeling hot, etc. Undertaking an experiential reading of the body represents a move away from the subject constructed in an overarching set of codes or categories (that is the body read for signs that signify a person) to an embodied body-subject. For example, thinking of a tattoo of the Union Jack in an embodied way makes it not an emblem or symbol of the self that links the individual with a wider set of cultural practices, but is an extension of the self. The next section examines the body-subject.

## The Body Being

This section is concerned with what the body does. It moves away from the seen and seeing towards actions and feelings, some of which are expressed through the performing body. In using Mauss's concept of body techniques, it moves into the body *habitus* of the tourists, and thus into the theoretical perspective of phenomenology.

Body techniques, as defined by Mauss (1979), have to be learnt. The concept is used as an ordering or categorising device. Many techniques are referred to in the section on the performing tourist – speed, loudness, strength, control. Bourdieu (1979) continued the line of thought about *habitus* in his work on differences in 'class' taste. *Habitus* is used to understand how the external environment is differently absorbed, or interpreted, from the perspective of the subject as a member of a social group. It identifies a socialisation process by which the individual is culturally incorporated into, according to Bourdieu, their class *habitus*. This process of cultural reproduction is connected to an inherited, historical 'cultural capital' and operates as a dynamic process. Bourdieu's work is particularly useful in that it provides a link between the body gaze and the body being. That is, it recognises the outward appearance of the body as a sign of, in his example, class; but also suggests that this is a manifestation of a way of being in the world that is linked to a phenomenological approach to the body.

For theorists such as Jackson (1989) and Gell (1996), human experience is grounded in the movement and way of being of the body, which is itself set within the framework of the material or social environment. Thus, an examination of body uses and experiences gives an indication of ideas about the world. According to Jackson, there is a psychophysical relationship with the world. He cites the example of a fall, which, he says, occurs both in mind and body. He further suggests that a disruption in environment results in changes to bodily dispositions. In trying to understand an apparent role reversal between men and women during a Kuranko initiation ceremony, Jackson (1989: 129) argues that it is the change in *habitus* that gives rise to the change in actions and thus 'lays people open to possibilities of behavior [sic] which they embody, but ordinarily are not inclined to express'. In the case of the fat body, it is possible to suggest that the unfettered, unbuckled body is the embodiment of the apparent free licence to indulge and consume, and to cross boundaries of 'morality' pertaining to codes of dress and public–private displays of the body. Further, given that the disrobing of the body takes place primarily on the beach (a place associated with liminality and spaciousness, compared to the tightly, densely packed, enclosed spaces of the built areas of Magaluf and Palmanova), the unleashing of the body creates a sense of well being in the body-subject that contributes to a feeling, or atmosphere, of ease in the resorts that form part of their product as a tourist commodity.

In Merleau-Ponty's phenomenology, the body is considered as a meeting place of the past, present and future. The 'habitual body' is its learned historical way of being and the 'present body' is how the body is experienced and experiencing in the present. Thus, the *habitus* of Mauss and Bourdieu can be linked to the 'habitual body' – the way of being in the world governed by past experience. The future referred to is derived from the idea that patterns of behaviour are determined by present experience that immediately becomes the past, and influences the future. One technique of the body that is dominant in Magaluf and Palmanova is dancing.

## Dancing

For many of the tourists visiting Palmanova and Magaluf, dancing is an integral part of their holiday experience. This is particularly true of the younger tourists who frequent the bars, fun pubs and nightclubs that are mainly found in Magaluf. This is not to say that older age groups do not dance,[9] but their participation in the late night clubbing activities is less prominent. Much of the music played by the club DJs is popular music found in the UK charts and is suitable for discos. For example, in 1999, music featured on the compact discs and tapes sold in nightclubs included, among others, songs from Vengaboys, Britney Spears, Steps and the Spice Girls. The Car Wash club, however, specialises in 1960s and 1970s music, and other clubs are known for playing house or garage music. Many of the nightclubs, including Bananas, Car Wash, Tokio Joes and Heroes, use paid male and female dancers, with the aim of encouraging customers to dance. These dancers are on raised platforms or podiums. The physical elevation of the dancers heightens their positions as dance leaders, and they appear, to use a religious analogy, like high priests or priestesses. The music is always loud[10] and the tempo invariably fast. In addition, there are pulsating coloured lights, and sometimes strobe lighting. In some ways, there is an increased awareness of the body, but at the same time a loss in consciousness of the body as its rhythms are mirrored by the pulsating lights and the beat of the music, and so the body merges with the surrounding environment. Rather than dancing, the dancer is the dance.

I visited the fun pub Cheeks in Palmanova on several occasions, sometimes alone and at other times accompanied. The visit described here is an accompanied visit. We start off by sitting outside, but eventually move into the building where the music being played is 'It's Raining Men' and 'I'm Horny'. People are either in groups, pairs of friends or in couples. Most of the clientele are young (the outside seating area attracts older people and those with families). There are three or four young women dancing together, along with a couple of young men. They are all in their early to mid twenties. Two of the women have dyed blond hair and they all wear make-up. They are dressed in bootlace strap tops and short skirts. One of the women is wearing a short white lacy dress under which is a white bra top and a pair of close fitting white shorts. She dances with her back to one of the men, who is wearing jeans and a long sleeved shirt. He puts his hand around her waist and slips it down to her crutch. She moves his hand away. Later, they leave the fun pub together. At one point, one of the other women lifts her skirt up to reveal a pair of white lacy knickers. The other man is dancing with all the girls in turn. In one dance, as he moves, he works his way down her body and simulates oral sex. The group of girls sing the words of the songs together and dance with the same actions to the songs. In another group, a man dances between two women and later one of the women dances between the man and the woman. There is an overt display of sexuality and acting out sexual intercourse. They share each others' bodies, responding to each other with intimacy and their bodily rhythms together, via the music, work to tell them they are 'horny'.

I visit the Britannia pub in Magaluf with Nancy, a worker in the resort. On entering the pub, it is very crowded with middle-aged men and women on a golfing holiday.[11] As we walk around the bar and through the crowd, Nancy bumps into one of the younger males in the crowd. Everyone is dancing. One couple is engaged in a continual kiss, even when they dance, although at one point he lifts her into the air. A man falls over and hits his back as he goes down. Later, another man falls on his back, he bends his knees up over his chest and other members of the crowd spin him around. One man keeps coming up to me and tries to get me to dance. At one point, he gestures towards his penis. Eventually, he takes off his belt and starts pulling it in-between his legs, rubbing himself. The dancing continues and everyone is swaying and heaving together. At one point, I feel as though I am on a boat. The movement seems to be quite fast and there is an intensity and excitement about the atmosphere. Nancy dances with the young man she bumped into and he buys her two red roses. Suddenly, one of the other men grabs me and I try to extricate myself from his grip, only succeeding when one of the bar men intervenes.

Benny Hills is another fun pub in Magaluf. It also plays disco music and has pulsating coloured lights and videos of people having accidents or animals doing 'amusing' things. People are given garlands to wear made from brightly coloured plastic. Sometimes they are worn around the neck or twisted several times around the wrist. The interior of the pub is decorated with football scarves from various teams, both British and Spanish, along with statues imitating those that might be found in ancient Greece or Rome. The pub's clientele is composed of a mixture of age groups. People are dancing together. The notable thing is that the group of dancers is made up of smaller groups of friends but everyone comes together in the dance. There is one group of six or seven young men. One of them encourages an elderly woman to get up and dance with him, and another starts to dance with a young woman. The latter is stopped with the appearance of the woman's partner and she re-orientates her body towards him in the dance. On the whole, however, there is evident enjoyment of the dancing and there is an air of excitement in the pub.

The ease of movement and the fluidity of the body, associated with dancing, is in contrast to the way in which the body is usually held in position – e.g. sitting at a desk or driving – and points the way towards a naturalness or flow in the establishment of relationships. Dancing is a means of display and of testing out potential partners' bodily compatibility or to show off one's own body. For example, in one nightclub a young male dancer spins himself around across the whole dance floor. At the same time, a group of women are dancing. They are a mixed age group from early twenties to forties. One of them wants to encourage everyone to dance. She comes up to me and tries to pull me up to dance, 'come on, we're all women, no problem'.

The element of display associated with dancing is also borne out in the 'podium dancing' undertaken by some of the younger tourists. I witness this several times in Banana Joes Nite Club. The area in a corner of the club where the DJ is stationed is surrounded by a shelf, about 30 cm wide and approximately 1 m off the ground (the shelf runs along the back wall of the club and is used primarily for standing drinks on). Young women (sometimes men) climb onto the shelf in front of the DJ to dance (Figure 6.1 and Figure 6.2). Only four people are allowed at one time. Some of the lads on the dance floor try to look up the women's skirts and dresses. Sometimes, the men lie on the floor underneath the girls, and have their photographs taken.

The crowd in Banana Joes Nite Club is mainly, but not exclusively, young. During 1 week, the club is frequented by a group of 16 lads

**Figure 6.1** Male tourists dancing on the DJ's shelf

**Figure 6.2** Female tourists dancing on the DJ's shelf

from Yorkshire. Except for one or two, they are wearing football shirts emblazoned with the word 'Brownies' on the front and their names on the back. Two of them are trying very hard to 'pull'. They kiss girls full on the lips and then try to get them to dance. One of the young women is quite short; she has long black hair and is running around in the crowd without looking where she is going. At one point, she is lifted into the air and onto the shoulders of one of the lads and they dance around like this for a while, as if carrying a trophy. One night, two of the lads do a 'Full Monty'. With their backs to the rest of the crowd, they take their trousers off and then take their boxer shorts down. They then turn to the others and hide their penises in between their legs, which somewhat detracts from the 'Full Monty' idea. Prior to this, another male had stripped down to his boxer shorts. In both cases, their penises remain hidden, which in some respects is neutering, the penis is only referred to. At the same time, the lads are teasing and remaining in control, enacting the idea that male genitalia should remain hidden.

Displays of parts of the body that are normally hidden can be interpreted as an act of defiance. However, the crossing of boundaries and the freedom of exposure can also be understood in the same way as the unfettered fat body – the literal, as well as metaphorical, hanging out and relaxation associated with the holiday. In this particular case, the constricted nature of the tourist experience is recognised in the hiding of the penises. The penis is not actually displayed and therefore cannot be an act of defiance, but, rather shows constraint. In another club, a man begins to strip but is stopped by bar staff. In Pirates Adventure, three of the male Pirates start to strip but stop before removing any clothes. Men, unlike women, can show constraint when it comes to displaying their bodies. This too is a conventional attitude. In the Garden of Eden, woman is the temptress who cannot control her urges to eat the forbidden fruit and leads man astray. Men, however, can portray their power and dominance through exposure of non-sexualised parts of the body – the chest and beer belly, which are indicative of strength and courage.

During one evening in Banana Joes Fun Pub, one of the waiters is encouraged by a group of female tourists to remove his shirt. One of the young women carries it like a trophy. This incident is in contrast to the others cited, where men are expected to show constraint and not become objects of the female gaze and subject to their consumption, in the way that women are asked to do for men. The case that exposure is sanctioned and encouraged in women has already been made.

The fluency of the body in the disco dance is in contrast to other forms of dancing found in the resorts. For example, in Banana Joes Fun Pub,

**Figure 6.3** Tourists doing the Conga

there are times when everyone follows instructions from the DJ on how to dance. He plays music that requires particular actions – e.g. *YMCA*, *Star Trekking* and *The Music Man*. On other occasions, Frank Sinatra's *New York New York* is played and tourists line up, link arms and do leg kicks in time to the music. At other times, we are instructed to do the conga, (Figure 6.3) the circuit of which includes going outside, down the road and back again. This also forms an act of display, becoming objects of attention for those not involved. People clearly enjoy doing something silly. The enforced touching involved in forming a conga line brings individuals physically closer together. It brings about a bodily experience of sharing. Although the dancing is orchestrated, the feeling of community still exists and the atmosphere is infective. It becomes automatic to join with others in telling the DJ to 'fuck off' as part of the rapport he tries to develop with the crowd. The singing and dancing together is exciting and the pulsating lights and heat create a feeling of sensuality. The shouting of 'fuck off' and joining in the dancing are spontaneous, rather than calculated reactions.

Dancing as a way of building social relationships operates at a broad level, that is, among strangers as well as at a more localised level within the family. Fathers dance with their little girls, they carry them as they move around the dance floor in a mock waltz. One father in Banana Joes Fun Pub explains to me that he and his teenage daughter have been to

BCM and Planet Rock dancing. He says 'I'll dance all night with her if that's what she wants. I've shown her how to have a good time without drinking excessively. We haven't drunk that much when we've been out. This is our first holiday abroad and I've shown the children [he also has a younger teenage son] how to holiday abroad. It's their turn now to organise their own holidays'.

The ease of movement associated with dancing and the building of social relationships or (re)affirmation of them has resonance with the imitative rites of Australian Aborigines described by Durkheim (1915: 358). He asserts that ceremonies in which the totem animal – kangaroo, emu, etc. – is imitated in movement 'does not limit itself to expressing this kinship; it makes it or remakes it ... Therefore, these leaps, these cries and these movements of every sort, though bizarre and grotesque in appearance, really have a profound and human meaning'.

## Summary

This chapter has examined the ways in which judgements are made about the body in relation to its abilities and the way in which bodies, which are seen to be less than fit and able, are judged to be a nuisance and a burden to the individual as well as the collective. Part of this relates to the fat body. However, appearance can also be used to make a defiant gesture. In the case of the 'fat bastard', he both embodies his self-confessed obnoxious personality and is a symbol of it.

Many of the judgements surrounding the body are based on how it functions and what it can do. In short, how well it can perform. A number of the games that involve tourists performing, pick-up on normalising aspects of the body, e.g. conventional male and female sexual relationships, strength, stamina and speed. The competitive nature of the games and displays that the tourists are involved in not only serves as reflexive activities, but reminds them of their role as consumers and their place within the capitalist system. They are performing as individuals and, as Bauman (1997a: 39, emphasis in original) notes, 'consumption is a thoroughly *individual* activity: it also sets individuals at cross purposes, often at each others' throats'. In many of the games played, there is an emphasis on sex either through simulating its performance or by innuendo. Again this links the tourists firmly to consumer culture as observations by Featherstone (1991) suggest.

Throughout both this and the previous chapter, references are made to the body that moves beyond the symbolic realm and the body as object, to an understanding of the body as a feeling, doing entity rather than couched within a set of codes or structures. One particular feature of this is dancing. Most of the dancing in Magaluf and Palmanova encourages free movement of the body in relation to the music, it is not about consciously moving this arm and that leg. It links people together as they share the same space and sense of the music. Thus, dancing is an embodiment of the social aspect of the holiday and the sense of ease and freedom that is felt to accompany the tourists' experiences. At the same time, the movements often both express and embody the sexualised nature of the holiday for some of the tourists. The idea that Magaluf is Shagaluf is enacted in the body movements of some of the dancers.

In this chapter, demarcations are made between male and female; the fit and unfit. In the case of the former, attention is drawn to conventional gender roles. To be different would establish the person as an outsider and thus a threat to the in-group. This confirmation of identity, which is manifest in the idea of uniform approaches to gender, helps to create a sense of security both for the individual, as one is not left to one's own devices, and for the group, because there are no unknown entities threatening to undermine the in-group. The conventionalising of gender differences calls on the nostalgic views of the way that Britain used to be.

Such ideas have resonance with the notion of the loss of power in post World War II Britain. Other societal changes, which have altered some of what it means to be British, are, for example, the perceived threats from the European Union and immigration. The latter are both understood as outside forces, which are seen to threaten the security found in national identity and the ability to control one's own fate. The idea of harmonisation that these ideas suggest again links to the market, the requirement to join in. The inability to do so, either through lack of means (monetary or bodily) or in the case of the bar crawls, a lack of control, is punishable. At the same time, the idea of the imperfect tourist leads to marginalisation; these people are not in control of themselves but are dependent on others. Thus, a particular group of people are not only stigmatised as different, they are ridiculed for their inability to participate, and they are objects of derision as they are seen as a drain on the resources of the fit and able. At the same time, they serve as reminders of the dangers of non-conformism, of being excluded from participation in the market. Again, this points to a tension between the offer of freedom in consumption practices and the need for regulation. The message is that in order to be a full member of the nation collective one must be a consumer, and be under the impression that consumption practices are an exercise in choice and agency.

The body in Magaluf and Palmanova cannot be avoided; it is both a vehicle of expression as well as a means of identifying the experiential features of the holiday. How it feels, reacts and is used helps to create the spaces of the resorts. In the next chapter, I will consider how particular consumption practices make the tourists.

## Notes

1. It is not the case that all of the men had bodies that appeared taut and attenuated but none would be described as fat or flabby.
2. A sad fact is that during the 1998 low season, a mentally impaired man went missing during a holiday to Magaluf and was later found dead in the surrounding countryside.
3. Julius Caesar Act 1, Sc. 2 191. Shakespeare.
4. On WWW at http://www.healthcarerepublic.com/news/934442/Cost-obesity-NHS-England-rise-62-billion/. Accessed 11.10.
5. However, in extreme cases of slimming disorders, it is self-destructive and repressive.
6. The marshalling of people between the bars also has a practical purpose in that the reps have to keep order. That is, they must not allow the tourists to wander outside the group onto the road. If this should happen, the reps are liable to be fined by the local police.
7. 'Transced' was what it sounded like the rep were saying.
8. The idea of free drinks seems incompatible with the fact that the tourists have paid to go on the bar crawl.
9. During the winter months, 'ball room' dancing is an integral part of the holiday experience for many of the elderly tourists.
10. The volume is actually metered and subject to inspection by the police. It is possible to override the meter but at the risk of being caught and fined. At midnight, the volume is supposed to be turned down.
11. One point about 'golfing holidays' is that they are often used by men as a cover for extra-marital relationships, according to one informant. It is therefore not clear if the women would describe themselves as being on a golfing holiday or if they were the partners of the men.

# Chapter 7
# *Consuming Tourists*

Cooking and eating can be a way of travelling to foreign countries.
(Kuper, 1997: x)

## Introduction

The main purpose of this chapter is to show the relationship between what is consumed and constructions of national identity. The discussions of space and the body have explored the symbolic and phenomenological aspects of tourism in Magaluf and Palmanova. This chapter on food and drink will follow a similar pattern.

The quote from Kuper suggests that the consumption of food[1] is a way of experiencing the other, of tasting and ingesting the essence of other places. In Palmanova and Magaluf, however, although the tourists have travelled to another country, their consumption practices are a way of remaining at home, and keeping the other at bay. I will demonstrate that what is ingested says something about the identity of the consumer. By relating practices of consumption to place, I will show that consumption practices have a spatial element. For example, a 'proper' cup of tea is 'proper' in the context of The Willows café-bar because it is served by English people in an English establishment with cups and saucers. The chapter will also relate to the body. Firstly, the old maxim 'we are what we eat' speaks for itself, as Bourdieu (1979: 190) notes, 'tastes in food also depends on the idea each class has of the body and of the effects of food on the body'. Secondly, I will pick up on the connection between the appearance of the body and consumption habits. I begin with the discussion's theoretical framework.

## Theoretical Framework

The study of food and drink has been an important aspect of social anthropological enquiry since the discipline's earliest beginnings (e.g. Frazer, 1993 [1922]). Evans-Pritchard (1940) demonstrates that in order to comprehend Nuer society, it is necessary to understand the relationship between the people and their food. Such an interdependent relationship with food in modern societies has been discussed by Beardsworth and Keil (1990: 149) as, 'increasingly remote from everyday experience'. Nevertheless, they claim that there is a mutual dependency of people, animals and plants in which networks of relationships influence what is eaten and the physical nature of the world that humans inhabit.

For many in western Europe there is a wide range of sources of food and drink from which to choose. Given this observation, it is reasonable to suggest that the choices exercised over the utilisation of food and drink are indicative of who we are, and our relationship to the world at large. Thus, food and drink are media for the symbolic expression of social relationships and us as individuals; they provide insights into cultural and social values and elucidate notions of identity and difference (Douglas, 1984; Mars, 1987; Gusfield, 1987; Gurr, 1987; Caplan, 1994). In addition, Caplan (1994: 28) argues, 'keeping one's own food traditions are an important way of maintaining boundaries'. This remark is highly relevant to the current context because in the resorts the choice of food available is predominately 'British'.[2] Food is noted by Douglas (1984) to be a field of action, and, as such, the meanings of food and drink cannot be divorced from the social context within which they are consumed. The values placed on food have been argued by Barthes (1975: 49) to arise both from personal idiosyncrasies as well as what he describes as the 'collective imagination'. Food, therefore, is 'a system of communication, a body of images, a protocol of usages [sic], situations, and behavior [sic]' (Barthes, 1975: 50).

No analysis of food and drink would be complete without a consideration of their preparation, as preparation itself is symbolic or suggestive of social relations (e.g. Lévi-Strauss, 1964, 1997; Barthes, 1975; Selwyn, 1980; Valentine, 1999). The relationship between what is eaten, from where it is derived and its preparation has been explored by Archetti (1997) in his consideration of the guinea pig in Ecuador. He describes the way in which the keeping, circulating and cooking of guinea pigs, while not separate from material needs, articulates social relations in terms of status, occasion, service and reward.

In terms of gender, sets of binary oppositions have been noted by Bourdieu (1979) in suggesting that some food and drink consumption practices are indicative of gender and class distinctions embedded in the *habitus*. The concept of *habitus* does, however, allow for individuals to negotiate with *a priori* constructs, challenging and subverting existing structures. Consumption choices can then be either a way of changing or maintaining the self. The presence of so much 'British' food in the resorts and the choice exercised by the tourists to consume these, betray an allegiance to a national identity in the rejection of the other 'Spanish' food.

This sense of self-maintenance is all the more established given the appropriation of the physical space of the resorts, highlighted in Chapters 3 and 4. The confirmation of the *habitus* is thus both spatial and alimentary.

The question of the symbolic expression, or signifying, of identity through food has been examined in depth by a number of scholars (e.g. Barthes, 1993; Fiddes, 1991; Varney, 1996). There is also an aspect of food and drink consumption that places it within a phenomenological framework that examines food and drink rituals. For example, dressing up for dinner, the use of the same establishment for drinking and what is done with food. It is linked to the body through the concept of *habitus*, that is, who people are and what they eat impacts on their appearance (Bourdieu, 1979: 190). This, in turn, relates to techniques of the body, which Appadurai (1993) suggests require habituation and repetition to be developed, i.e. drinking in the same bar and sticking to the same food routines of what and when things are eaten. Tourists develop habits even in the short time of their holidays – drinking in the same bar everyday and the need to maintain the same routines as at home. For example, one elderly tourist recounted his disappointment at having missed lunch 'at the appropriate time'.

The connection between food and body shape is also directly related to space. Consumption habits demarcate cultural boundaries and give form to spatial scales. In addition, the size of our bodies determines how much space we physically occupy. Our sense of place is also informed by food choices, e.g. the connection between fast food and modern urban environments versus the quaint, quiet tea-room of the rural locale (Bell & Valentine, 1997).

In terms of the relationship between food and the body, Caplan (1997) has suggested that weight loss diets only occur in times of plenty. The choice and quality of food available as well as what is eaten and the lack of attention to diets are popular points of conversation for tourists. The abundance of food and drink available without 'work' (although it has been worked for in the home world through jobs and savings), is indicative of ideas relating to paradise, and because this is a time of plenty, in which dieting is not undertaken, it is also redolent of feasting.

Feasting has been observed by Caplan (1997) to suggest two things. Firstly, it can be seen as a leveller in which social relations are fostered by the sharing of food and drink between social groups (cf. Mauss's [1954] classic exploration of the potlatch in *The Gift*). Secondly, Caplan suggests that feasts can also be indicative of greed, gluttony and ostentation, as well as, in some circumstances, highlighting 'class' differences between those that have and eat 'rich' foods, and those who do not. In terms of tourism, both of these scenarios might be seen to apply.

Tourism has been described as a social leveller because it is seen as providing a sort of 'anonymity' to the participants, in that the status enjoyed (or not) in the home world is left there and tourists of all social class or status mix equally in the holiday environment (Wagner, 1977). Examples of such levelling in the current ethnography include the use of 'small-talk' among tourists in hotel lifts, and demonstrations of camaraderie in helping each other with the logistics of the toasters in hotel dining rooms. It is also the case that although I categorise the tourists as 'working class', their perceptions of themselves may not meet this description, although it may be extended to their fellow travellers. In this respect, tourism offers the opportunity to affirm differences between people, which can be explored in what and where they eat. For example, one young woman staying in the Cala Blanca Hotel in Palmanova tells me that the hotel is, 'one of the most expensive in this area' and, in recounting her daily routine, which usually ends with a drink in one of the bars along Passeig Maritim de Son Maties, she comments, 'it's quite posh really'. She distinguishes herself and her holidaymaking from that found in Magaluf by linking her experience to that of seeking Spanish culture, as opposed to those tourists staying in an apartment in Magaluf. 'I didn't want to be surrounded by hometown and watch *Only Fools and Horses* surrounded by cans of beer. You can do that at home'. This serves to illustrate the association of particular consumption practices with place.

The idea of ostentation and display is evident in the manner in which tourists describe how they have left their diets behind, and eaten and drunk more than usual. Paul describes how, in one hotel, he witnessed tourists piling their plates high with food, to the point that it seems the food would tip over. Similar activities are observable in other hotels. Another dimension to feasting and tourism is that explored by Schwimmer (1979), who reacts to the idea that the advent of tourism has been attributed with endangering the tradition of feasting. He adopts Van Gennep's *Rite of Passage*, suggesting that *communitas* present in feasting only occurs in tourism when there is intercultural exchange between 'hosts' and tourists. Given that the holiday to Magaluf and Palmanova does not fit this pattern, other observations by Schwimmer on the same topic appear more apposite:

> The "trooping the colour" aspect of tourism arises where the essential transactions are not between tourists and hosts but by a group of tourists coming together to further a common cause whose ultimate success depends, however, on common efforts that will follow after the tour or feast. These common efforts are, of course, more often

political or economic or cultural rather than military. Metaphorically, however, such gatherings may be regarded as war councils.
(Schwimmer, 1979: 232)

If what is ingested is a way of maintaining boundaries, as Caplan (1997)
implies, and tourists' experiences in Magaluf and Palmanova are interpreted as an enactment of a particular type of 'Britishness', then the feasting
relates to a 'common effort' of maintaining this 'Britishness'. In this sense,
tourists' experiences are a confirmation of ideas pertaining to Durkheimian
social facts rather than a search for the other that tourism is often claimed to
be. I proceed with an exploration of the connection between tourists'
consumption practices and expressions of national identity.

## Eating and Drinking Home

This section analyses the ways in which the diets of the tourists in
Palmanova and Magaluf keep the home world in mind and body. The
connection between food and national identity is well rehearsed, e.g. Bell
and Valentine (1997), Doving (1999) and Ohnuki-Tierney (1993). The
latter's exploration of rice in Japanese society highlights the role of the
home-grown crop symbolising a 'pure' kind of 'Japaneseness', which
was used during World War II as a call to arms. At stake was the
maintenance of the production and consumption of 'pure white rice'
(Ohnuki-Tierney, 1993: 131). The impure other had to be kept at bay.

Drinking water in Magaluf and Palmanova is linked to ideas of purity
and danger. Tourists are advised not to drink tap water. Some tourists
heed this advice by checking the source of water-based produce, e.g. ice.
The desire to avoid contamination links firmly to ideas of boundary
maintenance, highlighting a tension between freedom and constraint. On
the one hand, the tourists are sold the idea of freedom, the fantasy of
plenty, yet, on the other, warnings of drinking foreign water serve to
restrain and reaffirm boundaries. In this respect, the need to maintain
other practices of 'Britishness', including queuing for dinner or eating at
a set time of day, as well as what is eaten, become more easily
understood. For example, one tourist, now residing in Jamaica, explains
that although he feels a greater sense of freedom in his new home, which
enables him to 'live life how I want to live', he does miss British culture,
which he describes as 'the theatre, entertainment, beer, bacon and
sausages'. During discussion with two other tourists, Jill, feeling hungry,
wishes to return to their hotel because 'I want to be first in the queue'.
However, her partner Craig says he does not want to queue 'because it
shows you are British'. Standing in a line is indicative of order, and lines

of attack and, by corollary, defence. Discipline is required to maintain the queue with everyone keeping their place and taking their turn. As such, one must know one's place and stick to it. Not only is keeping order related to militarism, but maintaining discipline (especially on holiday) is conformist.

The link between food and national identity is an important aspect of alimentary life in Palmanova and Magaluf. What is consumed and what is rejected and the acceptability of such speaks directly to the idea of the creation of an other. Drinking water provides an example in which a binary opposition demarcating difference is established. In Magaluf and Palmanova, tourists drinking fresh cold water is almost taboo. However, its use in the making of tea and coffee is not. The former beverage is understood as quintessentially British and the pursuit of a 'proper cup of tea' is an oft-remarked upon activity by tourists.

## A proper cup of tea

Tourists arriving as part of a package deal are met at the airport by a tour operator representative (rep) and escorted to their relevant hotel or apartment. During the journey from airport to accommodation, the rep gives a talk imparting practical information: resetting watches, the importance of attending welcome meetings and a warning not to drink the local water. The combination of reminders about time changes, along with jokes about the weather, highlight the differences between home and Mallorca, which are reinforced by suggesting that the water is not safe to drink. In this context, the other becomes threatening. Tourists take up this advice and are aware, regardless of whether they have arrived as part of a package or not, that the water is different.

For example, during one afternoon's bar stop, Bill and Trevor are trying to persuade their partners Pat and Dawn to have another drink. In the face of refusal, Trevor suggests that they should have an ice-lolly. Dawn declines based on the fact that 'it would be made from their water'. Other tourists will enquire whether ice provided at bars is made from tap water or bottled water, and reject it if the former.

The other drink that is given a similar treatment is tea. Although no-one ever questioned the source of the water from which it was made, the ability to obtain what is seen as a 'proper' cup of tea is important. Tea can be seen to be definitively British. Although it links the UK to her colonial past and the present day African and Asian continents, tea has been incorporated into 'British' culture to such an extent that it is representative of the country and (some of) the people (Paxman, 1998; Parr, 1998, 2000).[3]

During a conversation with two women on the beach, they decide to go and get some refreshments. They were gone for quite some time. On their return, they explain their prolonged absence: 'we stopped in McDonald's for a proper cup of tea'. Speaking to an elderly man, he tells me that he and his wife had walked to The Willows. He explains, 'it's a nice little English bar, the food's English and they speak English'. Here, 'you can get a proper cup of tea'. On another occasion in the bar of the Son Maties Hotel, two couples are discussing aspects of the hotel, one tourist comments, 'they [the Spanish staff] don't know how to make tea properly', although another claims that at breakfast it is possible to make a decent cup, when the tourists make it for themselves. Another member of the group says that they have found 'a place to have a proper cup of tea' and that in addition 'you can get Nescafe coffee in great big cups [and] ooh it was lovely'. However, the search for a proper cup of tea is not always approved of as one expatriate bar owner advises. She is embarrassed by the behaviour of the British tourists because they make no attempt to speak Spanish and are always moaning about the lack of a 'proper cup of tea'.

The idea of a proper cup of tea is undoubtedly and in the first place connected to the way it tastes. It (i.e. a 'proper cup') will taste differently from tea made in the UK since the water is naturally different. The actual tea used in the brewing is also different, although some café-bars use familiar UK brands. However, a 'proper cup of tea' is also derived from the context in which it is drunk. McDonald's is a far cry from the image of a quaint cosy country cottage tea-room in which one might expect to find a proper cup of tea. However, McDonald's is a ubiquitous feature of the British urban environment; it is therefore familiar and established. In this respect, it carries a sense of authority in being able to provide a 'proper' drink.

Similarly, The Willows café-bar has the ability to serve a proper cup of tea. Unlike some café-bars, but by no means all of them, The Willows serves its tea in small white china teapots, with matching small white china milk jugs, and white china cups and saucers. Here, refinement is associated with the tea, and there is a degree of autonomy over it, to the extent that customers are left to their own devices in pouring it, thereby determining its strength. Further, The Willows is attractive because it is owned and run by English expatriates and the language spoken is English.

The connection between tea and water brings into focus the idea of purity and danger. The importance of tea is not just reliant on its association with Britishness, but also in what is symbolised through the use of boiled water. Water in its natural state represents the Mallorcan other, coming directly from the land of the other. To digest it uncooked would be to ingest the other. The symbolic importance of keeping non-boiled water away reflects Douglas's (1966: 151) assertion 'that food is not likely to be polluting at all unless the external boundaries of the social system are under pressure'. In the case under discussion, here the boundaries of national identity need to be affirmed in the face of being in the land of the other. As Douglas (1966: 152) also suggests, '[b]efore being admitted to the body some clear symbolic break is needed to express food's separation from necessary but impure contacts. The cooking process ... provides this break'. In Palmanova and Magaluf, the source of the water is unavoidable, but the boiling process breaks the contact – even more so if it is within the environment of, for example, The Willows or McDonald's – the boiled water is safe to digest, acting as a boundary to the other.

## 'A bucket of vindaloo'[4]

Curry has become part of the British culinary landscape (James, 1997). It is often associated with the practice of going to the pub for beer to be followed by a curry. The ability to drink large volumes of the former and eat the hottest of the latter, are testaments to manliness, strength and holding one's own. During the 1998 football World Cup, the English 'anthem' for the competition was a song called 'Vindaloo'. The ditty's chorus is 'Vindaloo, Vindaloo', the strains of which are audible through-out the resorts (Andrews, 1999).[5]

However, perhaps the most evocative depiction of the idea of being able to stomach something hot is in the following incident that occurred by a beachside drinks kiosk. The barman, Pascal, has a good rapport with his clients, encourages drinking, administers advice about overcoming hangovers and applies penalties for misdemeanours such as spilling one's drink. One afternoon, a young man approaches the kiosk; he is completely inebriated. He is squinting, unable to open one eye and his skin is red. He informs Pascal and all the patrons that he is a jockey. Then he claims that he is a Club 18–30 rep and has only been on Mallorca for one day. He continues 'last night I had a shag ... I had a shag last night', at which point he farts, which is a punishable offence. The penalty is a shot of spirits containing a chilli, which has to be downed, or eaten, with the drink. He accepts the drink, downs it but refuses the chilli. Other customers start to goad him, 'call yourself an Englishman' and 'Thought you said you were English'. Still he refuses to consume the chilli, and

Pascal comments 'I've never known an Englishman to say no to the full penalty'.

During bar crawls, tour operator reps also play on the tourists' ability to stomach strong things. One bar in Magaluf, Pachas, is known for its 'deadly' cocktails: The Fireball, The Parrot and The Killer. According to one rep, drinking The Parrot is a marker of being a rep in Magaluf. Tourists are taken to the bar as part of bar crawls. The cocktails are promoted as being very strong and they have to be drunk in a certain way. The Fireball, for example, involves having some of the liquid lit in the mouth. The Parrot requires inhaling fumes from the drink before drinking it down. One of the reps demonstrates how to drink The Parrot. The tourists are told that anyone who can drink all three of the cocktails in succession and not be sick, 'will be a legend... will leave the bar and island a legend'. A young male tourist takes the bait, after drinking the third cocktail he immediately rushes out of the bar as if to be sick; he is not sick, but is now very drunk. The next bar on the crawl is Heroes.

The appeal to manliness associated with these cocktails and their statement of identity, in sealing the status of a tour operator rep and proclaiming people to be legends, is also exemplified in the challenges laid out by the DJ in Banana Joes Fun Pub. Pints of cocktails are available and Dave frequently encourages tourists to buy them by introducing a competitive element. For example, can they be drunk in one go? Dave explains the take-up of the challenge thus: 'because they think they're a man', although in reality they are drunk by women too.

The ability to consume large amounts of alcohol and stomach the hottest curries is linked to a sense of identity in terms of gender and nation. Such associations have a long history. For example, Bishop (1991: 31) notes that eating beef and mutton was seen as an important aspect of the English diet and gave the strength for the victories at the battles of Crécy and Agincourt. In a further link between what is eaten, and landscape and ideas of Britishness, Bishop notes that the paintings of John Constable, particularly *The Cornfield*, unites all three. At the beginning of the 19th century, fears were expressed by William Cobbett that Britishness was being threatened by the ubiquitous use of potatoes as opposed to bread; and so, just to depict corn growing was interpreted as a patriotic activity. The foregoing discussion has demonstrated that through practices of food and drink consumption, boundaries concerning identity are established and maintained, contributing to the sense of place in the resorts. The next section focuses on particular dishes that form part of the tourists' diets.

## Home Cooking

There is a paucity of Spanish and Mallorcan food in the resorts. Although it is possible to buy tapas, paella, Mallorcan soup and some dishes that have been cooked in a Mediterranean style, they are not prominent and tend to be spatially marginalised. The majority of the food on offer in the two resorts is recognisably 'British'. That is, they are dishes associated with Britain, including: roast beef, fish and chips, steak pie, potatoes and peas and the British breakfast or fry-up. It is not just the case that the dishes available appear to be typically British by name, but the content of the meals is also British. Many of the food outlets make an issue of the derivation of their food. It is therefore possible to eat Weetabix and cornflakes with British milk. Other imported foods include bacon, bread and fish.

### Fried pigs and tourists

The most popular dish is the fry-up or full breakfast. The meal consists of bacon, sausage, egg and beans. Extras include tomato, chips, toast, fried bread, mushrooms and bread and butter. It is normally accompanied by tea or coffee. Some café-bars only serve breakfast until midday, others the whole time they are open. It is therefore possible to eat a fry-up round the clock. It is often advertised alongside depictions of the Union Jack (Figures 7.1 and 7.2). Part of the attraction of eating the breakfast is its cheapness,[6] familiarity and the speed at which it can be delivered to the table. All these aspects are practical concerns, but the importance of the meaning of the breakfast lies in its signalling of the identity of the eaters and the way in which they inhabit the social world.

Speaking to the owner of one bar, he tells me that 'It is just comfort food. People don't have time to cook the breakfast at home so they eat it here, it's the only place they get it apart from their mother's'.[7] The significance in what he is saying lies in the link between the food and the mother. In an environment in which tourists are made in some contexts to be infants, or play the part of infants, the fry-up as food associated with mum gives insight into its popularity.

That the breakfast is special on holiday and forms a marker of the hiatus in life that the vacation can represent (Graburn, 1989) is expressed by some tourists. An elderly woman comments, 'we wouldn't normally eat breakfast, well my husband likes it, but it's in the hotel so it's so tempting'. Another couple note, 'we've been having the fried breakfast, we don't have time at home'.

**Figure 7.1** Advertising 'Great British Breakfast'

**Figure 7.2** Advertising the Fry-up

That food provides comfort or can be used as a method of placating people is evident when it is offered as compensation to complaining tourists. In one hotel, some tourists are seeking recompense for what they see as a ruined holiday. Along with alternative accommodation, the manager offers them free breakfast every morning. In a separate incident, in which some tourists claim the theft of items from their room, the family is offered a free meal in the hotel.

An understanding of the self as self, and as distinct from the other, requires a comprehension of where differences lie. In the case of the fry-up, it occurs in the contents of the dish, when the ingredients are not British, and in the way in which it is cooked. One woman opines, 'the food in the hotel is very good'. She comments on the variety available and says that if people are dissatisfied, 'I don't think you could be pleased, ... but the only thing is they [the Spanish staff] don't know how to cook bacon... sometimes they have ham instead which is not the same'. Douglas, who is staying in a different hotel, grumbles that the breakfast is not very good, 'the toast is lacking in texture and the bacon and sausages are not like the English versions. The sausages are like the ones in hot dogs'. In the case of the breakfast, the demarcation that occurs is based less on fear (as in the case of fresh water) but rather on the difference in the taste of the food and a dislike of the way it has been cooked. The origins of the ingredients, and the way in which they are cooked, serve to mark ideas of differences between 'us' and 'them'.

The presence of familiar food provides a feeling of security. It does not challenge ontological security because it is a known entity. Hamish, a tourist from Dundee explains, 'I like somewhere commercial. I've been to Tenerife and Torremolinos ... they are all the same really. When you come to Spain you know what you are getting. I like to come to a place where I know I'll be able to get a fried breakfast'. He is demonstrating that his liking and experience of place is linked to the food available. He enjoys being able to consume and engage with a commercial setting, commenting that he would not like to go to India because it is too underdeveloped, but that he has been to Los Angeles and Vegas.

The idea of comfort alluded to in connection with the fry-up is also found in its value after a heavy night's drinking. If it is possible to stomach food, a full breakfast can be very satisfying. There is an urban myth that the contents of the meal are a good hangover cure, probably due to the fat soothing the lining of the stomach. The idea of soothing one's innards is also related to comfort. In regard to the body, a fat body with folds of flesh to nestle into, is more comforting than a thin, hard, bony one. Barthes (1957) has discussed external body creams as signifiers of a soothing effect. What is eaten can occupy a similar symbolic space.

The pig, like the breast, is an ubiquitous image in Palmanova and Magaluf, appearing on postcards, in the form of ornaments, fridge magnets and toys engaging in sexual intercourse (Figure 7.3). In one postcard entitled 'Lovingly Yours', a pair of breasts has been altered into the faces of two pigs. The link between pigs and comfort could not be made more explicit.

The symbolic significance of pigs can be found in their deep-rooted role in British food and farming practices and their use in the symbolic economy of the social world. At one time, the keeping of a cottage pig was an integral part of cottage life and although this practice diminished with the advent of industrialisation and urbanisation (Malcolmson & Mastoris, 1998), nevertheless, pigs still carry symbolic significance.

The symbolic role of pigs is complex and contradictory, occupying both a 'positive' and 'negative' position in the symbolic world. Pig images have been used to connote 'unacceptable' behaviour, e.g. being a glutton, lazy and greedy (Haddon, 1996; Malcomson & Mastoris, 1998). On the other hand, piggy banks are associated with savings and, therefore, building a future, as their proliferation among banking advertisements would indicate. The ambivalence of attitudes towards pigs largely stems

**Figure 7.3** Pig figure souvenirs (Photo Montage: Les Roberts)

from their liminal status, in that they are neither of the house nor of the field (Leach, 1964).

In February 2002, the meat company, Walls, advertised its sausages and bacon on huge billboards around London. One showing cooked sausages and bacon carried the wording 'Sunday Morning Worship'. Here the connection to some kind of special feast day and honouring of a particular food is obvious. It further demonstrates (although clearly a promotional drive by Walls) that pig produce occupies a special place in the lives of some British people. Obviously, those who are non-pork or non-meat eaters are excluded. The advert acts as a binding mechanism for the included in that it feeds into the imagination a shared experience in much the same way as Anderson (1991) describes a nationalist sentiment based on an 'imagined community'.

I am suggesting that one of the reasons for the popularity of the fry-up in Palmanova and Magaluf is related to its symbolic role based on the contents of the meal. Some tourists referred to their consumption activities on holiday as making them appear to be like pigs. For example, in discussing the food in her hotel, one tourist reports, 'it's very good ... you have to stop yourself or you become a bit of a pig'. Another tourist, Bill, recounts the story of an excursion to the other side of the island that involved some wine tasting, during which he says, 'I made a bit of a pig of meself really'. He is on holiday with his wife Pat and two friends Dawn and Trevor. The latter claims that his diet has 'gone out of the window'. As Williams (1997) notes, the holiday is often a time for relaxation of dietary restrictions practised at home. In addition, the vacation is a time associated with not undertaking work, of lying around, frying oneself in the sun and being lazy. Another tourist explains about her holiday, 'I've had a real sense of freedom ... I don't know if it's because we both have demanding jobs. I haven't missed doing the dishes and cooking'.

Berger and Luckmann (1966) argue that a necessary part of an understanding of the self is reflexive activity, and that it is in the behaviour of others that the self is mirrored. It is necessary to objectify one's behaviour in order for it to be viewed and comprehended. Given the symbolic associations of pigs and their importance in the landscape of the home world for some it seems reasonable to suggest that when faced with a fry-up, tourists find themselves objectively displayed. The conclusion from the words of Barthes (1993: 62) that 'whoever partakes of it [steak] assimilates a bull-like strength' is that whoever partakes of bacon and sausage assimilates pig-like qualities.

## Fish and chips

This dish is also readily available, and popular, in Magaluf and Palmanova. Chips in themselves are particularly favoured. Indeed, one of the complaints of the hotel entertainer, Eric, is that tourists are unwilling to try Spanish food, preferring chips instead. However, the potato is a solid, no fuss food, and while it can be adulterated, with the addition of salt and vinegar, its presentation as a chip has not required much alteration, apart from the peeling and frying processes. Chips are honest, comforting and filling. A family of four are all eating chips in one of the café-bars and discussing, with the proprietor, a group of tourists (all young males) who have allegedly left Magaluf before the end of their holiday, because they are not enjoying it. The mother proclaims, 'don't understand how anyone couldn't like it here ... must be hard to please'.

As discussed, at one time potatoes were seen as a threat to Britishness; but more recently, according to Priestland (1972), chips (and fish) are associated with a sense of British national identity. Indeed, Walton notes (2000: 1), '[f]ish and chips is generally recognized as a great and quintessentially British institution'. He goes on to note that past associations of the fishing industry with searching the Arctic seas for fish links the dish to 'the notion of Britain as a gallant seafaring nation whose little ships do battle with the elements and the foreign enemy to feed and protect the people' (Walton, 2000).

In the latter half of the 20th century, fish have been increasingly linked to politics. The 1970s saw the so-called 'Cod Wars' between British and Icelandic fishermen. More recently, the introduction of fish quotas by the European Union has, in some cases, undermined the British fishing industry. Latter-day disputes have arisen between Spanish and British fishing fleets. Quotas for the former are deemed to be unfair from the British perspective and the Spanish are also portrayed as not playing to the rules. A somewhat extreme view is expressed by the newspaper columnist Richard Littlejohn (2000: 95), '[t]he British state ... has connived by its passivity in the ruin of thousands of British fishermen and farmers by accepting the schemes of the European Union to advance the interests of others'.

The idea that the ingestion of certain foods allows one to absorb the characteristics of the derivative animal has been explored. So, too, has the connection between beef, the strength of the bull and the courage and power of the British in times of trouble. The link between beef and 'Britishness' in the two resorts is evidenced in that it, like the full breakfast, is often advertised under the banner of the Union Jack flag.

One aspect that has yet to be addressed is the appearance of roast beef in terms of the meal as Sunday roast. In this respect, it allows other roast meats to be thought about in a similar way because it is not the content that is of concern, but rather the method of cooking, and the associated idea of what makes a meal.

## Roast meat

In her essay, *Deciphering a Meal*, Douglas (1975a) explores the reason why some food and how it is cooked is deemed to be more acceptable as a family meal than others. She concludes that the serving of a hot meal is associated with familiarity, closeness and the warmth of the family, while to serve a snack, or just to offer drinks, keeps people at a distance. The association of roast dinners with a particular day of the week – Sunday – marks it as one in which the sharing of a meal with close family or friends is made. Traditionally, in European Christian societies, Sunday has been the day of rest, a time to spend with the family rather than with one's work colleagues. Roasting is a lengthy process compared to frying and boiling and thus speaks of leisurely activity. Following Lévi-Strauss's (1997) analysis, roasting is at the luxurious, wealthy end of cooking. The availability of roast food on a daily basis allows tourists to re-create, if they so desire, the Sunday feeling of time and luxury and togetherness every day of the week. Trevor kept to the 'traditional' time for eating his roast. One Sunday he advises 'it's Sunday, I've gotta have a roast dinner' as he sets off for an establishment that he knows to be serving roast beef.

The connection between a sense of national identity and the eating of beef in relation to the 15th-century Battle of Agincourt and the 14th-century Battle of Crécy has been made. However, in order for beef to still have a symbolic value it must have meaning in the contemporary home world. The mythology of the Battle of Agincourt is kept alive by Shakespeare's play *King Henry V*, depicted in both stage and film performances. Post Shakespeare, the imagery of beef was used to great effect to distinguish between the English and French by the 18th-century British artist Hogarth in his painting *The Gate of Calais*. Such is the association between the British and roast beef that the French nickname for the British is 'Les Rosbifs'. The connection between the British and beef in art, according to Davidson (*Guardian* Saturday Review, 25 March 2000: p. 5) continued in the 20th century through the work of Damien Hirst and his cows in formaldehyde.

Hogarth's painting formed the central work in an exhibition at Tate Britain in the summer of 2000, entitled 'England: Roast Beef and Liberty'.

The basis of the exhibition was a collection of 18th-century ceramics and prints that illustrated the way in which food was used to define English and French national identities. The English, often represented as bodily well rounded, and therefore nourished, are contrasted to the French who eat chicken (a lesser meat) and appear as skinny, whimpish and somewhat affected. The beef eater by contrast is a solid, red, (full) bloodied individual (usually male, e.g. 'John Bull') made of strong stuff, who eats his unadulterated roast beef with the hottest mustard.

The BSE (or mad cow disease) crisis among British farmers (and beef-eating members of the public) at the end of the 1990s escalated when the French refused to concede to the lifting of the ban on British beef exports to Europe in what became known as 'The Beef War' (Rawnsley, *The Observer*, 31 October 1999). Calls to boycott French food-stuffs were made alongside the promotion of home-grown produce in supermarkets and shops under the banner of the Union Jack. Marr (*The Observer*, October 31 1999) observed that intense emotions were stirred due to the ban and that this resulted in '[an] outburst of beef-patriotism, a strong strain in English politics for 250 years'. James (1997: 72) also notes 'the continuing crisis over BSE threatens; not merely an outrage to the British meat industry, it menaces a core symbol of national identity'. Further, a joke among the meat and livestock industries ran 'that BSE actually stood for "Bloody Stupid Europeans"' (Bell & Valentine, 1997: 167). The conclusion is that beef remains a potent symbol of identity for many members of the British population, while, at the same time it excludes other members who do not eat beef. In addition, it is used to articulate the relationship between Europe and the UK in connection with the idea of a changing world based on Europeanisation, and attempts by Brussels to take control.

The foregoing discussion has demonstrated the link between food and drink choices and a sense of Britishness. It has done this by examining the role that the contents of the meals have in the home world, e.g. the symbolic role of pigs and the long history associated with the consumption of roast beef. At the same time, the analysis has highlighted aspects of the 'national character' associated with some of these meals. Roast beef and the ability to stomach the hottest food are signals of strength in adversity and stamina. The indulgence, luxury or comfort connected to other dishes also says something about the holiday experience. For example, the holiday as a time to relax and indulge the self both as a time away from the home world of work and bills; but also the health advice given out by various government agencies.

I continue with the issue of consumption and its relevance to creations of identity, social structures and the nature of the holiday experience.

Closer links between the body and consumption practices will also be made in consideration of the role and appearance of the female breast. The breast is both an object of desire and a source of nourishment. Following a semiological approach, I will discuss the breast in relation to desire and explore its connection with the idea of mother and nation. I begin by considering consumption practices more generally and their connection to the body and constructions of gender.

## Consuming Women

The representation of women in some of the postcards for sale in both Palmanova and Magaluf is illustrative of the way in which relationships between men and women are seen in terms of power and control in which women are portrayed as commodities. For example, one card, entitled 'Special Hamburger', shows two pairs of women's buttocks as the meat in hamburgers. From the top of the postcard there is the burger bun with lettuce and cheese, followed by one set of buttocks placed on a slice of tomato, more cheese and lettuce. This layout is followed by more bread, lettuce and tomato, another pair of buttocks set on tomato, cheese and lettuce supported by the other half of the bread bun.

Another postcard with the caption 'Typical "Breakfast"' shows a pair of breasts with droplets of moisture on them poking through a number of ensaimadas.[8] Yet another postcard, called 'Spanish Barbecue', shows a pair of breasts through various stages of a suntan. The first picture, named 'Fresh Meat', depicts pale breasts partially hidden beneath a denim jacket. By the time they reach the final picture, having gone through 'still raw', 'medium', 'well done', 'very well done', they are fully exposed and darkly 'tanned'. The breast is a dominant image in the landscapes of Palmanova and Magaluf, appearing as it does in many forms: on postcards, aprons (Figure 7.4), souvenirs, topless sunbathing and the request for women to 'get their tits out for the boys' (Andrews, 2009b).

In another postcard called 'Isla de Mallorca', the head of a bearded man pokes above the sand, the rest of his body is buried. He looks hot and with mouth open, tongue hanging out, and eyes closed, he appears thirsty. Two breasts dangle provocatively above him. Apart from sexual titillation, the breasts also offer a possibility, albeit just out of reach, of nourishment.

Female breasts are multi-vocal symbols linked to ideas of dependency, availability, power, sexuality and consumption. The breast, Yalom (1997) argues, is the defining part of the female body. In her exploration of the

**Figure 7.4** Breast apron souvenir

history of the breast in Western culture, she demonstrates how its symbolism has been contradictory and manipulated in different situations. For example, she claims that in both Jewish and Christian traditions the breast is honoured as the provider of milk, important for the survival of the Hebrew people and the suckling Baby Jesus. As such, the ability to nourish infants has been used allegorically for the care of whole religious or political communities. This view found currency in the French Revolution in which breast feeding became a political choice linked to republicanism. The Republic itself was likened to a bounteous mother whose breasts were available to all. The breast symbolised liberty, fraternity, equality, patriotism, courage, justice, generosity and abundance, all of which were portrayed in the depictions of an ideal citizen called *Marianne*, often shown as bare breasted, and sometimes, lactating (Yalom, 1997).

In addition, the breast connotes something more. It is both a provider of an item of consumption and an object of commercial practices, ranging from items of clothing to lotions and surgery. As such, in an environment that is highly predicated on consumption practices, the function of the breast signifies both the commercial context of consumer capitalism, and the very consumption practices (in the form of sucking milk) that are a prerequisite for capitalism's survival.

Other aspects of the exposed female breast in Palmanova and Magaluf include those of resistance and celebration. This situation comes about, for example, when the spatial and temporal boundaries regarding codes of dress are crossed. As already noted, bare-breasted women are acceptable on the beach during the day, but it is very rare, and a subject of comment, to find public displays of naked breasts off the beach during the day. When it does happen, the disregard for the 'rules' constitutes an act of resistance as in the case of the young woman outside a bar who kept exposing her bottom and confessed to happily exposing her breasts.

Celebratory associations with the breast are found in the aftermath of an England football win against Columbia during the 1998 World Cup tournament. The *Majorca Daily Bulletin* reported on the post-match celebrations in Magaluf: 'It was a night which Magalluf [sic] and the fans will not forget, especially one girl who bared all for England while being carried on a friend's shoulders' (Eatwell, *Majorca Daily Bulletin*, 28 June 1998 p 11). The paper also carried an illustrative photograph. Here the display of the breasts is linked with victory and pride. It is reminiscent of the actions of Anne Chapel, a popular French singer, who, on the liberation of Paris at the end of World War II, jumped up on a car, revealed her bosoms and sang the French national anthem (Yalom, 1997: 123).

Also of importance is lactation, a function that carries its own significations. Milk speaks of kinship and creating relationships. For example, under Islamic Law, people are related by blood, marriage and milk (Khatib-Chahidi, 1992). Milk is also indicative of nature and abundance. The ubiquitous presence of the breast, and by association milk, suggests that the holiday is about relationships, the creation of new encounters and opportunities to build on existing familial and friendship connections. Milk as the first food infantilises the tourists. The idea of plenty comes to mind along with the satisfaction of want. The breasts depicted in the postcards are always available and ready for sucking. They do not appear to be the 'bad' breast described by Klein that frustrates and angers as it is withheld and unavailable for lactation (Yalom, 1997). Thus, the breast and its milk become signifiers of the satisfaction of needs, desires and wants that exist at a most basic level.

However, as a verb, milk has a different meaning – to bleed, drain, draw off, exploit, extract, manipulate and impose on. Thus, it speaks of the manipulation of tourists by tour operators and supports the idea that the holiday is about gaining a maximum profit. In effect, the tourists are being 'milked' for their money. This feature appears in the way that the tour operators attempt to get more money from the tourists, over and above that which has already been paid out for the package. Via the 'welcome meetings', they encourage further expenditure and, by providing entertainment in the form of bar crawls, seek to promote themselves as 'like' the tourists and thus their friends, thereby encouraging the tourists to purchase day trips and other night-time entertainment (Andrews, 2000).

Both tourists and tour reps recognise that the role of the latter is to attempt to increase tourist expenditure. One man, complaining about his family's holiday experience, tells me 'they herd you in like sheep take your money and then give you a bad package'. One rep explains: 'management are interested in money, money, money not customer care'. He goes on to say that the tourists are 'set-up on the holiday', and feels that they know that they are sold trips 'that rip them off' and 'money . . . that's what the bosses like'.

In UK antenatal clinics, breast feeding is promoted as providing 'fast food'. No preparation is required (other than a biological one) to deliver milk directly to the baby. Milk is the first food, and once again the strong presence of the breast, and by implication milk, is a reminder of the child-like state that tourism can evoke. In psychoanalytic terms, an obsession with the breast is indicative of arrested babyhood and regression to that state (Yalom, 1997). Such an analysis fits well with the idea of the tourist as child. Indeed, Dann (1996a: 105) notes, 'Cazes (1976: 17) also talks about the "infantile regression" of the tourist... when he speaks of the tourist returning to the bosom of mother nature'. In other respects and linked to the idea of the nation, the breast is a reminder of the values of home: love, intimacy and nurturing, all factors that the disorientated tourist needs to feel secure. The appeals to the infant tourist are present in the food advertisements that proclaim 'Mom is cooking here!', 'Cooking like mum' and that food is home cooked and British (Figures 7.5 and 7.6). One advert for a café called Natalies shows a portly cartoon-like figure of a woman, with her breasts clearly defined, holding a plate of steaming hot food in both hands. The advert claims that it is the 'Best British Food in Mallorca' and also features a Union Jack (Figure 7.7).

**Figure 7.5** Cafe sign proclaiming 'Cooking like Mom'

The imagery discussed thus far has predominately featured women. Two postcards that show men continue the theme of plenty and availability attached to the presence of food and drink in the resorts. Both postcards are entitled 'Mallorca'. One features the muscular upper torso and head of a man. He is holding two jug glasses above his head with his face turned up towards them, mouth open. He is tipping the beer, in the glasses, over himself. It splashes onto his face and cascades down his body. The other postcard shows a man lying, presumably

**Figure 7.6** Cafe sign proclaiming 'Home cooking just like Mum's'

asleep, on the beach beneath a parasol. In the foreground of the photograph, there are several empty drinks bottles that once contained gin, campari, rum and brandy. The postcards are indicative of the availability of drink. In the latter card, variety is shown and one assumes that the man is sleeping off the effects of having drunk too much, and mixed his drinks. It is luxurious in that he can spend time drinking alcohol and then spend time sleeping it off. The first picture is more celebratory in nature and the male figure is evidently enjoying himself. This enjoyment of the alcohol is immediate. The male celebrates its presence as well as the attractiveness of his own body. Here, drink is falling from the skies and there is so much available he can shower in it. The drink goes beyond its function as thirst quencher since it can be wasted. Several of the postcards discussed have sexual connotations. The connection between food and eroticism is continued in the next section.

## Erotic Food

This brief section carries forward the connection between food and sex, thereby making the link to the idea of sex as a form of consumption. A postcard entitled 'Mallorca' on the front, and referred to as 'the friendship post card' on the back, features a rather sinister-looking cartoon banana lying on a sunbed on the beach, shaded by a parasol. It is

**Figure 7.7** Sign for Natalies cafe, Palmanova

drinking a cocktail, wearing dark sunglasses and has a wide, toothy grin. To its right is the rear view of a real woman with her vulva visible. Quite obviously, the picture is about sexual arousal and intercourse. The banana stands for the penis. The postcard is an example of the way in which parts of the body are likened to, or described metaphorically as food, especially those parts of the body that are sexualised.

One example is a souvenir in the form of a penis sandwich. It takes the shape of a plastic representation of a penis sandwiched between two slices of bread. Not only is this an obvious statement that places the penis as edible, and therefore consumed, it also links the sexual consumption to oral sex, and to actual sexual positions. A sandwich refers to the woman occupying a central position during simultaneous anal and vaginal penetration; the buttocks in the hamburger postcards also make this suggestion. The penis sandwich souvenir is an inversion of this scenario. Another example of the penis being likened to food in the resorts is as a vibrator in a carrot-shaped case. These items are used as part of the joking that occurs in a bar between tourists, the in-house DJ, and, at one time, a barman.

The penis in a sandwich, as a carrot, and as a banana places it in a similar position to the breasts in the 'typical Mallorcan breakfast' as a consumable item. All the images link sex with consumption practices, the ingestion of the male or female other. The images doubtless have associations with the bawdy humour often associated with British seaside resorts (Howell, 1974). However, they also speak of a fetishism of the body, in a broad sense, within consumer society. Women are portrayed as readily available for sex, the pursuit of pleasure and satisfaction, but the images do not display the power relationships between genders, which is hinted at in Pirates Adventure when the female pirate is put below deck to take up her rightful place in the domestic duty of washing up. The penis, however, can be withdrawn, it can hide in the sandwich or banana skin, it can be withheld and hidden as restrictions on male bodily exposure previously discussed show. Many of the images described suggest the easy availability of food and drink and women and men as items of consumption. Such notions are concomitant with ideas of fantasy and magic, which I will explore in relation to some of the drinks available.

One group of drinks called 'Magic Cocktails' (from a standardised menu that appears in many of the resorts' bars) carry names that allude to sexual excitement, e.g. 'Love on the Beach' and 'Free Passion'. In addition, these names suggest an easygoing satisfaction of the desires to which they refer. Such allusions are found in other cocktails throughout the two resorts. For instance, Sex on the Beach[9] and Orgasm.[10] In one bar in Magaluf, called Manos, the cocktail menu lists the following drinks: Between the Sheets, Slow Comfortable Screw, Screaming Orgasm, Harvey Wallbanger and Slippery Nipple. The content of some of the drinks is not really the issue and, in fact, Sex on the Beach is not very strong (although obviously the measure by which it is taken will have some bearing on this). Rather, it is the titillation of requesting an Orgasm, a Slow Comfortable Screw or Sex on the Beach that is important. It is about giggling, being a bit naughty and childish, as well as linking sexual intercourse with the act of consumption. The names of many of the cocktails therefore relate to sexual relations, they feed into the notion of Magaluf as 'Shagaluf', and the idea of several available partners for sexual indulgence.

Names of the other 'Magic Cocktails' include 'Vodka Sun', 'Colorado', 'Love on the Beach', 'Free Passion', 'Volcanic Islands', 'Tequila Rise', 'Pina Tropic', 'Caribe Dreams' and 'Coco Magic'. The names conjure up ideas of the exotic and have direct associations with warmth, the sun, fantasy and mystery. The reference to fantasy and magic is evident elsewhere in Magaluf and Palmanova. Tourists can play 'Golf Fantasia' or visit the Fantasy Island Bar in Magaluf. The language of the tourists also echoes ideas of fantasy. The word 'fantastic' appears in the descriptions provided by the tourists of food, and of the environment in general – in the words of one young male tourist, 'this is fucking fantastic', as he refers to the warmth of the sun and the openness of the beach. One tourist, Emma, says of Mallorca, 'we call it fantasy island'. She and her husband are regular visitors to Torrenova (she has a clear idea that she is not staying in Magaluf), visiting for the warmth and the sun. She explains that there is a sense of freedom about the area. Usually, they travel with their 11-year-old daughter, who, on this occasion, has been left with relatives in the UK. When her daughter is present, Emma feels that 'there is so much freedom for her she can go up and down the beach and we know it and we don't need to worry'. Emma's husband is drunk and the conversation moves to the amount of alcohol that is consumed. Referring to expatriates, she says, 'people who have lived here for a while go back to the UK as alcoholics, but it's not called that here, it's called socialising'.

## Socialising

The comments made by Emma concerning the idea that drinking large amounts of alcohol is considered 'socialising' appears to be fundamental to the act of consuming in the resorts. Although Emma is initially referring to the lifestyle of British expatriates, the socialising aspect of drinking is also evident among tourists. The point is that drinking together is inextricably linked with bonding, or being part of a particular group. Accepting a drink from someone means that the receiver is accepting and internalising that person as the drink becomes a gift in the Maussian sense as standing for that person. In addition, drinking is essentially a social act and gives structure to social life (Douglas, 1987).

Similar points are made by Seymour (1983) in relation to eating a meal, in that she asserts that the sharing of a meal is a social process allowing the boundaries of a particular group to be continually reaffirmed and redrawn.

The food, and particularly drink in this context, becomes a form of totem around which people can collect and feel some sort of solidarity. A member of a mixed gender group of young tourists complains about one of her travelling companion's refusal to join in. 'She doesn't want to do anything, she won't drink, go on the bar crawls or to Aquapark. All she wants to do is lie by the pool and sunbathe. ... She drinks in England but won't drink here'. It is unacceptable not to want to join in, and especially not to want to drink. In another instance, Clare, a woman in her mid-forties, points out a couple whom she has tried to engage in conversation, but has given up because she 'got nowhere'. Clare is an exception, in that she is holidaying alone (most people are travelling in a group of friends or family, or as couples).

The importance of being able to share food and drink is outlined by Lucy. She says that she would not like to come on holiday alone. She feels that she would be able to occupy herself during the day, and that eating breakfast alone would be 'ok'; but 'I wouldn't like to eat dinner on my own or be on my own in the evening'.

One of the attractions of drinking is its ability to relax (and, the link with losing control). I speak to Fred, a retired labourer from Luton, who describes his old job as 'digging shit and laying bricks'. He says that he wants to 'get pissed all the time' and 'meet someone on the same wavelength as me'. He advises that he has been married for 45 years, and when the plane took off from the UK, he began crying, thinking 'here we go again' as he is next to an empty seat and his wife is not there. He says, 'I've come here to go swimming and get pissed [and] to give the wife a bit of peace'. He says that in Luton, 'I know everyone... go around all the pubs but can't speak to people [but that here there is] someone different I can talk to them'.

I am speaking to Fred at midday, he is very drunk on Bacardi and Coke, the Bacardi being virtually neat. He tells me that his ambition is to drink in every bar in the world, and that if he could find someone on the same wavelength as himself, he would build a house on the moon for them. The next time I see Fred, he is drinking coffee and is apologetic about his previous behaviour. Fred's broken conversation with me, when he was drunk, suggests a deep dissatisfaction with his home life and the relationship with his wife, someone that he says he cannot communicate with. The sheepishness that he then exhibits when sober suggests that without drink he would not open up in such a way, and that his ability to speak to me, a complete stranger, was largely governed by the fact that he had been drinking. Of course, the credibility of what Fred said in his inebriated state is open to question. However, it clearly demonstrates a loosening of some kind of restrictiveness, and a recognition that through drink he is able to talk to people more than in his home environment. The hotel entertainer, Eric, comments that the British are 'anally retentive' only 'breaking' once they have had a drink.

The sharing of drinking, and of getting drunk, is used as a method to ease the passage of social relationships towards sex. This will, of course, depend on the make-up of the group involved, but the connection between drinking and sex, particularly in Magaluf, is very strong, indeed inextricably linked, as some of the names of the cocktails indicate. Peter, one of the tour reps, tells me that 'all the tourists are out to get laid, drink and have a good time'. He claims that this is easy because there is no-one to judge their behaviour and that for a male the aim is simply to have sex, 'it doesn't matter if the girl is fat or thin'. Although Peter might be correct, in that tourists want to have a good time, have sex and get drunk, the notion that no-one is around to judge their behaviour is somewhat strange. As already observed, a tourist holidaying alone is an exception, the presence of the home peer group either as family or friends is usually still there. The clue to the acceptability (although not in all cases) of the behaviour lies in the disruption of the *habitus* (Jackson, 1989; Gell, 1996) that the holiday brings for the individual and their peer group (Andrews, 2009a). The change in *habitus* that appears to facilitate social and/or sexual relationships is also something that is shared by the tourists. Thus, the bonding and boundary marking come about in a shared set of experiences.

Jamie, a male tourist on holiday with his brother, describes an example of sharing leading to sexual fulfilment. Discussing a fellow tourist, Jamie describes her as a 'slapper', having slept with her on the first night of his holiday. She had invited him to her room for a cigarette, which led to them lying on the bed together, her naked, lights out. The encounter ends in sex. Jamie claims that he would be ashamed to tell his mates at home about the incident. Although Jamie's latter comment does support Peter's statement that there is no-one to judge behaviour on holiday, it is not strictly the case that the tourists are left without some kind of assessment, which may be as Jamie's reflections indicate, self-assessment. Jamie's peer group, apart from his brother, is absent and would not apparently have approved of his actions. At the same time, fellow tourists become a peer group and exercise judgement about behaviour. For example, a young female tourist from Essex describes the scene in a bar in which a lad had been sick all over one of the tables. She says, 'I know you're on holiday and you want to enjoy yourself, but not that much'. Her comments suggest that there is a need to limit consumption and maintain control over, in this case, bodily functions and fluids. Although the drink has caused the letting go, the young woman's comment indicates it has gone too far, and the young man has been anything but retentive.

Being out of control and being sick is not restricted to the younger members of the tourist population. Nor is the lack of control entirely manifest in being sick. Help with walking is often needed by some tourists from their friends or family when they have got too drunk – a situation noted by both Passariello (1983) in her micro-ethnography of Mexican tourists, and referred to in my discussion of Pirates Adventure. In addition, a crucial aspect of getting inebriated is that, although it initially liberates, it eventually constrains. Sexual activity for men is prevented and the senses are dulled; there cannot be a much more docile body (Foucault, 1977) than one that is asleep or unconscious. A middle-aged woman from Aberdeen is holidaying with her married friends. They are staying in Magaluf and spend all their evenings drinking. They do not very much like the hotel in which they are staying. The man in the group has not been able to sleep very well because of being disturbed by noise. However, the two women have not found this a problem, as one says, tapping her glass of alcohol, 'too much of this'.

In a different incident in Magaluf, an elderly couple are walking down Punta Ballena. They are both very drunk. She is bare foot. She falls over and the man bends down to help her up, swearing at her. She falls over again, at which point other people intervene to help her to sit down. The couple want to get a taxi and the incident has happened next to a taxi rank; but the drivers, having been called 'bastards' by the man, are refusing to take the couple.

In his study of drinking in American society, Gusfield (1987) claims that the sociability that the sharing of alcohol brings about engenders a sense of *communitas*. Drinking also acts as a temporal marker between leisure and work. As such, it is a mood setter, that, in the current case, speaks of fun and play, rather than serious graft. In addition, alcohol defers responsibility, as it becomes an excuse for 'bad' behaviour. To return to Peter's comments that the absence of a judging peer group allows unusual behaviour, it is reasonable to suggest, given the link that he makes with sexual activity and drink, that it is the alcohol rather than the absence of like fellows that permits the actions.

In the opposite way, extreme drinking brings about anti-structure (Gusfield, 1987) in which the framework of social organisation is undermined. Thus, although in Fred's case there is self-expression in which he is vocal about some intimate aspects of his life, the case of the elderly couple on Punta Ballena demonstrates the risks and dangers that surface with a lack of control. Also, the idea of fantasy links with myth, which, in a semiological approach, has been used to examine the way in which a tourist world is constructed in tourism brochures and tourist activities (Uzzell, 1984; Dann, 1996b; Selwyn, 1996b). This would appear to introduce an element of control, in that fantasy is being fuelled by the machinations of the tourism industry.

## In the Land of Cockaigne[11]

The idea of availability and immediacy of both food and drink in Palmanova and Magaluf is often a topic of conversation with tourists. In many ways, this is not surprising given that the need for food and drink and the practices of their consumption are things that they all have in common. As such, even if they did not directly share food and drink, they are socially linked in the practice of consuming the fare available. It is possible to drink and eat 24 hours a day in the resorts. Clare, the middle-aged woman holidaying alone, claims that during her week's break, she has drunk far more than she would at home, spending approximately £360 on both food and drink. Clare sees this as a reward for her recent weekend and evening overtime in her job as a banker, which she describes as 'boring'.[12]

Other tourists notice the availability of food and drink in terms of its variety and abundance. Lucy says of her hotel, 'the best thing about the hotel is the food. The choice is tremendous'. In addition, 'the salads are wonderful' and there is a choice of three starters and lots of fruit including cherries, melons and bananas. Both Ruth and Jill describe the food in their respective hotels as 'fantastic'. On another occasion, Jill relates her visit, with her husband, to the evening entertainment of Son Amar, during which they have a 'fabulous time'. She tells me 'the food was great' and describes rows of suckling pigs, and chickens on spits. Here, the food is given a sense of luxury and decadence. Roasting on a spit is slow and indicative of waste (Lévi-Strauss, 1997). The abundance of food is evident as there are rows of things cooking and there is plenty to spare. Jill explains that a fellow tourist had found a hair on their plate, and, on drawing this to the attention of the tour operator rep, had had the whole meal replaced with a new plate of food. Jill is impressed that the whole dish is changed, rather than just the hair being removed.

For Bill and Trevor, the two middle-aged men on holiday with their wives Pat and Dawn, previously mentioned in Chapter 5, much of their holiday revolves around drinking alcohol. They spend every night drinking and drink regularly during the day. What they drink and how much they imbibe is a topic of conversation with other tourists when recounting their own drinking tales. Bill's party has a favoured venue – Rafalillos – where they invariably sit at the same table. Again, other tourists comment on the regularity of their presence in this bar. The group's actions are an example of Appadurai's (1993) notion regarding the repetition of body techniques.

The ideas of abundance referred to in the discussions about food and drink by tourists as well as in their consumption practices, link to notions of display. The next section considers the theme of large quantities and the links to display by focussing on the way that some drinks are offered for consumption.

## More buckets[13]

The opportunity to buy pints (imperial measures are advertised and used) of cocktails is well advertised in Magaluf, and found in some bars in Palmanova in the pursuit of game playing. In addition, the use of buckets in Magaluf and enormous glasses[14] in Palmanova to serve sangria is also evident. These containers are not for individuals, but for groups of people. In addition, the containers used to serve the refreshments also carry connotations about the context in which the consumption takes place.

The receptacles appear in different places, the glass in Palmanova and the plastic bucket in Magaluf. The latter calls to mind infants who are given plastic eating and drinking utensils, not only because they cannot be broken but also to prevent harm to self or others. The infantile treatment of tourists demanding buckets of drink (and being offered buckets of drink) fits in with Dann's (1996a) assessment of the tourist as child and the regression associated with childhood scenes. Buckets and spades are also associated with children on the beach. An element of play is present in plastic and in many contemporary childhood toys, a characteristic of the ludic post-modern world. The tourists play up to the image of being child-like in a resort in which much of the activity is highly mediated by, among others, tour operator reps attempting to create a situation of dependency, as the child needs its mother (hence also the abundance of breasts). The use of a bucket allows those tourists involved to play up to the role of child.

However, buckets have other connotations. The connection of food or drink with buckets conjures up the provision of slops in the trough. It is indicative of waste and therefore 'low' quality, unwanted food and drink that is unfit for human consumption. It is associated with cheapness or getting a bargain that is linked with package holidays, the notion of getting one's money's worth. The idea that British tourists demand 'cheap' food and drink is commented on by one waiter. One afternoon, I see a Spanish family eating a fish soup, which smells and looks delicious. I look for it on the menu but cannot see it listed. Upon enquiry, the waiter explains that this dish, typical of Spain, does not feature on the regular menu, but is on the *a la carte* menu. Asking if it is ever requested by the British, his reply is, 'the English eat mainly burgers, sausages and chips ... they don't have the money for this [fish dish]'.

The association of buckets with cheapness is further exemplified in the 'bucket-shop'. Of American provenance, the term originally referred to places where liquor was obtainable by the bucket. It later became associated with the purchase of small amounts of stocks and shares without the services of authorised dealers (SOED, 1983). This irregularity associated with buckets (which even if it did not have this etymological history, it is still outside the norm to drink from a bucket) gives tourists' experiences, for those participating in this activity, something different from the normally inhabited quotidian world.

Buckets also call to mind being sick, since they are often used as a receptacle for vomit. They are also associated with prisons and the act of slopping out human waste from the previous night. The supply of a bucket can be interpreted as a precautionary act, to provide what might be needed later on, or even to suggest that what the bucket contains has the potential to make the drinkers sick in terms of quality and quantity. By requiring a bucket, an allusion to the ultimate aim of the evening is made. A determination to be sick not only indicates and displays self-indulgence and excess (as denoted in the bar crawl oath that calls on tourists to get drunk, be sick and drink some more), but also appears as an act of resistance in rejecting and vomiting, on being treated like a child, and vomiting on the 'cheapness' of what is provided.

In addition, and in the wider scheme of mass consumption in advanced capitalism, that which is produced en masse is associated with poor quality, since it implies lack of care, haste and an absence of skill and craftsmanship. As Rykwert (1997) notes, 'real' food is associated, by the middle classes, with rough, uneven textures (e.g. coarse cuts and bran) made by hand, as opposed to the machine-finish smoothness and regularity found in pre-packaged foods, or the standardised Fordist production of KFC chicken portions and McDonald's burgers.

The provision of sangria in plastic buckets in Magaluf adds to the sense of place and thus the spatial understanding of food and drink consumption. This linkage is possible because, in contrast to the plastic of Magaluf, the large volume of sangria served in Palmanova is in an oversized glass. Plastic, as already indicated, is redolent of childhood; it is also man-made. The suitability of plastic to the sense of place of Magaluf lies in its resistance to being broken and therefore suitable for rough handling that may arise from being hurried or pressurised to consume and the possibility of violence erupting (of which vomiting is also a symbol). By contrast, glass, a natural product of less durability, symbolises a more leisured and refined experience that is associated with the less frenetic Palmanova. Glass speaks of delicacy and care; it connotes trust, in that it will not be broken. Its transparency mirrors the openness and feeling of spaciousness that accompanies Palmanova as opposed to the oppressive, enclosed space of Magaluf.[15]

Drinking from the same vessel connotes sharing and community, and is thus suggestive of bonding and fraternity. The notion of sharing is here exaggerated in the use of a bucket or a large glass. It is also indicative of intimacy, because although straws are used to drink the beverage, there is still a connection with the mouth being in contact with the same vessel, and the possible resultant exchange of bodily fluids. Further, the large volume of liquid available speaks of plenty and the ability to consume more than the usual measure. It evokes ideas of being able to have more than is desired, of need and desire not only being satisfied but pleasure *ad libitum*.

The idea of display is not just restricted to the volume of food and drink consumed by tourists, but also in the payment for these items. In the majority of cases, whenever I am engaged in conversations with tourists in café-bars, they insist on buying my drinks, and refuse offers of reciprocity, unless severely pressed. It is difficult to refuse drinks because refusal is interpreted as non-participation, which is, in some cases, extended to the type of drink; for example, mineral water, for some, is unacceptable as a 'drink'. This attitude may be for reasons other than demonstrations of generosity or 'wealth', e.g. acknowledging my lone status, wishing to afford me some sort of care and not impose, what might be seen as, an unequal financial payment (the tourists were usually in pairs or groups). However, at the same time the impression formed is that buying an additional drink is of no consequence because money is of little concern.

In a totally different situation, the issue of payment for some drinks entails a protracted performance. One evening, in the lounge of the Cala Blanca, there are two British couples. The men sit together watching a World Cup football match and the two women sit separately, they are discussing a knitting pattern that one of them is working on. The two women decide that it is too warm to sit inside and want to go outside. On advising their partners, it is also decided that they will all have a drink. The men have control of the money and one is going to pay for all the drinks. He issues three separate sets of instructions to his wife on how to pay for the drinks, during which time a Peseta bill is held in the air and the woman has to make three trips to her husband's seat to receive the directions. In the first case he says, 'here take that and buy Lulu a drink, then tell the barman to come in here and get our order'. Then, 'you get yourselves a drink and buy ours and get the barman to bring it in here'; and finally, 'order your drinks, and ours and get him to come in here and we'll pay for them'. The women show no means of paying for the drinks independently, and, apparently, have no method of developing their own payment plan.

This section has explored the way in which consumption practices can be turned into practices of display and sharing. In the first instance, the availability of enormous measures of sangria link back to the ideas of fantasy and Cockaigne. That is, the drink is available in abundance. At the same time, the containers invite sharing and therefore connect with the idea of food and drink as a way of socialising and forming or confirming relationships. The use of buckets, as opposed to glass, identified in the two resorts gives a spatial context to the practice of consumption and reinforces the perceived and practised differences between Palmanova and Magaluf.

## Summary

The main purpose of this chapter has been to discuss the constructions of identity through the food and drink choices made by the tourists in the resorts of Palmanova and Magaluf. One of the attractions in the food and drink decisions made by the tourists is its familiarity. At the same time, much of the food is advertised as British. Many of the dishes have a long history in the home world, beef for example is associated with 14th- and 15th-century military victories, and the idea of conflict, in more recent history, in relation to the disputes over beef imports by parts of continental Europe. Fish and chips, another 'typically' British meal, also has associations with conflict as another example of Europeanisation in the form of fishing quotas demonstrates.

The main conclusion to draw from this chapter is the way in which the practice of consumption choices exercises a desire to keep the other at bay. The choice of the familiar in the seeking of British milk, bacon, bread, etc. and the rejection of the other in the form of water, all serve to form boundaries between self and other. The drinking of 'a proper cup of tea', one of the few times that local water is permissible having undergone a cooking process, and the ingestion of white fish, uncontaminated by too much salt,[16] help to maintain the self as pure in the face of danger from the polluting other.

As suggested in previous chapters, the polluting other is represented by the European Union and immigrants. The latter may not only take the form of nationalities other than those known collectively as British, but also between the regions and individual countries of the nation. Some of the food chosen by the tourists further links back to ideas of competition and greatness in the face of the enemy. Thus, the relationship with the other is characterised by aggression either in an attacking way or as a defence mechanism to maintain boundaries. The desire not to drink local water is not an act of attack in the way that Pirates Adventure, for example demonstrates, but it is an act of maintaining boundaries, and keeping the other out. It connects to other forms of boundary maintenance, e.g. the use of Union Jack towels on the beach or the flying of a national flag from a hotel balcony. The latter is not just demonstrative of laying claim to territory, but also erects a barrier to those who do not subscribe to its symbolic meaning. In the context of the two resorts, this might be interpreted as a message to the Spanish, French or German other, or, in the case where individual UK country flags are flown, as a message to the other countries composing Great Britain.

The availability of 'British' food and drink in Palmanova and Magaluf, whether it has been specially 'flown-in' or exists in name only (i.e. The British Breakfast made from raw Spanish materials) gives the tourists the opportunity to buy into ideas of what it is to be British. The meals on offer are seen to be what the British eat and have deep roots in the nation's imagined, collective military history, as well as finding resonance in present day conflicts with the European Union. Thus, the British maintain their sense of self-autonomy. In addition, given that for the majority of the tourists their meals are shared experiences with family or friends and often within the context of a larger group sharing the hotel dining room (and at similar times across the resorts), there is again a sense of uniformity, a socialisation into, and imagined sharing of what it means to be British.

## Notes

1. Although at first sight food and drink appear as distinct categories because they are differentially consumed and internalised, they both become integral to the symbolic (and biological) identity of a person. They both lead into the innermost parts of the tourists. Indeed, in his analysis of Indian inter-caste food transactions, Selwyn (1980: 301) refers to a typology of food that includes non-vegetarian, vegetarian, raw, cooked, drink, smoke, *kacca* and *pakka*. (*Kacca* refers to food cooked in water and *Pakka* to food cooked in ghi, which is clarified butter.)
2. Bishop (1991) suggests that there is no such thing as 'British' food *per se* given the diverse origins of much of what is eaten (there is instead what Bell and Valentine [1997] describe as naturalised or hybridised foods), but that there are associations between certain dishes and a particular type of 'Britishness', an idea that will be explored further in the chapter. In addition, James (1997: 81) notes that the British diet contains creolised elements. For example, 'pasta is now seen as British, rather than Italian' and that it is attitudes towards the food that mark them to be British – 'concern with saving time and money, creolised food is ironically, a kind of foreign food which characterises what is truly British about contemporary food consumption in Britain' (James, 1997: 84).
3. *A Canterbury Tale* (Powell & Pressburger, 1943) was a film made to the stipulations of the Ministry of Information for propaganda purposes during World War II (Aldgate & Richards, 1999). The aim of the film, underlain by the idea of modern day pilgrimage, was to provide a distillation of the values of the British/English to demonstrate what was being fought for. During one scene, a British and an American soldier are engaged in a conversation about tea in which the latter expresses his dislike of the beverage. The reply from the former is 'don't forget the Nazis and Japs have knocked down every country they tried to except the tea drinkers – China, Russia and England. So long live tea drinking'. This does not allow for what happened after the film was made which is that the Japanese, also great tea drinkers, were themselves 'knocked down'.
4. The main lyrics of the song Vindaloo are 'Where on earth are you from, we're from Engerland. Where you come from do you put the kettle on? Kick it... Bonjour Monsieur. Can I introduce you please to a lump of cheddar cheese? Knit one, purl one, drop one, curl one. Kick it ... Me and me mum and me dad and me gran we're off to Waterloo. Me and me mum and me dad and me gran and a bucket of vindaloo. Bucket. Vindaloo (repeat). We all like vindaloo. We're England. We're gonna score one more than you. England'. The theme of buckets will be examined further in Chapter 8.
5. Although this song was the English football anthem, it was sung by all British tourists including Scottish fans present for their own football fixtures with Spanish clubs after the World Cup contest.
6. In 1998–1999 prices ranged from 375 ESP to 550 ESP.

7. Williams (1997) has demonstrated through research with British holiday makers in the UK that the fry-up is associated with the holiday and not eaten at home.
8. A sweet pastry typical of Mallorca.
9. Composed of vodka, peach schnapps, orange juice and grenadine.
10. Made from a mixture of Baileys, Cointreau, rum and milk.
11. Cockaigne is an imaginary land of medieval times. It refers to a dreamland on earth where food and alcohol are always readily available. For example, roasted pigs roam around with knives in their backs waiting to be carved and grilled geese fly directly into one's mouth (Pleij, 2001). Here, there is the link between the idea of the holiday and the 'better way of life' explored in Chapter 1. A more up-to-date version of the Cockaigne myth can be found in episodes of *The Simpsons*. In one dream sequence, Marge dreams about the Garden of Eden in which there is a pig that readily offers up its own ribs for food without damaging itself. In another story, Germany is referred to as the land of chocolate. In his imagination, Homer sees himself skipping through this place in which everything presented to him – lamp posts to rabbits – is made from chocolate and available for his consumption.
12. In another conversation, she advises that she is bored with her holiday, but has not been prepared to tell that to her husband, who is still in the UK.
13. This title follows on from A Bucket of Vindaloo discussed in Chapter 7.
14. Both are able to hold approximately a gallon of liquid.
15. I do not wish to suggest that the 'quality' of the sangria in Palmanova is superior to that of Magaluf. What I want to stress is that there is a difference in atmosphere between the two resorts that is reflected symbolically in the materials used for providing enormous quantities of sangria.
16. A claim made by the son of a local fish and chip eatery is that 'British' cod needs to be imported because the 'cod' in the Mediterranean are too salty to be used. The reality is that there are no cod in the Mediterranean.

## Chapter 8
# Conclusion: The Great Escape

## Introduction

In this chapter, I will pick up on issues referred to in the introduction to reaffirm the theoretical lineage that underscores the ideas explored in the book. I will then demonstrate how the themes raised at the beginning, with the theories, inform the findings detailed in the ethnography. The discussion will be further augmented by a consideration of the 'mega-themes' that arise from the analysis, in terms of national identity, practices of consumption and the role of women.

What the book demonstrates is why the expression of national identity appears to be so important in Magaluf and Palmanova. One reason is that, in the context of the two resorts, it is one thing that the tourists have in common, a sense of their nation, whether it is Scottish, Irish, Welsh or English, but often conflated and represented as British. Further, the tourists are in the presence of the foreign other and vulnerable to the manipulation of their fears, insecurities and anxieties by the commercial exploits of tour operators and others seeking to gain a profit from tourist activities. The idea of the collective nation around which tourists can congregate is exploited, and controlled, primarily for the purposes of the market.

The background against which this takes place is a world in which threats to identity and sovereignty are perceived to come from outside forces, mainly in the guise of the European Union, immigrants and asylum seekers to the UK. At the same time, the home world is also characterised by changing employment patterns, which have inculcated a sense of insecurity, the weakening of collective representation in the form of unions and the increased erosion of the welfare state. As Bauman (2002) notes, 'the plebeian' no longer needs to be controlled by daily management, but with the process of globalisation the threat of being able to withdraw the means to live, through 'downsizing', 'outsourcing' and 'streamlining', is enough. In terms of the welfare state, he suggests it is no longer seen as 'sharing and caring', but rather welfare provision is 'seen as the birthrights of the citizen rather than a handout for the invalid and indolent' (Bauman, 2002: 15).

A further element to the framework within which the tourists' world is situated is that of the process of globalisation. A feature of globalisation is argued to be the dissolution of boundaries, which are seen as a way of asserting and maintaining identity (Chan & McIntyre, 2002). For example, food consumption practices have been noted as ways of establishing and affirming demarcations, thereby maintaining boundaries. The idea that globalisation undermines many boundaries also suggests the opposite. As Chan and McIntyre (2002: xix) contend, '[i]f boundary dissolution characterizes major changes in the world, the other half of the equation is boundary reassertion and reconstruction'.

The claim for increasingly pluralist societies, which have given rise to a new '*Homo Sociologicus*', with a number of different cultures living side by side, has been made by Krausz and Tulea (2002: xii). One of the results, they argue, is that each culture within the pluralist society will want to assert its own exclusiveness, which will inevitably lead to confrontation with other cultures. As Chan and McIntyre (2002) suggest, confrontation requires difference and boundary marking. Attempting to fix boundaries and assert them is an identifiable process in Magaluf and Palmanova. In the face of the undermining of boundaries, which are what all the perceived threats (of the European Union and immigrants) amount to, as well as the idea of the threatening other abroad, the tourists assert their identity by buying into the practice of a particular type of Britishness. For example, the experience in Pirates Adventure allows them to participate in a fantasy world of British greatness. The flying of the Union Jack (and other country flags) allows them to be reminded of their British identity, as well as territorial acquisition, and they keep the other at bay by rejecting local water and seeking out familiar food stuffs.

Globalisation is seen as initiating change. This is on a large scale and adds to the uncertainty that is felt on a more micro-level in the constant changes of the free-market and consumption patterns found in, for example, everyday shopping experiences. Chan and McIntyre (2002: xvi) also concede the point made earlier that it is because of change that nationalism is given prominence: '[i]n a time of change and uncertainty, people are turning to nationalism'.

This turn to nationalism can be interpreted as a need or desire to belong. Belonging can best be understood as being linked to a fixed entity and Bauman (2002: 15) contends that the vagaries of the market, as a result of globalisation, have 'increased [the] value of place'. A feeling of belonging to somewhere in particular, comes back to the feeling of being in the right hotel, and the feeling of being, or having the right to be, in the physical space of a nation. In the home world of the tourists it seems that, for many, the needs of the European Union (e.g. in terms of fishing quotas), immigrants and the disabled appear like cuckoos in the nest, ousting or threatening the position of the rightful occupants and, by corollary, access to nourishment by the mother. Instead the 'rightful occupants' are left to fend for themselves.

Creating one's identity alone, however, is insecure and risky and thus,

> the precariousness of the solitary identity building prompts the identity-builders to seek pegs on which they could hang together their individually experienced fears and anxieties and perform the exorcism rites in the company of the other, similarly afraid and anxious individuals. (Bauman, 2002: 19–20)

If globalisation and consumerism have increased the construction of identity on an individual basis, and this is a frightening experience, then one peg on which individuals can all hang together is national identity; even more so given that the mother is seen as refuge and pacifier of fears and anxieties. As Brown (2000a: 24) notes, '[i]f the nation is conceived as a natural kinship community of common ancestry (as the parental family writ large), then it is more likely to evoke the feelings of security which the infant found in dependence on the mother'. Tourists' experiences in Magaluf and Palmanova offer the opportunity for like-minded people to come together and be provided with a (somewhat false, short-lived and precarious) sense of security and identity based around the idea of a commonly held identity in the form of the nation. One characteristic of the nation that takes prominence is its existence and portrayal as female, a feature I will return to below. The next section will fit the above discussion into the present context, linking it back to the statement at the start of Chapter 1, that tourism is often thought of as a search for something.

## Show me the Way to go Home

The purpose of this section is to further frame the discussion and provide more context to the direction taken by the book. It suggests that the everyday world of the British charter tourists no longer feels like 'home'; that Britain has changed, for some, into a place they do not recognise; but when they get to Magaluf and Palmanova, they are presented with aspects of Britishness that represent, or fulfil the imaginings, of a world that is British in a particular and meaningful way. The following excerpts, taken from conversations with two different tourists, illustrate the point: 'England isn't really England any more' and

'I said to him "can't we go and live in Spain? I feel more at home here than I do in England"'. The latter quote strongly conveys the impression that there is lack of feeling of belonging in the home world.

A feeling of belonging is noted to be an important element of identity. Indeed, '[p]eople may feel that they belong to a piece of territory, to a community, or to a state. Normally they will also have a good idea who else rightfully belongs to this their own authentic context, their home' (Hedetoft & Hjort, 2002: viii). This links to ideas of Gemeinschaft (Tönnies, 1957 [1887]) and mechanical solidarity (Durkheim, 1933) in which the 'authentic in-group' is clearly defined in terms of group and kinship ties. Losing a feeling of belonging and therefore identity – through perceived threats to the collective – leads to feelings of loss of control. As Juergensmeyer (2002: 15) notes, 'a loss in a sense of belonging leads to a feeling of powerlessness'. For example, tourists, who felt themselves to be 'not posh' felt out of place, suffered an identity crisis, of sorts, when placed, due to overbooking, in what they saw as a posh hotel. Being out of their normal *habitus* could give rise to new possibilities of being for the tourists in general (Gell, 1996; Jackson, 1989), but the attendant insecurity this brings is used by others, such as the tour operators, to encourage a seeking of the familiar.

The book began with the premise that many people carry with them a yearning, or longing, for a better life. The resultant search invariably takes the 'traveller', metaphorically, imaginatively or literally elsewhere. The superior life is based on imaginings of a peaceful world char-acterised by plenty and total satisfaction. These places are usually mythical and magical and hard to find. Similarly, some religions offer a route to such a place and hold out a promise of a better life ahead. What this observation does is to establish the principle of the need to journey elsewhere to find happiness and fulfilment. At the same time, it also instils the notion that a sense of dissatisfaction exists in the here and now. The quotes lamenting the loss of England and the need to move elsewhere to regain it illustrate this point.

The idea of searching for something that has been lost has found its way into tourism studies, principally through the work of MacCannell (1976). The tourist, MacCannell argues, leads a fragmented and alienat-ing existence in the home world, and uses the holiday to recover the missing sense of wholeness. Indeed, '[f]or moderns, reality and authen-ticity are thought to be elsewhere: in other historical periods and other cultures, in purer, simpler lifestyles' (MacCannell, 1976: 3). The alienation that MacCannell refers to comes about through the processes of industrialisation, rationalisation and the division of labour. However, this book has gone beyond MacCannell as it dispels the notion that the holiday is a search for authenticity in the life of the 'exotic' other, based on a need for difference. The tourists to Magaluf and Palmanova seek a sense of self in the familiar, although it becomes 'other' in so far as it is distinct from the alienated home world.

At the beginning of the book, I suggested that for many people in the UK their sense of what it is to be British is being undermined. One example is the erosion of the manufacturing base of the economy as the case of shoe making in Northampton demonstrated. Another example is found in the process of Europeanisation, which is seen to threaten daily life. As Cinnirella (2000: 42) notes, '[t]he 1990s saw many political debates about European integration. British politicians and the mass media portrayed the European Union and its ardent supporters as a potential threat to British sovereignty and national identity'. A threat that is exemplified, for instance, by the changes to the content of British sausages in line with European Union regulations and the requirement to use metric weights and measures in the purchase of food and drink. Such events have implications for the very conduct of peoples' lives.

On top of these sorts of concerns is the issue of immigration and asylum seekers, constantly played out in the tabloid press and the rhetoric of politicians. For example, a story reported in *The Sun* newspaper (19 May 2003: p. 1)[1] claimed that one of its journalists had posed as an asylum seeker and managed to smuggle his way into the UK, whereupon he was promptly given 'free housing, food, travel expenses and Home Office ID'. The full story 'will shock a nation already enraged by the asylum crisis', *The Sun* (19 May 2003) claimed. The item was presented alongside another proclaiming that Britain is in danger of being 'swamped' by immigrant criminals. The idea that Britain is somehow being taken over by outsiders is an area of concern for some of the tourists in Magaluf and Palmanova. One informant describes his region of England as being 'infested with them'. Linsell notes, in connection with the perceived 'influx' of immigrants,

> [o]ne of the consequences of bringing people with very different cultural values and perceptions together... is that it stimulates defensive communal instincts. Communal competition and conflict leads to communal insecurity and pressure for greater internal conformity, which in turn leads to a reduction in the scope for personal choice, not an increase. (Linsell, 2000: 69)

The importance of Linsell's observations (albeit somewhat extreme as there is also the potential for cultural exchange) in the context of Magaluf and Palmanova, is that competitive rivalries are acted out in the resorts, as evidenced in the games played and some of the entertainment provided. Furthermore, within these enactments there is an emphasis on conformity.

The notion that the 'British way of life' is under threat from the European Union also finds currency in *The Sun*. With reference to a European Treaty regarding the establishment of a European Constitution, the paper ran a news report under the banner 'Save our country' (*The Sun*, 15 May 2003: p. 1). The main issue was that the then Prime Minister Tony Blair was 'surrendering' the UK, a country that had successfully repelled any attempts by Europeans to invade since 1066, to Europe. Thus, 'we saw off the Spanish', 'we saw off the French' and 'we saw off the Germans' (*The Sun*, 15 May 2003). The 'threat' of the Germans, Spanish and French is constantly played out in the resorts of Magaluf and Palmanova, through the language of night-time entertainment, the thoughts and feelings of some of the tour operator representatives (reps) about their fellow German reps, and the representation of the local people and amenities. So, local buses are full of pickpockets, water is unsafe to drink and certain attractions are discouraged because they are 'full of Germans'. In addition, the 'seeing-off' of the foreign other is celebrated in some of the names ascribed to café-bars in Magaluf and in the night-time entertainment of Pirates Adventure.

The point in bringing these issues to the fore is to demonstrate that the sense of loss of Britishness referred to in the introduction is ongoing, and that the defence of this is decidedly militaristic and aggressive. These characteristics point towards components of what it is to be British in the context of Magaluf and Palmanova. Furthermore, what these issues – sausages, shoes, asylum seekers', 'handouts' and European integration – do is suggest that the holidaymaker to Magaluf and Palmanova, rather than looking for reality and authenticity in the lives of the other, as MacCannell suggests about tourists in general, seek that which is authentically and 'really' British. This is ostensibly because authentic Britishness is perceived as being endangered in the home world. Many of these tourists, then, are not in search of a better life elsewhere, but of a life that is based in the home world, and that this home is one in which their imaginings of what it is to be British can be lived out and constructed in a very particular way.

A feeling of competition, particularly from feelings of uneven distribution of the 'food' of the nation (welfare provision, houses, etc.), is also engendered and given expression in Magaluf and Palmanova. If people are like children in relation to the mother nation, they become competitive for her attention, nurturing and nourishment. These issues are important in the resorts because there is a competitive element to the environment in games played and in some of the entertainment offered. The feeling of conflict is also expressed in national rivalries between the nations of the UK, most markedly between the English and Scottish.

The issue of choice and conformity raised by Linsell is also noted by Hagendoorn and Pepels (2000). They argue that national identity is reinforced by homogeneity (in terms of Anderson's imagined community, this links to the idea of access to a common daily newspaper) reliant on symbols in the form of flags, war, etc. (cf. Billig, 1995). These elements contribute to a common national identity, and to socialisation through group pressure. This argument's relevance to the context of Magaluf and Palmanova is that there is much to suggest conformity of identities, limited choice in terms of consumer goods available and attempts to conventionalise and uniform relationships are evident. For example, the promotion of heterosexual, conventional women's roles and the need for fit, able bodies (the disabled being another out-group, albeit within the in-group, they are seen as a threat to the fit, healthy nation).

One feature of the tourists' experiences is that there is an attempt to inculcate a sense of community – laying claim to the territory through flying national flags, naming places in a familiar British fashion and so on. In addition, there is the idea of sticking together, e.g. 'we all sit together at night-time entertainment', 'this is a British hotel' and the outward disapproval of anyone who does not want to join in. How can someone not be happy with what Magaluf offers? How can they just want to sunbathe and not go clubbing, or spend money on one of the many excursions? To not join in is to be seen to be different, which earns the disapproval of one's companions. The representation of the British in Pirates Adventure as winners, and therefore better than the French (and by inference the Spanish and Germans), again instils a sense of community.

I therefore demonstrate that the 'search', so to speak, of the British charter tourists to Magaluf and Palmanova brings them into an encounter with a form of 'effervescent-Britishness', rather than with a difference or an exotic other. The characteristics of this Britishness are represented and lived through composites of social life, namely, space, the body and food and drink. These elements form the core of the book and allow an exploration around questions of identity and an understanding of the experiential nature of tourism, for these tourists, to be examined.

Part of the purpose of this chapter is to summarise the theoretical perspective underlying the ethnography. The chapter will demonstrate how the theory and data lead to the assertion that the British charter tourists to Magaluf and Palmanova 'escape to Britain'. In order to understand how the contention that tourists to Magaluf and Palmanova encounter an effervescent Britishness, it is necessary to examine the nature or characteristics of the world that the tourists finds herself/himself in.

## Flying the Flag

This section examines the way that Magaluf and Palmanova can be understood as 'Britain' as it looks at the characteristics of the resorts, which gives them their sense of a British identity. It does this by thinking about the totems or signs and symbols of Britishness that are present in the two resorts. For example, the Union Flag (or Union Jack, as it is colloquially known) along with the country flags of Scotland, England and Wales can be seen flying from balconies, on advertisements for food and drink and on beach towels and bags used by tourists in both resorts. The flags are one example of a number of objects that can be interpreted as signalling or symbolising aspects of Britishness. The flags fly alongside other representations that speak of Britishness. These include food and drink, the use of pounds sterling, the way in which the space of the resorts is constructed, understood and used by the tourists, and through the use and representation of the body both as an expression of these ideas and as an embodiment of them.

The flagging up of identity in the way described owes its theoretical lineage to Durkheim, and it is this inheritance that provides the theoretical underpinning of the book. The basic tenet of the argument is that in order to understand inner thoughts and feelings, and express our sense of who we are to ourselves, it is necessary to externalise the inner world. As Durkheim (1915: 228) proposed, 'in order to express our own ideas to ourselves, it is necessary ... that we fix them upon material things which symbolize them'. This material expression can take many forms and in Durkheim's language is known as a totem. In trying to understand social relations, Durkheim noted that a totem could represent a whole group of people and was used to separate them out from other groups with different totems. The totem is a symbol, it stands for something other than what it literally is and can take different forms. Importantly, it is an expression of identity.

As the introduction demonstrated, the threads of Durkheim's work can be followed through Mauss (1954), Lévi-Strauss (1969), Barthes (1993) and Bourdieu (1977, 1979). The ideas are not fixed in totemism or religious practices per se, but are in the concept that material objects stand for or send messages about who we are and who we are not. Thus, for Mauss, a gift is a representation of the giver. For Lévi-Strauss, being able to understand what the material objects stand for is a method of ordering and structuring the social world. They become a form of language through which ideas are transmitted. As Berger and Luckmann (1966: 55) point out, 'symbolism and symbolic language become essential constituents of the reality of everyday life and of the common-sense apprehension of this reality'. According to Barthes, the reality of every-day life contains inherently mythological language. The objects of the quotidian world contain signs and symbols that refer to much greater ideas than the objects themselves. Wine, for example, stands as a totem of the French, and steak, linked as it is to the bull, tells us that the eater is, among other things, strong, stubborn and aggressive. Thus, people become 'types' that do not necessarily have any bearing on reality.

The legacy of Durkheim also finds resonance in the work of Bourdieu (1977, 1979). Bourdieu acknowledges that identities find expression through a variety of mediums, e.g. the food eaten or the way in which the body is used. Building on Mauss's (1979) concept of *habitus*, who we are and our way of being in the world is embodied. This is a key concept because it attempts to make a bridge between a structuralist perspective and that of phenomenology. That is, it acknowledges, in the Durkheimian sense, that '[w]e speak a language that we did not make; we use instruments that we did not invent; we invoke rights that we did not found; a treasury of knowledge is transmitted to each generation that it did not gather itself' (Durkheim, 1915: 212). At the same time, however, Bourdieu (1977: 79) allows for the agency of the individual in working with the embodied aspects of the *habitus*: '[t]he virtuoso finds in the *opus operatum* new triggers and new supports for the *modus operandi* from which they arise, so that his discourse continuously feeds off itself like a train bringing along its own rails'. That is, society reproduces itself through the embodiment of the *habitus* but it is in practice, its experiential formation, that it can be manipulated, negotiated reinforced and/or rejected.

In a similar vein, the theories of Lefebvre (1991) are also key. Using a spatial 'triad', the social relationships present in space can be examined. The way in which space is constructed acknowledges the presence of predetermined structures. That is, by encoding Magaluf and Palmanova with symbols of Britain in the form of place names and food, for example, the tourists are brought immediately into a British imbued world. However, by allowing for the resistance to, negotiation and practice of these signs, a Lefebvrian-based perspective brings an experiential understanding and dimension to the situation. Thus, in the contested spatiality of quotidian experience, how the tourists live the signs or not, tells us how the meaning is understood and, at the same time, feeds into the perpetuation or rejection of the message.

The approaches outlined by Lefebvre and Bourdieu are important because I seek to bridge the gap between a purely structuralist interpretation of the resorts and that of a phenomenological approach; thus ensuring that the experiences of the tourists are represented. That is, it is possible to identify many flags of Britishness in the two resorts; but it is necessary to understand how they are flown, and waved by the tourists. This theoretical background informs the technique and methodology that has been undertaken to study the tourists. The desire to understand how the symbolic is manifest in the experiential has meant that it was necessary to engage with the tourists and take part in their activities, to share with them their symbolic home.

## At Home with the British

This study is unique in that it is the first ethnography of British charter tourists abroad. The main field methodology used was that of participant and non-participant observation. This basically involved joining in and sharing the way of life that was being practised in the two resorts. Taking part means to inhabit the same space, use the body in similar ways and eat the same food, as one might when visiting another's home. The question to ask is what does this involve? This section proceeds with a summation of the main aspects outlined in the ethnography around the central themes of the book. Given the theoretical background in terms of the use of semiotic analysis and that more akin to phenomenology, this section will re-visit the nature of the symbolic world and move on to examine the experiential nature of the codes, as they exist in the two resorts.

I explore the symbolic economy present in the tourists' world via space, the body and food and drink. All of these are separate categories of social life; however, all inter-link with each other. For example, the nature of what is eaten can have an influence on body shape, which, in turn, will influence the way that space is inhabited or perceived.

The signing or flagging of British identity in Magaluf and Palmanova appears through a variety of symbols. Some, as already suggested, are quite obvious, the use of flags, for example, speaks immediately of national identity and a sense of belonging to a particular socio-cultural group. On its own, the flag does not display what is *meant* by this particular identity. Such an understanding comes about through linkages (or webs of significance to use Geertz's [1973] term) to other signs. Thus, for example, the display of the 'Union Jack', as part of the advertisements for food; but, especially in connection to the fry-up, give the meal an identity that goes beyond that of merely being an arrangement and amalgamation of ingredients to satisfy hunger. The dish itself is marked or coded as being British. In this instance, the nature of being British is of someone who eats meat, and specifically pork; the vegetarian and non-pork eater are excluded.

To continue the semiological analysis further, the pork content of the fry-up links to the presence of the representation of pigs in both resorts. They appear on postcards, as toys simulating sex and as ornaments. By understanding the significance of pigs in the home world (symbols of laziness, greed, gluttony, heroes and saviours) it is possible to gain an even deeper understanding of the nature of British identity within the context of the holiday. That is, as tourists they can lie around, eat and drink as much they want, indulge in copulation, while at the same time, because of the presence of other signs, they are reminded of their status as heroes. The idea of 'the hero' will be returned to again in the following discussion.

In terms of food- and drink-related flags of Britishness, these appear in the presence of other meals including roast beef and Yorkshire pudding, both associated with their own meanings. The nature of cooking the roast, in Lévi-Straussian (1997) terms, signifies waste and extravagance, and the content of the meal again, through the association of British military victories at Agincourt and Crécy, with that of being a hero. The ideas of waste and extravagance also fit with a notion of a tourist identity in terms of self-indulgence, and the 'abundance of money'. This interpretation is given as tourists will save for their holidays so that they can have additional spending money.

The use of imperial measures to sell cocktails and British-branded beers is another sign of the establishment of British identity. Similarly, the acceptance of pounds sterling also flies in the face of the European Union. Here, on the soil of another's nation, the British stand by their use of imperial measures (outlawed by European Union legislation but hotly contested by the likes of Littlejohn's so-called 'Metric Martyrs') and use

British money.[2] Clinging on to the currency (especially in light of debates about joining the Euro and perceived threats to British sovereignty) and imperial measures is, in effect, giving two fingers up to both the Spanish and European Other.

The heroic element of British identity is evident in the encoding of the space of Magaluf, particularly with names that are familiar both in terms of having derived from the home world and, at the same time, make reference to a British military past, e.g. The Lord Nelson and Duke of Wellington. Although these names make reference to events that occurred nearly 200 years ago, they are still of significance to the construction of British identity; both men are commemorated in the home world and Nelson has been used in anti-European rhetoric as the feature in *The Sun* (15 May 2003) demonstrates. The celebration, or memory, of British militarism has a more contemporary feel with references to the Falklands, in both the name of a shop and by reference to the conflict with the Argentineans during some of the evening entertainment.

Names such as Robin Hood, for example, speak of a different kind of heroism from the military, suggesting a different set of characteristics. The liminal status of the semi-fictional character of Robin Hood links the tourists with the idea of an in-between state that tourism is often claimed to induce (Graburn, 1989). The idea of being on the edge of society, which Hood also signifies, could also, in this context connect to the ideas of the UK being on the edge of Europe, both geographically and in terms of the Euro. The location of Pirates Adventure (where reference to Britain's antagonistic relationship with continental Europe is acted out) is also spatially on the edge. This 'little England', as one tourist referred to it, is like a crucible for the emotions and attitudes towards the European other (particularly in the guise of the French and Germans) to come to the fore in the form of an effervescent Britishness. The characteristics that Robin Hood refers to include a sense of fair play, loyalty and strength in adversity. In the fable, Robin Hood and his men are resisting someone who poses a threat to the sovereignty of the nation, someone who (as in the perception of Europe and immigrants) is trying to take over and impose his/her will, or get something out of the hard-working citizens for nothing.

Other facilities are also signed with names that are taken from the home world, including The White Horse, The Oak and Willows. The latter two speak of a connection to the soil, solidity, strength and longevity. Other names, e.g. The British Chippy, Eastenders and the Dudley Tavern, again remind the tourists that what they are eating is marked with a British identity. This is brought home further by references to the mother.

The use of slogans such as 'cooking like mum' or depictions of soft, comfy mother-like figures refers the tourists back to the nation, in the form of reference to the mother. The signing of Magaluf and Palmanova with allusion to the mother is most pronounced in the form of the breast.

The appearance of the breast as a symbol in the two resorts is very potent. It is a multi-vocal symbol and stands for many things of which the mother is one. Part of its power is derived from its various meanings and its ability to appeal to virtually all people. Another aspect is its ubiquitous presence in the two resorts. It appears on postcards, aprons, on the beach, in nightclubs and as souvenirs. It is present in its actual bodily form and in representation. To reveal the breast off the beach, during the day, is considered, by some, to be 'not nice' or indicative of a lack of morals. At night, its revelation can be taken as fingers up to authority, and titillation, in the form of objects of desire, for men. This latter point fits alongside the way in which the breast is depicted on postcards, which themselves belong to a range of material displaying women as consumable items, and reinforcing ideas of heterosexuality. Thus, the breast appeals as a source of comfort and nourishment, which link it to the child, as well as making it an object of sexual desire.

The above are examples of signs or symbols that code Palmanova and Magaluf. The fry-up is an example of encoding via food, the place names are a way of organising the spaces of the two resorts into a 'British-esque' landscape, or a heterotopia to use Foucault's (1986) terminology. The breast, a part of the body, is used as a sign of sexual titillation, the mother and by extension, in this context, the nation. All of these symbols interweave with each other to form, along with all the other signs referred to in the ethnographic chapters of the book, a 'web of significance' (Geertz, 1973). They are examples of ways in which space is encoded and forms the *habitus* into which the tourists are born, so to speak. They are the bricoleurs' (Lévi-Strauss, 1969) building blocks.

The 'flags' of Britishness discussed in the preceding discussion began with some observations about the food available and how it is marked up as being British. The reluctance of the British to engage with the foreign other is seen in the seeking out of British food. Even in simple business terms, the abundance of facilities selling this type of food testifies to the actions of the tourists in seeking it out. Thus, when the German proprietor of a café-bar in Palmanova noted that 'when they hear English being spoken next door they go there', she was speaking of the tourists' actions in seeking out the familiar. Similarly, one hotel manager explained that when his hotel tried to promote Mallorcan culture via the food available,[3] 'the British look at the sausage and walk straight by'. In terms of the fry-up, there are sausages that taste like 'hotdogs', 'ham instead of bacon' and 'they don't know how to cook it'; as well as the inability to get 'a proper cup of tea', and the desire not to drink 'their water'. All of these suggest that the tourists want the familiar, and, what is familiar is that which they know from home. Some of the tourists also attest to seeking the familiar and claim that it is part of Mallorca's attraction. They consume what they understand and identify with. Thus, they will not drink the local water (in part because they have been advised not to as part of the tour operators' attempts to keep the tourists under their control) unless it has been boiled, and a 'proper cup of tea' exists in the familiar world of McDonald's and Willows, the latter with its horse brasses and white china.

The whole act of consumption is a manifestation of many of the facets of being British in this context. Eat British to keep out the other, engage in competitive consumption activities to show that you are the best, or a hero, as in, for example, many of the games played during the evening entertainment organised by hotels, or as part of bar crawls. Who can consume the most (especially of alcohol) testifies to strength and the ability to hold one's own, to be the best. In the case of the tourist who was told he would 'leave this island a legend' if he could consume three strong cocktails in a row and remain standing, he was acting in the face of adversity – the potency of the drinks was working against him. The comments by the tourists to the man who refused to take his penalty drink (a shot with a chilli) berated his lack of strength and questioned his nationality, 'call yourself an Englishman', and the bartender's comment, 'I've never known an Englishman not to do a penalty'.

Being strong and being the best both link to the battle theme identified in the signs of British militarism explored earlier. In experiential terms, this is acted out literally in Pirates Adventure, and the jokes used by some entertainers to which the tourists respond, sometimes with fervour. The aggression to which these acts refer sometimes spills out into actual fighting by tourists, or is expressed in the violence of some language used. For example, the reference to a hawker as 'nig-nog', and bartering with him to the lowest point which is 'fuck off' both act out the distrust and combative attitude towards the other. This is further heightened in acknowledging the difference between 'us' and 'them' as the comments about food suggest.

War is a contest, and while the encoding of Magaluf refers to this, and the behaviour of some of the tourists attests to this, the idea of competition is prevalent in the games played. The emphasis is on who can win, who can be the best, whether it is to shout the loudest, drink the most or be the funniest, all speak of rivalry. Sometimes, demarcation is between nationalities, as in the case of games played in the hotels. In similar locations, sometimes the matches are between male and female and on other occasions between male and male or female and female. Very often, the games make use of, or focus on, the body, e.g. sexual positions or the biggest breasts. Even seeking to ascertain where the tourists come from has an element of challenge to it, as they are invited to shout for their hometown or region, in some cases the loudest wins a prize. The effect of this is to fix the tourists not only in terms of national identity but also in terms of regional identity. Gender is highlighted by the matches between male and female and in reference at other times to the differences between the two sexes – women called 'skirts' or 'heels', and men called 'trousers'.

The body as a whole is the focus of the nature of the tourists' experiences. It can also be read for signs. For example, a bulldog with a Union Flag tattoo can be identified as symbolising Britishness on someone's arm. However, at the same time, the wearer has literally embodied that idea, they are that identity. To fit this thinking with one of the sets of symbols referred to above, the semiotic reading of some of the place names in Magaluf and Palmanova speak of an appropriation of another's land. To imprint these names on to the two resorts literally marks them as British, taking over, having free reign. The unbuckling of the body by the tourists embodies these ideas. The folds and ripples of skin occupy more space, as they are not constricted by clothing, the tourist on holiday is letting it all hang out, relaxing and freeing their bodies. They are spreading themselves (in sunbathing quite literally) over another's land.

This section has explored some of the elements to emerge from the main themes of the ethnography. It began by highlighting some of the ways in which semiotic analysis – signs, symbols and codes – can be used to understand the nature of the structure of the home of the tourists in Magaluf and Palmanova. It then went on to examine the ways in which some of the ideas represented in the signs are performed by the tourists. For the sake of clarification, the different aspects have been treated separately, but in practise they all interconnect to form a whole. It is clear that a form of British identity is inscribed onto Palmanova and Magaluf, and is underwritten by regional and gendered identities. These are responded to and manipulated by the tourists in their lived experiences of the two resorts. The findings suggest that the nature of this British identity is based on repelling the other, of being the best and maintaining a child-like competitiveness in consumption practices. It is underpinned by an emphasis on being white and heterosexual. Two key themes emerge from this discussion: that of the importance of consumption, and secondly the role of women in the idea of nation.

## Consumption

The practice of consumption in the two resorts is intimately linked to the feeling of belonging outlined at the beginning of this chapter. Inherent in this is a tension between the idea of the free market, that is the ability to construct individual identities through consumption practices (which assumes equal access to the means of consumption) and the insecurity this engenders, which Bauman (2002) identifies as a problem for people left to their own devices. The tension is further exacerbated in that the promise of freedom, held out through the idea of individual choice, is in reality met with a lack of choice. However, that there is limited choice undermines the idea of post-Fordism. In reality, we are living in an accelerated Fordism where there is more choice, but that in itself is limited and conformist. In Magaluf and Palmanova the choice in the shops is limited, hotels operate in fairly standard ways, and behaviour is not open to approved individual expression. Indeed, you will be a consumer, you will get your tits out for the boys, and you will enjoy yourself.

The world of the tourists is thus characterised by 'the complex ambiguities inherent in the relationships with the external modern world, and also of the disintegrative incoherence of the inner, psychological world' (Brown, 2000a: 24). The external world of the tourists can be understood in terms of issues of globalisation and perceived outside threats as well as the ambivalence connected with consumption practices. The inner world is held to be objectified, and externalised, which links the theoretical lineage of this work to Durkheim (1915) and the expression of the subjective through totems. Brown (2000a) contends that reconciliation of the external and internal is evinced (in Kleinian terms) by a retreat to childhood, and, as Sceats (2000: 5) notes, '[t]he modern world manifests an overwhelming human yearning for wholeness, oneness or integrity, a yearning apparent in oral appetites, sexual desire, religious fervour, physical hunger, "back to the womb" impulses'. The idea of the desire to be reunited with the maternal figure is a fantasy of return 'to the wholly fulfilled infant at the breast, or even *in utero*. This might almost be said to be the ur-longing a desire to be reunited with the block off which we are a chip' (Sceats, 2000: 5). In terms of physical hunger and sexual desire, efforts are made to satisfy these in

Magaluf and Palmanova; this idea of union with the mother the ur-longing, the block being the nation, and its association with roots and identity positions the tourist as child (Dann, 1996a).

The longing for wholeness, a sense of creating oneness by denying difference, and of belonging to a kinship group, which is natural, are portrayed in the idea of the nation as a single entity composed of a group of people with a common ancestry. Thus, there is a link, and a form of dependence; but, at the same time, nationalism requires independence to be able to stand alone without need of the other. In Magaluf and Palmanova, this ideal is thwarted as attempts to prevent independence are made, via the tour operators, and in many cases independence is not looked for. Although independence might be an attribute of nationalism, and resistance to Europe would attest to this, in the two resorts it is being used as a way of encouraging people to buy into a particular set of practices. Therefore, it is the ideal of standing against the other that is tapped into, although the individual cannot be independent or free. So, this is where nationalism is manipulated, the pull of that in the face of all these other crises of identity is exploited in an attempt to perpetuate the market. National identity gives a sense of temporal and historical continuity, and differentiation against the other (Guibernau, 2001). The importance of ensuring that people are consumers is summed-up by Bell and Lyall (2002: 153), '[c]onsumption is essential to industrial capitalism ... Citizens can be replaced as workers, but as consumers they are irreplaceable. The global economy has utter dependence on continuing discretionary consumption'.

Writing about US consumerism, David Brown (2000b) notes that in return for giving up certain welfare rights after World War II, the masses were given greater consumer power (ability to buy cars, houses, etc.). Consumer rights were seen as a way of placating the citizenry, and a way of regulating behaviour. Although at a later historical period, in the UK it is possible to note that during the 1980s, with Thatcherism and the selling of public utilities and the disempowering of the unions, consumerism took a greater hold. The collective and its responsibilities in terms of the welfare state were severely undermined. In its place was the freedom to get money to participate in consumption activities. David Brown says of the USA,

> [t]he States has used consumption ... as a viable tool to regulate the behaviour of its citizens in order to produce desired outcomes. Consumers themselves have facilitated this process by punishing non-conformists through psychological weaponry of social ostracism

on one extreme and subtle public ridicule on the other. (Brown, 2000b: 10)

In the UK, the housing market is an example. The importance placed on the ownership of one's own home inevitably excludes a section of the population. Although consumerism promises freedom of choice, it is only available if there is the money to exercise that choice, for many people this simply does not exist. Also, once one has bought into the system it becomes difficult to get out of – failure to keep up mortgage repayments leads to repossession and loss of home. Therefore, there is a need to keep working, and accept what is on offer, because failure to do so limits one's ability as a consumer.

In Magaluf and Palmanova consumption activities are normalised – drink as much as possible, purchase items, but abide by the rules. Do not dare not to join in because lying by the pool and not wanting to buy an excursion or activity will result in stigmatisation as odd. To be a consumer requires conformity: bar crawls, for example, play with normative ideas of gendered, heterosexual relationships, which appear to serve the purpose of reinforcing conventional roles. Forgetting the rules applied to the games is punishable. The perversion is that they are forgotten because the consumption is too much, hence the need to punish and humiliate. Therefore, do not have more than is good for you. To be able to fully appreciate the freedom of the market requires unlimited supply of money. The inadequacies of most people's consumption practices are demonstrated in fuelling their desires for more (via such expensive items as yachts) and showing their inability to properly control or deal with their fantasies. This leads to another contradiction inherent in consumption. In the book, I noted that the fulfilling of desire may become a torture, more than one can handle (hence being sick), thus, although consumption is held out as a promise of satisfaction, it has a 'darker' side. Indeed, 'the most rapturous form of shopping, for example clothes purchasing on unlimited credit in a shopping mall, may equally turn into the most tortuous as the shopper tires, the clothes don't fit, the car park is cramped and so on' (Edwards, 2000: 5).

The tension between the idea of freedom through the market and the control and conformity it actually brings is further exacerbated in that the holiday holds open a promise of freedom against a backdrop of home where one must go to work to survive, one is told not to eat or drink too much, or of certain things, and sovereignty is being threatened. The holiday freedom promise is one of self-determination to drink or eat yourself sick (as a baby might), be overweight, and show it, and indulge in your fears (expressions of dislike or suspicion) of the other, and fears of yet more change in the home world. The main way that individuals experience national identity is as a community of culture through unity of meaning. However, this cannot be allowed to drift, as Guibernau (2001: 77) notes: '[a]s a collective sentiment national identity needs to be upheld and reaffirmed at regular intervals'. These occur in symbols, even at, as Billig (1995) suggests, the banal level, and, in the case of the holiday to Magaluf or Palmanova, a more elevated level. This does not necessarily mark the holiday out as a time of difference in the Graburn (1989) sense, but it highlights and gives a sense of effervescence to the sentiments expressed through symbolic and actual discourse. This does, without making it a sacred journey, connect to religion in the Durkheimian sense – a group of people coming together to uphold commonly shared beliefs or convictions.

What is evident in the foregoing discussion of consumption and the feeling of the need to belong is that there is a strong link to the idea of a return to childhood in order to be linked to the mother. It is because of these associations, along with the predominance of images of women (and particularly naked ones) in Magaluf and Palmanova, and the discourse associated with them that the nation is seen as female and maternal. It is this aspect of the nature of tourism in the two resorts, which is explored in the next section.

## Being with Mother

I have discussed the preponderance of images of nude women, but especially the exhibition of breasts, linked consumption practices with the idea of woman, and, thus, the idea of the nation. It is the association of the woman with motherhood, family, and tradition that links her to nation (the idea of ancestry), and, as such, the nation is often represented in female form. For example, as White (2003) contends women reproduce the nation biologically, culturally, and symbolically. Drawing on research undertaken in Russia, White (2003) argues that the mother figure is important because she is seen as the person to turn to in times of distress, and as more affectionate than a father figure,[4] and while children may feel disappointed at times by their mothers, they would continue to love her. Bauman (2002) contends that society is becoming increasingly abstract and distant due to the undermining of welfare provision. If welfare provision is also associated with the idea of a caring nation, which I contend that it is, and the nation is accepted as being represented by the female, maternal form, following White's example, the nation can still inspire feelings of loyalty and affection.

Further, Cusack notes,

> women have often been given a special symbolic status in relation to the nation, while being distanced from active membership of the polity. Women in particular have been used as "cultural markers of the nations" identity ... strongly associated with the family and tradition, and this has militated against their roles as modern citizens. (Cusack, 2003: 7)

Indeed, it is the symbolic role of the woman as nation that has made her vulnerable to nationalist discourse that tends to sexualise and eroticise the nation. Women's bodies become a part of a collective body, e.g. the use of rape as a way of violating the nation. As Valerius (2003: 43) contends, '[t]here is a close correspondence between the nation and women's bodies, whether they are material bodies biologically reproducing the nation ... or targets of ethnic rage and humiliation'.

Sexualising the idea of the nation links to desire. There is desire for other territories, the desire to acquire other lands – linked to male desire for the woman – to possess, to control. In the case of the nourishing mother and the ability to withhold milk, she is in the controlling position, subjugating women reverses that. In Magaluf, emphasis is on possession through winning at Pirates Adventure and the way in which aspects of the resorts are named, linking back to empire and taking of other's lands.

To return to the feeling of loss and emptiness, much is made in Magaluf and Palmanova of the opportunity to eat and drink, and fulfil one's sexual appetite. Big appetites are according to Sceats (2000) indicative of an inner emptiness (both literally and metaphorically). The lack of a state of wholeness links to the idea of a fundamental insecurity (all supposed to be conditions of being British and expressed in some ways by some of the tourists). The idea of going back to the womb, or seeking the mother in the nation, has been characterised as regressive; but, as Sceats (2000) points out, it might also be thought of as a part of development and/or of a form of spiritual growth. For example, promoting the nation might be understood as furthering a love of self, an overcoming of the self-loathing that might be attached to the idea of loss of self-esteem or importance. Aldridge (2003) argues that contemporary society is characterised by narcissism (a theme explored in this book in connection to tourists' bodies), which arises from a combination of consumerism and sexual permissiveness. This is manifest in Magaluf and Palmanova through treating the self, indulging and admiring the self. The self-admiration is evident in the presence of many mirrors in the tourists' facilities. The idea of looking at oneself, in this context, is about love of the self (nation), promoting past battle victories, for example, a means of proclaiming the nation's greatness. In short, to paraphrase Geertz (1973), it is a story being told by the British about themselves. As Crossley (2001: 144) notes, 'the existence of mirrors and other reflecting surfaces adds to the basic 'mirroring' from others and potentially intensifies the relationship which an agent may enjoy to their self *qua* embodied being'. At the same time the desire to assert independence, be separate from the mother (or the surrogate or stepmother in the form of the EU) may be understood as part of self-development.

The woman as nation and nurturing mother accords her a powerful function. At the same time, she is dis-empowered because of the serving nature of her role. Thus, for example, we are reminded of the domestic duties of women in Pirates – 'put her below stairs there's washing up to be done' that is her correct role, not as a warring pirate.[5] In addition, women are humiliated in the axe throwing 'game', the most intimate parts of their bodies are exposed and used for entertainment, and their bodily functions mocked. During one evening's entertainment, for example, a man is hypnotised into thinking he is giving birth, in another – a drag act – one of the female characters is shown menstruating. In addition, there is the joy of seeing women engaged in lesbian sex (here it is all right for like to consume like [Douglas, 1975b], which in this context is perverse because it is against the 'norm' and so the women are further degraded). This is almost like a constant carnivalesque of upturned order, but nastier because it contains an air of misogyny that McDowell also noted is present in workers in the City of London financial district. As one of her informants reported, '[t]hey had a blow-up woman that they used to kick around the floor' (McDowell, 1995: 83). Again woman as powerful in being a provider and causing dependence needs to be overturned. All of the above examples do that. Even a grandmother figure does not command respect, as the 'Fat Bastard' talks about his octogenarian grandmother being 'shagged'.

As already suggested, consumerism is seen as a way of countering problems and women are linked to this activity through the breast. It is suggested by Stearns (2001: 56) that consumerism is used to placate children and that growing up with it accords it a normalcy, it is part of the socialisation process: '[t]he more consumer expectations were planted in childhood, the fuller their expression once adulthood loomed. Consumerism, in other words, was by this point feeding itself'. This gets reconfirmed in Magaluf and Palmanova – fulfilment of desire comes with good behaviour as if the tourists are children, hence the emphasis on food, drink and sex. If the sense of loss (threats from the EU or immigrants) and insecurity about identity is there, then consumerism offers a way of dealing with this, as Stearns (2001: 138) comments, '[c]onsumerism helps people deal with confusions about social status and with challenges to established patterns because of foreign influence'.

The link between women and consumption activities and their ability to withdraw or withhold their bodies in the gratification of desires initially puts them in a powerful position. With reference to the ability of the mother to socialise a child's diet Sceats (2000: 11) argues, '[m]aternity provides a figure of limitless, irresistible authority'. The mother is connected, therefore, to food and love. On holiday in Palmanova and Magaluf, the idea of nourishment on a 24-hour basis is present. The welcome drink given during the welcome meeting symbolises this idea. It is indicative of (false) love to make the tourists think they are wanted and cared for (Andrews, 2000). The hotels and tour operators take on the role of the mother in the face of the distant nation, in terms of space, and the perception of her 'natural' offspring that they no longer receive their due gratification.

One way to overcome the power of women is to make them commodities, and Stearns (2001) notes that women are increasingly commodified. If something can be made into a commodity it implies ownership and with that control. So you will get your tits out for the boys (as we tell you in Pirates) and you will be ready for sex, as the postcards that present your vulva to the world state. This can also be seen as a way of demanding nourishment as sex and food are often conflated, both can be discussed in terms of satisfying an appetite and the body symbolised through food – fruits for breast, asparagus for penis (cf. Sceats, 2000). You will not have that ability to hold back from us as you do as a mother withdrawing the breast, or as the nation withdrawing welfare support. As Stearns (2001:138) notes, '[c]onsumerism also, relatedly, allows ... challenges to hierarchy, in terms of social class, gender, even parental authority'. Thus consuming women challenges them. This does happen in the reverse, but to a lesser extent. The penis is presented as food in the form of the plastic sandwich but images of male genitalia either as food or presented alongside food, do not abound in the resorts. In addition men are not invited to get their penises out for the girls, male homosexual sex is not permitted, and no mockery is made of male bodily functions. For example, no pretend sperm filled condoms are produced for entertainment purposes, and audiences are not invited to laugh at impotence or testicular cancer.

De-robing women, stripping them of culture (clothes being markers of culture) and highlighting their natural bodily functions debases them, they are shown in an animal element, in effect less than human. As Sceats (2000: 62–63) notes, '[t]he "Dominating body", almost invariably male, acts through a sense of lack, seeks "Subhuman enemies" to fight'. This links back to the idea of the male as the conqueror, taking over virgin, compliant territories through colonialism for his own gratification and nourishment.

The tourists in Palmanova and Magaluf can be seen to be caught up in a number of forces that impinge on the construction of their identities. For one, there is the societal changes in the home world characterised by the demise in the welfare state and the perceived 'influx' of immigrants. Next, there is the perceived threat to sovereignty from the European Union, and other facets of the globalisation process. Consumption activities are offered as a way of forming identity or providing a collective around which people can congregate. However, these practices are themselves inadequate and in a world where collectivities compete for prominence, one that provides a commonality for the tourists in Magaluf and Palmanova is that of a national identity. Consumption is seen as a way of placating fears and satisfying wants. The idea of the nation as providing and keeping safe is linked to such an ideal; a role also attributed to the mother. Thus, consumption in the guise of the free market has attempted to replace or usurp the mother (and or nation) but in turn needs to exploit the idea of both for its own self-maintenance. It does not satisfy a promise of freedom and in the case of women serves as a further form of subjugation.

Before drawing the book to a close, I wish to outline what the way forward with some of the ideas highlighted above might be. One question to arise from this research is how much of this identity highlighted here is a regional one? The majority of the tourists hailed from 'the north', and some showed open hostility to London. Indeed, one informant referred to the city as 'the arsehole of Britain'. A group of Londoners felt that, unlike Ayia Napa, Magaluf was geared to 'northerners'. Many of the owners of the facilities in the two resorts were, also, originally from northern England or Scotland, and it can be argued that they have constructed the resorts in their own likeness, and how they reflect on the nature of the home world from which they are now removed. Thus, future research in this area might be to, firstly, undertake a similar ethnography of a resort elsewhere in the Mediterranean, identified as being set-up for Londoners and thus obtain a comparison. Secondly, to undertake research into the ways that tourist destinations are marketed to different regions within the

UK, and what the expectations of those potential tourists might be and how they might differ. This would make a contribution to the understanding of constructions of British identity in a regional context in the home world. Third, research with the expatriate community contributing to the construction of the resorts to further ascertain their understanding of what it means to be British. A similar project was undertaken by O'Reilly (2000) regarding expatriate communities on peninsula Spain. An ethnography of those in Magaluf and Palmanova would offer a comparative study. This group of people, as well as the tourists, has been involved in a 'great escape' and it is with this idea, in relation to the tourists, that I conclude.

## 'The Great Escape'

The foregoing discussion has drawn on some examples from the ethnography that illustrated the ways in which Magaluf and Palmanova can be understood in terms of the encoding or signing of the resorts. In addition, it explored the practise of these codes by the tourists, which gives their analysis greater depth and meaning. The proceeding discussion will draw the preceding threads of discussion together and make the final concluding comments on the 'escape to Britain'.

The tourist journey is often described as one that seeks out difference, or looks for a better way of life in an other. For tourists travelling to Magaluf and Palmanova they do not find such a difference, not in the way in which it is popularised in much tourism literature. This is a myth of both the tourism industry, and tourism studies. What the tourists to Magaluf and Palmanova are presented with is a world of Britishness. It may be thought of as different in that it is a Britain that has, in some respects, been made ideal. The absence of (or indeed very low representation of) ethnic minorities serve to suggest that being British is to be white.

The tourists entering Magaluf and Palmanova are presented with a world characterised by signs of Britishness. Place names, food, drink, money, language, television programmes and other media, for example *The Sun* newspaper, entertainment, imperial measures, the Union Flag and flags of the countries that compose the UK, and familiar (albeit American) brand names both in terms of food outlets and material goods, McDonald's and Nike for example. Much of this Britishness is exclusive. That is, it refers to a military past, a history, not shared by all members of British society. The acts of consumption also rely on a foregrounding of particular expressions of Britishness. For example, the promotion of the fry-up caters for only a segment of the British population, but its association with Britishness is reinforced by its advertisement alongside pictures of the Union Jack. In addition, the heightened awareness of differences between men and women refers to a world in which divisions of labour are gendered, and women are objects for the use of men.

The representation of Britain in this context is not forward looking, it is a form of heritage that is referred to (undoubtedly not thought of much by the middle classes who, on the whole, do not frequent the resorts), which does not fully acknowledge a relationship with Europe and exhibits a fear of the other. In many respects it is a regressive attitude, which attempts to cling to an understanding of 'British culture',[6] which is perceived to be threatened by outside forces, be it the European Union, immigrants or globalisation. Rather, the nation, and all that stands for, and all that signifies it, is seen to be under threat. The source of comfort, sustenance and shelter is suffering from too many demands. In effect, the relationship between mother and child is under pressure.

The nation can also take on a different significance. It can be understood as that which provides rules and boundaries within which people are required to operate. Home, for some, can be a place of terror or problems. The holiday as freedom offers a temporary escape from bills and the strictures of work. The problem is that the holiday replaces the confines of the home world with a different set of limits and attempts to control. The promise of difference in freedom is an illusion.

Tour operators use the idea of difference to remind tourists of the presence of the foreign other – change your watch, do not drink the water, be careful in the sun, beware the local pickpockets, and do not visit such and such resort because it is full of Germans. The idea of being a stranger brings about a feeling of insecurity, and creates a dependency and yearning for the mother. All of this can be used and manipulated to great effect by the tour operators, and other elements of the tourism industry, who seek to exert as much supervision over the tourists as they can. Game playing and competitions allude to a child-like status. Fighting to be the best and gain the greatest attention is like sibling rivalry. The presence of the breast as a symbol of the mother (and therefore child) and its link to the nation, further infantilises the tourists.

The tourists, with some exceptions, travel in hope of difference and freedom, a time to be themselves. What this being themselves refers to is a particular construct of British identity that is white and heterosexual, in which the other is kept at bay. This may well represent some kind of authenticity, a perceived genuine or authentic Britishness. In Magaluf and Palmanova, the tourists are 'free' to express these elements of themselves. They interact with the signs of home, which they identify with, and continue to craft the resorts, via a dialogue with them, in their own image. They have 'escaped' to a place that offers them their understanding of what it is to be British. This understanding is based on the imaginings of a romanticised past in which Britain was Great, both on the world stage and in being able to fully nourish her children. In addition, men went to war and women knew their place.

## Notes

1. Not only is this Britain's biggest selling newspaper it is also readily available in Palmanova and Magaluf.
2. At the time of fieldwork this was instead of Spanish pesetas, but would now be instead of the Euro.
3. This was a poor effort on behalf of 'local' businesses.
4. In Russia, the father is more associated with the State and is perceived as remote, authoritarian and stern (White, 2003).
5. This may also go some way to understanding why Captain Scarlet, played by a woman, does not refer to real female pirates.
6. If such an expression can exist. I fully recognise the differences between countries and regions and thus the complexity of such a term.

# References

Abram, S., Waldren, J. and Macleod, D. (eds) (1997) *Tourists and Tourism: Identifying with People and Places*. Oxford: Berg.

Aitchison, C. (1999) Heritage and nationalism: Gender and the performance of power. In D. Crouch (ed.) *Leisure/Tourism Geographies: Practices and Geographical Knowledge* (pp. 59–73). London: Routledge.

Albrecht, G. (1999) Disability humour: What's in a joke? *Body and Society* 5 (4), 67–74.

Aldgate, A. and Richards, J. (1999) *Best of British: Cinema and Society from 1930 to the Present*. London: I.B. Tauris.

Aldridge, A. (2003) *Consumption*. Cambridge: Polity Press.

Anderson, B. (1991) *Imagined Communities: Reflections on the Origin and Spread of Nationalism*. London: Verso.

Andrews, H. (1997) Tourism policy in the municipality of Cavlia, Mallorca. Unpublished report for the National Tourism Organisation of Malta, London.

Andrews, H. (1999) We are what we eat. *In Focus* Summer No 3, 24–25. London: Tourism Concern.

Andrews, H. (2000) Consuming hospitality on holiday. In C. Lashley and A. Morrison (eds) *In Search of Hospitality: Theoretical Perspectives and Debates* (pp. 235–254). Oxford: Butterworth Heinemann.

Andrews, H. (2002) A theme park for the Brits behaving badly. *Times Higher Education Supplement* 19 July, p. 22.

Andrews, H. (2009a) Tourism as a 'moment of being'. *Suomen Antropologi* 34 (2), 5–21.

Andrews, H. (2009b) Tits out for the boys and no back chat: Gendered space on holiday. *Space and Culture* 12 (2), 166–182.

Appadurai, A. (1993) Consumption duration, and history. *Stanford Literature Review* 10, 11–33.

Archetti, E.P. (1997) *Guinea-Pigs: Food Symbol and Conflict of Knowledge*. Oxford: Berg.

Arnold, K. (1977) The introduction of poses to a Peruvian brothel and changing images of male and female. In J. Blacking (ed.) *The Anthropology of the Body* (pp. 179–197). London: Academic Press.

Augé, M. (2002 [1986]) *In the Metro*. Minneapolis, MI: University of Minnesota Press.

Bakhtin, M. (1984) *Rabelais and His World*. Bloomington, IN: Indiana University Press.

Bamforth, L. (1999) Letter: 'A fruitful experiment'. *The Evening Standard* 19 April, p. 22.

Barthes, R. (1975) Toward a psychosociology of contemporary food consumption. In E. Forster and R. Forster (eds) *European Diet from Pre-Industrial to Modern Times* (pp. 47–59). London: Harper & Row.

Barthes, R. (1983) *The Eiffel Tower and Other Mythologies*. NewYork: Hill & Wang.
Barthes, R. (1993) *Mythologies*. London: Vintage Books.
Bataille, G. (1987) *Eroticism*. London: Marion Boyars.
Baudrillard, J. (1988) Consumer society. In M. Poster (ed.) *Baudrillard, J – Selected Writings*. Oxford: Blackwell.
Bauman, Z. (1997a) *Postmodernity and its Discontents*. Oxford: Blackwell.
Bauman, Z. (1997b) The haunted house. *New Internationalist* April, 24–25.
Bauman, Z. (2002) Space in the globalizing world. In E. Krausz and G. Tulea (eds) *Starting the Twenty-first Century: Sociological Reflections and Challenges* (pp. 3–24). London: Transaction Publishers.
BBC Radio 3: Nightwaves (1997) Discussion: Britain in the 50s. I. Jack, J. Seabrook and J. Richards. *Radio Programme*, 9th January.
BBC Radio 4 Today Programme (2002) Friday 27 September.
BBC TV (2001) Homeground: Obesity. BBC2, 11 April.
Beardsworth, A. and Keil, T. (1990) Putting the menu on the agenda. *Sociology* 24 (1), 139–151.
Beckett, A. (1999) Bash thy neighbour. *The Guardian* 28 October, p. 2.
Bell, C. and Lyall, J. (2002) *The Accelerated Sublime: Landscape, Tourism and Identity*. London: Praeger.
Bell, D. and Valentine, G. (1997) *Consuming Geographies: We Are Where We Eat*. London: Routledge.
Bender, B. (1993a) Introduction: Landscape – meaning and action. In B. Bender (ed.) *Landscape: Politics and Perspectives* (pp. 1–17). Oxford: Berg.
Bender, B. (1993b) Stonehenge – contested landscapes (medieval to present day). In B. Bender (ed.) *Landscape: Politics and Perspectives* (pp. 245–279). Oxford: Berg.
Berger, J. (1972) *Ways of Seeing*. Harmondsworth: Penguin.
Berger, P. and Luckmann, T. (1966) *The Social Construction of Reality*. Harmondsworth: Penguin.
Billig, M. (1995) *Banal Nationalism*. London: Sage.
Bishop, P. (1991) Constable country: Diet, landscape and national identity. *Landscape Research* 16 (2), 31–36.
Black, P. (2001) Walking on the beaches looking at the bodies. In K. Backett-Milburn and L. McKie (eds) *Constructing Gendered Bodies* (pp. 104–119). London: Palgrave.
Boissevain, J. (ed.) (1996) *Coping with Tourists: European Reactions to Mass Tourism*. Oxford: Berghahn Books.
Bondi, L. (1992) Gender symbols and urban landscapes. *Progress in Human Geography* 16 (2), 157–170.
Bourdieu, P. (1973) The berber house. In M. Douglas (ed.) *Rules and Meanings: An Anthropology of Everyday Knowledge*. Harmondsworth: Penguin.
Bourdieu, P. (1977) *Outline of a Theory of Practice*. Cambridge: Cambridge University Press.
Bourdieu, P. (1979) *Distinction: A Social Critique of the Judgement of Taste*. London: Routledge.
Bourdieu, P. (1990) *The Logic of Practice*. Cambridge: Polity Press.
Bowman, G. (1995) The politics of tour guiding: Israeli and Palestinian guides in Israel and the Occupied Territories. In D. Harrison (ed.) *Tourism in Less Developed Countries* (pp. 121–134). Chichester: John Wiley.
Boyle, D. (2000) Director. *The Beach*.
Bramwell, M. (ed.) (1977) *Atlas of the Oceans*. Guildford: Colour Library Books.

Brewer, E. (1988) *The Dictionary of Phrase and Fable*. Leicester: Galley Press.
Brown, D. (1996) Genuine fakes. In T. Selwyn (ed.) *The Tourist Image: Myths and Myth Making in Tourism*. Chichester: John Wiley.
Brown, D. (2000a) *Contemporary Nationalism: Civic, Ethnocultural and Multicultural Politics* (pp. 33–47). London: Routledge.
Brown, D. (2000b) The dialectic of consumption: Materialism and social control in American history. *Culture and Consumption Religion and Public Life* 31, 1–11.
Brück, J. (2001) Monuments, personhood and power in the British neolithic. *JRAI* 7 (4), 649–667.
Bunce, M. (1994) *The Countryside Ideal: Anglo-American Images of Landscape*. London: Routledge.
Bungay, S. (1999) Keep your shirt on.... *Majorca Daily Bulletin* August 11, p. 9.
Burgess, R. (1984) Recording and analysing field data. In R. Burgess (ed.) *In the Field: An Introduction to Field Research* (pp. 166–184). London: Unwin Hyman.
Caplan, P. (1994) *Feasts, Fasts, Famine: Food for Thought*. Oxford: Berg.
Caplan, P. (1997) Approaches to the study of food, health and identity. In P. Caplan (ed.) *Food, Health and Identity* (pp. 1–31). London: Routledge.
Capra, F. (1937) Director. *Lost Horizon*.
Carpenter, E. and McLuhan, M. (1960) Acoustic space. In E. Carpenter and M. McLuhan (eds) *Explorations in Communication: An Anthology* (pp. 65–70). London: Jonathan Cape.
Carr, N. (1998) *Defining the Young Beach-Oriented Tourist: A Distinct Tourism Market*. Tourism Management Paper 5, University of Hertfordshire working paper series.
Carr, T. (1953) Director. *Captain Scarlett*.
Carter, E., Donald, J. and Squires, J. (1993) Introduction. In E. Carter, J. Donald and J. Squires (eds) *Space and Place: Theories of Identity and Location* (pp. vii–xv). London: Lawrence and Wishart.
Carter, S. (1997) Who wants to be 'peelie wally'? Glaswegian tourists' attitudes to sun tans and sun exposure. In S. Clift and P. Grabowski (eds) *Tourism and Health: Risks Research and Responses* (pp. 139–150). London: Pinter.
Cesarani, D. (1996) The changing character of citizenship and nationality in Britain. In D. Cesarani and M. Fulbrook (eds) *Citizenship, Nationality and Migration in Europe* (pp. 57–73). London: Routledge.
Chambard, J-L. (1980) *Atlas D'Un Village Indien. Piparsod. Madhya Pradesh*. Paris: Ecole des Hautes Etudes en Sciences Sociales.
Chan, J. and McIntyre, B. (2002) Introduction. In J. Chan and B. McIntyre (eds) *In Search of Boundaries: Communication, Nation States and Cultural Identities* (pp. xiii–xxvi). London: Alex Publishing.
Cinnirella, M. (2000) Britain: A history of four nations. In L. Hagendoorn, G. Cseppeli, H. Dekker and R. Farnen (eds) *European Nations and Nationalism: Theoretical and Historical Perspectives* (pp. 37–65). Aldershot: Ashgate.
Club 18–30 (1999) *Club 18–30 Main Edition Summer 1999 Brochure*.
Cohen, E. (1974) Who is a tourist?: A conceptual clarification. *Sociological Review* 2, 527–555.
Cohen, E. (1979a) A phenomenology of tourist experiences. *Sociology* 13, 179–201.
Cohen, E. (1979b) Rethinking the sociology of tourism. *Annals of Tourism Research* Jan/Mar, 18–35.

Cohen, E. (1982) The Pacific Islands from utopian myth to consumer product: The disenchantment of paradise. *Cahiers du Tourisme*, Série B, no 27.

Cohen, E. (1985) Tourism as play. *Religion* 15, 291–304.

Coleman, S. and Elsner, J. (1995) *Pilgrimage Past and Present in the World Religions.* London: British Museum Press.

Collins, E. (1968) *In the Land of Faraway.* London: Odhams.

*The Concise Mythological Dictionary* (1989) (2nd edn) London: Peerage Books.

Corsín Jiménez, A. (2003) On space as a capacity. *The Journal of the Royal Anthropological Institute* 9 (1), 137–153.

Crick, M. (1985) Tracing the anthropological self: Quizzical reflections on field work, tourism, and the ludic. *Social Analysis* August, 71–92.

Crick, M. (1989) Representations of international tourism in the social sciences: Sun, sex, sights, savings, and servility. *Annual Review of Anthropology* 18, 307–44.

Crick, M. (1994) *Resplendent Sites, Discordant Voices: Sri Lankans and International Tourism.* Reading: Harwood Academic.

Crossley, N. (2001) *The Social Body: Habit, Identity and Desire.* London: Sage.

Crouch, D. (1999a) Introduction: Encounters in leisure/tourism. In D. Crouch (ed.) *Leisure/Tourism Geographies Practices and Geographical Knowledge* (pp. 1–16). London: Routledge.

Crouch, D. (1999b) The intimacy and expansion of space. In D. Crouch (ed.) *Leisure/Tourism Geographies Practices and Geographical Knowledge* (pp. 257–276). London: Routledge.

Crouch, D. (2001) Spatialities and the feeling of doing. *Social and Cultural Geography* 2 (1), 61–75.

Crouch, D., Aronsson, L. and Wahltstrom, L. (2001) Tourist encounters. *Tourist Studies* 1 (3), 253–270.

Crouch, D. and Lübbren, N. (2003) Introduction. In D. Crouch and N. Lübbren (eds) *Visual Culture and Tourism* (pp. 1–20). Oxford: Berg.

Csordas, T.J. (1990) Embodiment as a paradigm for anthropology. *Ethnos* 18 (1), 5–47.

Cusack, T. (2003) Introduction. In T. Cusack and S. Bhreathnach-Lynch (eds) *Art, Nation and Gender Ethnic Landscapes, Myths and Mother-Figures* (pp. 1–11). Oxford: Blackwell.

Daniels, S. (1991) Envisioning England. *Journal of Historical Geography* 17 (1), 95–99.

Dann, G.M.S. (1988) Images of Cyprus projected by tour operators. *Problems of Tourism* 3 (41), 43–70.

Dann, G.M.S. (1989) The tourist as child: Some reflections. *Cahiers du Tourisme*, Série C, no 135.

Dann, G.M.S. (1996a) *The Language of Tourism: A Sociolinguistic Perspective.* Wallingford: CAB International.

Dann, G.M.S. (1996b) The people of tourist brochures. In T. Selwyn (ed.) *The Tourist Image: Myths and Myth Making in Tourism* (pp. 61–81). Chichester: John Wiley.

Dann, G.M.S. (2002) The tourist as a metaphor of the social world. In G.M.S. Dann (ed.) *The Tourist as a Metaphor of the Social World* (pp. 1–17). Wallingford: CAB International.

Dann, G.M.S. and Jacobsen, J.K.S. (2002) Leading the tourist by the nose. In G.M.S. Dann (ed.) *The Tourist as a Metaphor of the Social World* (pp. 209–235). Wallingford: CAB International.

Davidson, J. (2000) The beef that made John Bull. *The Guardian, Saturday Review* 25 March, p. 5.

Davies, D. (1988) The evocative symbolism of trees. In D. Cosgrove and S. Daniels (eds) *The Iconography of Landscape, Essays on the Symbolic Representation, Design and Use of Past Environments* (pp. 32–42). Cambridge: Cambridge University Press.

Desforges, L. (2000) Travelling the world: Identity and travel biography. *Annals of Tourism Research* 27 (4), 926–945.

Douglas, M. (1966) *Purity and Danger: An Analysis of Concepts of Pollution and Taboo.* Harmondsworth: Penguin.

Douglas, M. (1973) *Rules and Meanings: An Anthropology of Everyday Knowledge.* Harmondsworth: Penguin.

Douglas, M. (1975a) Deciphering a meal. In M. Douglas (ed.) *Implicit Meanings: Essays in Anthropology* (pp. 36–54). London: Routledge and Keegan Paul.

Douglas, M. (1975b) Animals in Lele religious symbolism. In M. Douglas (ed.) *Implicit Meanings: Essays in Anthropology* (pp. 27–46). London: Routledge and Keegan Paul.

Douglas, M. (1984) *Food in the Social Order.* New York: Basic Books.

Douglas, M. (1987) *Constructive Drinking Perspectives on Drink from Anthropology.* Cambridge: Cambridge University Press.

Douglas, M. (1996) *Thought Styles: Critical Essays on Good Taste.* London: Sage.

Douglas, M. (1997) Introduction. In J. Kuper (ed.) *The Anthropologists' Cookbook* (pp. 1–7). London: Kegan Paul International.

Doving, R. (1999) The Matpakke: The great Norwegian narrative about the family and the nation. Unpublished conference paper. First International Conference on Consumption and Representation: *Consuming Markets; Consuming Meanings.* University of Plymouth, UK, 1–3 September.

Drummond, J.C. and Wilbraham, A. (1958) *The Englishman's Food: Five Centuries of English Diet.* London: Jonathan Cape.

Dumont, L. (1970) Religion, politics and society in the individualistic universe. The Henry Myers Lecture. *Proceedings RAI*, 31–40.

Dumont, L. (1977) *From Mandeville to Marx: The Genesis and Triumph of Economic Ideology.* London: University of Chicago Press.

Durkheim, E. (1933 [1893]) *The Division of Labour in Society.* London: MacMillan.

Durkheim, E. (1976 [1915]) *The Elementary Forms of the Religious Life.* London: George Allen & Unwin.

Eatwell, A. (1998) English party in Magalluf. *Majorca Daily Bulletin* 28 June, p. 1 and p. 11.

Ebin, V. (1979) *The Body Decorated.* London: Thames & Hudson Ltd.

Edensor, T. and Kothari, U. (1994) The masculinisation of Stirling's heritage. In V. Kinnard and D. Hall (eds) *Tourism: A Gender Analysis* (pp. 164–185). Chichester: John Wiley.

Edwards, T. (2000) *Contradictions of Consumption Concepts, Practices and Politics in Consumer Society.* Buckingham: Open University Press.

Ellen, R. (1977) Anatomical classifications and the semiotics of the body. In J. Blacking (ed.) *The Anthropology of the Body* (pp. 343–373). London: Academic Press.

Evans-Pritchard, E.E. (1940) *The Nuer.* Oxford: Clarendon Press.

Falk, P. (1994) *The Consuming Body.* London: Sage.

Featherstone, M. (1991) The body in consumer culture. In M. Featherstone, M. Hepworth and B. Turner (eds) *The Body: Social Process and Cultural Theory* (pp. 170–196). London: Sage.

Fiddes, N. (1991) *Meat a Natural Symbol*. London: Routledge.

Fort, M. (2003) Fat's the way to do it. *Food Handbook, Guardian Weekend Magazine* 29 November, pp. 65–68.

Foucault, M. (1976) *The Will to Knowledge, The History of Sexuality: Volume One*. Harmondsworth: Penguin.

Foucault, M. (1977) *Discipline and Punish: The Birth of the Prison*. Harmondsworth: Penguin.

Foucault, M. (1986) Of other spaces. *Diacritics* 16 (1), 22–27.

Franklin, J. (1989) The liberty of the park. In R. Samuel (ed.) *Patriotism: The Making and Unmaking of British National Identity Volume III* (pp. 141–159). London: Routledge.

Frazer, J. (1993 [1922]) *The Golden Bough*. Ware: Wordsworth.

Garland, A. (1997) *The Beach*. Harmondsworth: Penguin.

Geertz, C. (1973) *The Interpretation of Cultures*. New York: Basic Books.

Gell, A. (1993) *Wrapping in Images*. Oxford: Oxford University Press.

Gell, A. (1996) Reflections on a cut finger: Taboo in the Umeda conception of the self. In M. Jackson (ed.) *Things as They Are: New Directions in Phenomenological Anthropology* (pp. 115–127). Bloomington, IN: Indiana University Press.

Gellner, E. (1983) *Nations and Nationalism*. Oxford: Blackwell.

Goffman, E. (1959) *The Presentation of Self in Everyday Life*. Harmondsworth: Penguin.

Gomme, A.B. (1964) *The Traditional Games of England, Scotland, and Ireland Volume 1*. New York: Dover Publications.

Gottlieb, A. (1982) Americans' vacations. *Annals of Tourism Research* 9, 165–187.

Graburn, N.H.H. (1987) Material symbols in Japanese domestic tourism. In D.W. Ingersoll Jr and G. Bronitsky (eds) *Mirror and Metaphor: Material and Social Constructions of Reality* (pp. 17–27). London: University Press of America.

Graburn, N.H.H. (1989) Tourism: The sacred journey. In V. Smith (ed.) *Hosts and Guests: The Anthropology of Tourism* (2nd edn) (pp. 17–31). Oxford: Blackwell.

Gray, J. (2003) Open spaces and dwelling places: Being at home on hill farms in the Scottish Borders. In S. Low and D. Lawrence-Zúñiga (eds) *The Anthropology of Space and Place. Locating Culture* (pp. 224–244). Oxford: Blackwell.

Greenwood, D. (1989) Culture by the pound: An anthropological perspective on tourism as cultural commoditisation. In V. Smith (ed.) *Hosts and Guests: The Anthropology of Tourism* (2nd edn) (pp. 171–185). Oxford: Blackwell.

Gruffudd, P. (1991) Reach for the sky: The air and English cultural nationalism. *Landscape Research* 16 (2), 19–24.

Guibernau, M. (2001) National identity and modernity. In A. Dieckhoff and N. Gutiérrez (eds) *Modern Roots Studies of National Identity* (pp. 73–92). Aldershot: Ashgate.

Gurr, L.A. (1987) Maigret's Paris conserved and distilled. In M. Douglas (ed.) *Constructive Drinking: Perspectives from Anthropology* (pp. 220–236). Cambridge: Cambridge University Press.

Gusfield, J.R. (1987) Passage to play: Rituals of drinking time in American society. In M. Douglas (ed.) *Constructive Drinking: Perspectives from Anthropology* (pp. 73–90). Cambridge: Cambridge University Press.

Gutiérrez, N. (2001) The study of national identity. In A. Dieckhoff and N. Gutiérrez (eds) *Modern Roots: Studies of National Identity* (pp. 3–17). Aldershot: Ashgate.

Haddon, C. (1996) *Pigs are Perfect: An Illustrated Anthology.* London: Headline.

Hagendoorn, L. and Pepels, J. (2000) European nations and nationalism: An introductory analysis. In L. Hagendoorn, G. Csepeli, H. Dekker and R. Farnen (eds) *European Nations and Nationalism: Theoretical and Historical Perspectives* (pp. 1–35). Aldershot: Ashgate.

Hammersley, M. and Atkinson, P. (1995) *Ethnography Principles in Practice* (2nd edn). London: Routledge.

Hanefors, B.M. (2001) Paradise regained Swedish charter tourists visiting the non-ordinary. Unpublished PhD thesis, University of North London.

Hanefors, M. and Selwyn, T. (2000) Dalecarlian Masques: One souvenir's many voices. In M. Hitchcock and K. Teague (eds) *Souvenirs: The Material Culture of Tourism* (pp. 253–283). Aldershot: Ashgate.

Hann, C.M. (1998) Introduction: The embeddedness of property. In C.M. Hann (ed.) *Property Relations. Reviewing the Anthropological Tradition* (pp. 1–47). Cambridge: Cambridge University Press.

Harrison, J. (2003) *Being a Tourist. Finding Meaning in Pleasure Travel.* Vancouver: University of British Columbia Press.

Hastrup, K. (1992) A question of reason: Breast–feeding patterns in seventeenth- and eighteenth-century Iceland. In V. Maher (ed.) *The Anthropology of Breast-Feeding Natural Law or Social Construct* (pp. 91–108). Oxford: Berg.

Hawkes, T. (1977) *Structuralism and Semiotics.* London: Routledge.

Hedetoft, U. and Hjort, M. (2002) Introduction. In U. Hedetoft and M. Hjort (eds) *The Postnational Self: Belonging and Identity* (pp. vii–xxxii). London: University of Minnesota Press.

Henley, J. (2003) Beef encounter. Prince does his bit for British meat. *The Guardian* 7 February, p. 8.

Hertz, R. (1973) The hands. In M. Douglas (ed.) *Rules and Meanings: The Anthropology of Everyday Knowledge* (pp. 118–124). Harmondsworth: Penguin.

Hilton, J. (1933) *Lost Horizon.* London: Pan Books.

Hirsch, E. (1995) Introduction. Landscape: Between place and space. In E. Hirsch and M. O'Hanlon (eds) *The Anthropology of Landscape: Perspectives on Place and Space* (pp. 1–30). Oxford: Clarendon Press.

Hobsbawm, E. (1983) Introduction: Inventing traditions. In E. Hobsbawm and T. Ranger (eds) *The Invention of Tradition* (pp. 1–14). Cambridge: Cambridge University Press.

Howell, S. (1974) *The Seaside.* London: Cassell and Collier Macmillan.

Hyman, T. (2000) *Carnivalesque: National Touring Exhibitions.* London: Hayward Gallery.

Jackson, M. (1989) *Paths Toward a Clearing: Radical Empiricism and Ethnographic Inquiry.* Bloomington, IN: Indiana University Press.

James, A. (1997) How British is British food? In P. Caplan (ed.) *Food, Health and Identity* (pp. 71–86). London: Routledge.

Jones, J. (2000) Scary masks and sausages. *The Guardian, Saturday Review* 13 May, p 5.

Jordan, Z.A. (1971) *Karl Marx: Economy, Class and Social Revolution.* London: Nelson.

Juergensmeyer, M. (2002) The paradox of nationalism in a global world. In U. Hedetoft and M. Hjort (eds) *The Postnational Self: Belonging and Identity* (pp. 3–17). London: University of Minnesota Press.

Keelan, S.H. (2001) Paradox in a postmodern paradise. In F. Lloyd and M. Roberts (eds) *Sex and Consumerism Contemporary Art in Japan* (pp. 57–97). Brighton: University of Brighton.

Kent, S. (1995) Comment on Smith, A. and David, N., the production of space and the house of Xidi Sukur. *Current Anthropology* 36 (3), 459–460.

Khatib-Chahidi, J. (1992) Milk kinship in Shi'ite Islamic Iran. In V. Maher (ed.) *The Anthropology of Breast-Feeding: Natural Law or Social Construct* (pp. 109–132). Oxford: Berg.

Kirby, L. (1997) *Parallel Tracks: The Railroad and Silent Cinema*. Durham, NC: Duke University Press.

Krausz, E. and Tulea, G. (2002) Introduction. Postmodernism and the cunning of reason. In E. Krausz and G. Tulea (eds) *Starting the Twenty-first Century. Sociological Reflections and Challenges* (pp. ix–xv). London: Transaction Publishers.

Krugman, H. (1968) Consumer behaviour. In D.L. Sills (ed.) *International Encyclopedia of the Social Sciences* (Vol. 3; 349–354). New York: Crowell Collier & MacMillan.

Kuper, J. (1997) Preface. In J. Kuper (ed.) *The Anthropologists' Cookbook* (pp. 8–13). London: Kegan Paul.

Lao Tzu. (1985) *Tao Te Ching* (R. Wilhelm, trans.). London: Arkana.

Lash, R. (1999) Rikki Lash Lazaar Show. *Majorca Daily Bulletin* 23 July, p. 24.

Leach, E. (1964) Anthropological aspects of language: Animal categories and verbal abuse. In E.H. Lenneberg (ed.) *New Directions in the Study of Language* (pp. 23–63). Cambridge, MA: MIT Press.

Lefebvre, H. (1991) *The Production of Space*. Oxford: Blackwell.

Lett, J.W. Jr. (1983) Ludic and liminoid aspects of charter yacht tourism in the Caribbean. *Annals of Tourism Research* 10, 35–56.

Lévi-Strauss, C. (1964) *The Raw and the Cooked*. Harmondsworth: Penguin.

Lévi-Strauss, C. (1969) *Totemism*. Harmondsworth: Penguin.

Lévi-Strauss, C. (1997) The roast and the boiled. In J. Kuper (ed.) *The Anthropologists' Cookbook* (pp. 239–248). London: Kegan Paul.

Lewis, C.S. (1950) *The Lion, the Witch and the Wardrobe*. Harmondsworth: Penguin.

Linsell, T. (2000) Nations, nationalism and nationalists. In T. Linsell (ed.) *Our Englishness* (pp. 49–73). Norfolk: Anglo-Saxon Books.

Littlejohns, G. (2000) Our English. In T. Linsell (ed.) *Our Englishness* (pp. 95–107). Norfolk: Anglo-Saxon Books.

Lunn, K. (1996) Reconsidering Britishness: The construction and significance of national identity in twentieth-century Britain. In B. Jenkins and S.A. Sofos (eds) *Nation and Identity in Contemporary Europe* (pp. 83–100). London: Routledge.

MacCannell, D. (1973) Staged authenticity: Arrangements of social space in tourist settings. *American Journal of Sociology* 79 (3), 589–603.

MacCannell, D. (1976) *The Tourist: A New Theory of the Leisure of the Class*. London: The Macmillan Press.

MacCannell, D. (1992) *Empty Meeting Grounds: The Tourist Papers*. London: Routledge.

Malcolmson, R. and Mastoris, S. (1998) *The English Pig: A History*. London: The Hambledon Press.

Marr, A. (1999) So what kind of England do we really stand for?: What's wrong with our food? *The Observer* 31 October, p. 22.

Mars, G. (1987) Longshore drinking, economic unity and union politics in Newfoundland. In M. Douglas (ed.) *Constructive Drinking: Perspectives from Anthropology* (pp. 91–101). Cambridge: Cambridge University Press.

Mauss, M. (1954) *The Gift: Forms and Functions of Exchange in Archaic Societies.* London: Routledge.

Mauss, M. (1979) *Sociology and Psychology Essays.* London: Routledge and Keegan Paul.

McDowell, L. (1995) Body work: Heterosexual gender performances in city workplaces. In D. Bell and G. Valentine (eds) *Mapping Desire: Geographies of Sexualities.* London: Routledge.

Meethan, K. (1996) Place, image and power: Brighton as a resort. In T. Selwyn (ed.) *The Tourist Image: Myths and Myth Making in Tourism* (pp. 179–196). Chichester: John Wiley.

Meethan, K. (2001) *Tourism in Global Society: Place, Culture, Consumption.* Basingstoke: Palgrave.

Mennell, S. (1991) On the civilizing of appetite. In M. Featherstone, M. Hepworth and B. Turner (eds) *The Body: Social Process and Cutlural Theory* (pp. 126–156). London: Sage.

Merleau-Ponty, M. (1962) *Phenomenology of Perception.* London: Routledge.

Merrifield, A. (1993) Place and space: A Lefebvrian reconciliation. *Transactions of British Geographers* 18, 516–531.

Morley, D. (2000) *Home Territories: Media, Mobility and Identity.* London: Routledge.

Morely, D. and Robins, K. (1993) No place like *Heimat*: Images of (homeland) in European culture. In E. Carter, J. Donald and J. Squires (eds) *Space and Place: Theories of Identity and Location* (pp. 3–31). London: Lawrence and Wishart.

O'Reilly, K. (2000) *The British on the Costa Del Sol: Transnational Identities and Local Communities.* London: Routledge.

O'Rourke, D. (1987) Director. *Cannibal Tours.* Canberra: O'Rourke and Associates.

Odhams (1961) *The Modern Encyclopaedia.* London: Odhams.

Ohnuki-Tierney, E. (1993) *Rice as Self: Japanese Identities Through Time.* Chichester: Princeton University Press.

Okely, J. (1994) Thinking through fieldwork. In A. Bryman and R.G. Burgess (eds) *Analysing Qualitative Data* (pp. 18–34). London: Routledge.

Overboe, J. (1999) "Difference in itself": Validating disabled people's lived experience. *Body and Society* 5 (4), 17–29.

Palmer, C. (1998) From theory to practice: Experiencing the nation in everyday life. *Journal of Material Culture* 3 (2), 175–199.

Palmer, C. (1999) Heritage tourism and English national identity. Unpublished PhD thesis, University of North London.

Palmer, C. (2003) Touring Churchill's England: Rituals of kinship and belonging. *Annals of Tourism Research* 30 (2), 426–445.

Parker, A., Russo, M., Sommer, D. and Yaeger, P. (eds) (1992) *Nationalisms and Sexualities.* London: Routledge.

Parr, M. (1998) Home truths (Photographs). *The Guardian Weekend* 4 April, pp. 16–24.

Parr, M. (2000) *Think of England.* London: Phaidon.

Passariello, P. (1983) Never on Sunday? Mexican tourists at the beach. *Annals of Tourism Research* 10, 109–122.

Paxman, J. (1998) The English: A Portrait of the People. London: Michael Joseph.

Perniola, M. (1989) Between clothing and nudity. In M. Feher (ed.) Fragments for a History of the Human Body Part Two (pp. 236–265). New York: Urzone.

Philips, D. (1999) Narrativised spaces: The functions of story in the theme park. In D. Crouch (ed.) Leisure/Tourism Geographies: Practices and Geographical Knowledge (pp. 91–108). London: Routledge.

Phillips, A. (1999) Down with pin-ups. The Guardian Education 26 October, 6–7.

Pitcher, M. (1991) Rock, reef and 'roos: A critical analysis of the role of images in Australian tourism promotion. Unpublished MA thesis, Roehampton Institute of Higher Education.

Pleij, H. (2001) Dreaming of Cockaigne. Chichester: Columbia University Press.

Poster, M. (1988) Introduction. In M. Poster (ed.) Baudrillard, J – Selected Writings (pp. 1–9). Oxford: Basil Blackwell.

Powell, C. (2002) How cool is Britannia now? The durability of national image. In J.M. Fladmark (ed.) Heritage and Identity: Shaping the Nations of the North (pp. 271–277). Shaftesbury: Donhead Publishing.

Powell, M. and Pressburger, E. (1944) Directors. A Canterbury Tale.

Powell, M. and Pressburger, E. (1948) Directors. The Red Shoes.

Priestland, G. (1972) Frying Tonight: The Saga of Fish and Chips. London: Gentry Books.

Rabinow, P (ed.) (1984) The Foucault Reader: An Introduction to Foucault's Thought. Harmondsworth: Penguin.

Rawnsley, A. (1999) Why the real losers are the Euro-haters: What's wrong with our food? The Observer 31 October, p. 31.

Reynolds, K. (1991) Director. Robin Hood Prince of Thieves.

Rodda, M. (1967) Noise and Society. Edinburgh and London: Oliver and Boyd.

Rolleston, T.W. (1985) Myths and Legends of the Celtic Race. London: Constable.

Rose, G. (1993) Feminism and Geography: The Limits of Geographical Knowledge. Cambridge: Polity.

Rose, G. (1995) Place and identity: A sense of place. In D. Massey and P. Jess (eds) A Place in the World? (pp. 87–118). Oxford: Oxford University Press.

Rousseau, J-J. (1973 [1762]) The Social Contract and Discourses. London: J.M. Dent and Sons Ltd.

Ryan, C. (1995) Learning about tourists from conversations: The over-55s in Majorca. Tourism Management 16 (3), 207–215.

Rykwert, J. (1997) On strata in the kitchen, or the Archaeology of tasting. In J. Kuper (ed.) The Anthropologists' Cookbook (pp. 58–63). London: Kegan Paul International.

Samuel, R. and Thompson, P. (1990) Introduction. In R. Samuel and P. Thompson (eds) The Myths We Live By (pp. 1–22). London: Routledge.

Sceats, S. (2000) Food, Consumption and the Body in Contemporary Women's Fiction. Cambridge: Cambridge University Press.

Schafer, R.M. (1985) Acoustic space. In D. Seamon and R. Mugerauer (eds) Dwelling, Place and Environment: Towards a Phenomenology of Person and World (pp. 87–98). Dordrecht: Martinus Nijhoff.

Schroeder, B. (1972) Director. La Vallée (The Valley Obscured by Clouds).

Schwimmer, E.G. (1979) Feasting and tourism: A comparison. Semiotica 27 (1/3), 221–235.

Seabrook, J. (1996) An English exile. Granta 56, 173–189.

Searle-Chatterjee, M. (1993) Christmas cards and the construction of social relations in Britain today. In D. Miller (ed.) *Unwrapping Christmas* (pp. 176–192). Oxford: Clarendon Press.

Selänniemi, T. (1992) A charter trip to sacred places – individual mass tourism. Unpublished conference paper presented at Le Tourisme International entre Tradition et Modernité – Colloque International (ISA WG05), Nice, 19–21 November.

Selänniemi, T. (1996) Beneath, between and beyond the paradigms – looking down on the tourist in the sociology of tourism. Unpublished conference paper presented at the International Sociological Association RC50, Paradigms in Tourism Research – Symposium, Jyväskylä, 4–7 July.

Selänniemi, T. (1999) The anthropology of charter tourists – ethnography and theoretical implications. Unpublished conference paper presented at the International Academy for the Study of Tourism: Building a Knowledge Base for the Next Millenium, Zagreb, Croatia, 27 June to 2nd July.

Selwyn, T. (1980) The order of men and the order of things: An examination of food transactions in an Indian village. *International Journal of the Sociology of Law* 8, 297–317.

Selwyn, T. (1990) Tourist brochures as post-modern myths. *Problems of Tourism* 13 (3/4), 13–26.

Selwyn, T. (1993) Peter Pan in South-East Asia: Views from the brochures. In M. Hitchcock, V. King and M. Parnwell (eds) *Tourism in South-East Asia* (pp. 117–137). London: Routledge.

Selwyn, T. (1994) The anthropology of tourism: Reflections on the state of the art. In T. Seaton *et al.* (eds) *Tourism: The State of the Art* (pp. 731–735). Chichester: John Wiley.

Selwyn, T. (1995) Landscapes of liberation and imprisonment: Towards an anthropology of the Israeli landscape. In E. Hirsch and M. O'Hanlon (eds) *The Anthropology of Landscape* (pp. 114–134). Oxford: Clarendon Press.

Selwyn, T. (1996a) Introduction. In T. Selwyn (ed.) *The Tourist Image: Myths and Myth Making in Tourism* (pp. 1–32). Chichester: John Wiley.

Selwyn, T. (1996b) Atmospheric notes from the fields: Reflections on myth-collecting tours. In T. Selwyn (ed.) *The Tourist Image: Myths and Myth Making in Tourism* (pp. 147–161). Chichester: John Wiley.

Sennet, M. (1912) Director. *The Tourists*, cited in L. Kirby. *Parallel Tracks* (pp. 135–136). Durham, NC: Duke University Press.

Sennett, R. (1994) *Flesh and Stone: The Body and The City in Western Civilization*. London: Faber & Faber.

Seymour, D. (1983) The social functions of the meal. *Journal of Hospitality Management* 2 (1), 3–7.

Shakespeare, W. (1982) Romeo and Juliet. *The Illustrated Stratford Shakespeare*. London: Chancellor Press.

Shakespeare, W. (1982) Julius Caesar. *The Illustrated Stratford Shakespeare*. London: Chancellor Press.

Shapespeare, W. (1982) Henry V. *The Illustrated Stratford Shakespeare*. London: Chancellor Press.

Shields, R. (1991) *Places on the Margin: Alternative Geographies of Modernity*. London: Routledge.

Shields, R. (1999) *Lefebvre, Love and Struggle: Spatial Dialectics*. London: Routledge.

Shilling, C. (1993) *The Body and Social Theory.* London: Sage.

Simmel, G. (1950) The metropolis and mental life. In K. Wolff (ed.) *The Sociology of Georg Simmel* (pp. 324–339). London: Collier MacMillan.

Simpson, J. and Roud, S. (2000) *Oxford Dictionary of English Folklore.* Oxford: Oxford University Press.

Smith, V. (ed.) (1989) *Hosts and Guest: The Anthropology of Tourism* (2nd edn). Oxford: Blackwell.

Soper, K. (1995) *What is Nature?* Oxford: Blackwell.

Stearns, P.N. (2001) *Consumerism in World History: The Global Transformation of Desire,* London: Routledge.

Stein, R. (2003) Let's live a little. *Food Handbook, Guardian Weekend Magazine,* 29 November, pp. 46–53.

Stoddard, S. (2003) *Paradise.* National Gallery Touring Exhibition, National Gallery, London.

Synnott, A. (1993) *The Body Social: Symbolism, Self, and Society.* London: Routledge.

Tambiah, S J. (1969) Animals are good to think and good to prohibit. *Ethnology* 8 (4), 423–429.

Tapper, R (2008) Who are the Kuchi? Nomad self-identities in Afghanistan. *JRAI* 14 (1), 97–116.

*The Sun* (2003) Blair surrenders Britain to Europe. 15 May 2003, p. 1, pp. 6–7.

Tilley, C. (1994) *A Phenomenology of Landscape: Places, Paths and Monuments.* Oxford: Berg.

Tönnies, F. (1957 [1887]) *Community and Society: Gemeinshcaft und Gesellschaft.* New York: Harper & Row.

Triandafyllidon, A. (2002) *Negotiating Nationhood in a Changing Europe – Views from the Press.* Ceredigion: Edwin Mellen Press.

Turner, B.S. (1996) *The Body and Society: Explorations in Social Theory.* London: Sage.

Turner, V. (1969) *The Ritual Process: Structure and Anti-Structure.* New York: Cornell University Press.

Urbain, J.D. (1989) The tourist adventure and his images. *Annals of Tourism Research* 16 (1), 106–118.

Urry, J. (1990) *The Tourist Gaze: Leisure and Travel in Contemporary Societies.* London: Sage.

Urry, J. (1995) *Consuming Places.* London: Routledge.

Urry, J. (1999) Sensing leisure spaces. In D. Crouch (ed.) *Leisure Tourism Geographies Practices and Geographical Knowledge* (pp. 34–45). London: Routledge.

Uzzell, D. (1984) An alternative structuralist approach to the psychology of tourism marketing. *Annals of Tourism Research* 11, 79–99.

Valentine, G. (1999) Consuming pleasures: Food, leisure and the negotiation of sexual relations. In D. Crouch (ed.) *Leisure/Tourism Geographies Practices and Geographical Knowledge* (pp. 164–180). London: Routledge.

Valerius, J. (2003) (Dis-)Embodying the nation: Female figures, desire and nation building in early twentieth-century Finland. In T. Cusack and S. Bhreathnach-Lynch (eds) *Art, Nation and Gender Ethnic Landscapes, Myths and Mother-Figures* (pp. 38–52). Oxford: Blackwell.

van den Berghe, P. (1994) *The Quest for the Other.* London: University of Washington Press.

Varney, W. (1996) The briar around the strawberry patch. *Women's Studies International Forum* 19 (3), 267–276.

Veblen, T. (1925 [1899]) *The Theory of the Leisure Class: An Economic Study of Institutions*. London: George, Allen & Unwin.

Veijola, S. and Jokinen, E. (1994) The body in tourism. *Theory, Culture and Society* 11 (3), 125–151.

Verhoeven, P. (1990) Director. *Total Recall*.

Wagner, U. (1977) Out of time and place – mass tourism and charter trips. *Ethnos* 42, 38–52.

Walton, J.K. (2002) *Fish and Chips and the British Working Class 1870–1940*. London: Leicester University Press.

White, A. (2003) Mother Russia: Changing attitudes to ethnicity and national identity in Russia's regions. In J. Andall (ed.) *Gender and Ethnicity in Contemporary Europe* (pp. 179–198). Oxford: Berg.

Wickens, E. (2002) The sacred and the profane: A tourist typology. *Annals of Tourism Research* 29 (3), 834–851.

Williams, J. (1997) We never eat like this at home: Food on holiday. In P. Caplan (ed.) *Food, Health and Identity* (pp. 151–171). London: Routledge.

Willis, R (ed.) (1993) *World Mythology*. London: Simon and Schuster.

Wilson, E. (1995) *The Body Social: Women's Bodies in Life and Art*. Video, Open University.

Wright, P. (1985) *On Living in an Old Country: The National Past in Contemporary Britain*. London: Verso.

Yalom, M. (1997) *A History of the Breast*. London: Harper Collins.

Yuan-Ming Tao (1985) The well in the peach blossom forest. In R. Wilhelm (trans.) *Tao Te Ching (Lao Tzu)*. London: Arkana.

## Web addresses

On WWW at http://www.guardian.co.uk. Accessed 21.11.03.

On WWW at http://www.dollynet.freeserve.co.uk/thatcher.htm. Accessed 3.04.

On WWW at http://despina.advanced.org/16438/fact/pirates/SirFrancisDrake.htm. 1999.

On WWW at http://www.atlanticonline.ns.ca/celtic/captmorgan2.html. 1999.

On WWW at http://ils.unc.edu/nc/Blackbeard.html. 1999.

On WWW at http://despina.advanced.org/16438/fact/general.htm. 1999.

On WWW at http://despina.advanced.org/16438/fact/pirates/jeanlaffite.htm. 1999.

On WWW at http://despina.advanced.org/16438/fact/general.htm. 1999.

On WWW at http://news.bbc.co.uk. Accessed 5.4.03.

# Index

German, 88, 110, 112, 118, 161-162, 336, 348, 363
Gesellschaft, 8, 55
Glass, 164, 324, 328, 332, 334
Globalisation, 340-343, 368, 382, 386
Graburn, Nelson, 17-19, 33, 125, 205, 293, 360, 374

Habitus, 45-47, 49, 61, 118, 127, 164, 239, 261, 263, 277-278, 322, 345, 354-355, 362
Heaven, 8
Hell, 31
Heritage, 55, 81, 159, 173, 386
Hero, 81, 98, 358-359, 364
Heterosexual, 6, 25, 77, 93, 102, 199, 243, 350, 368, 372, 387
Home, 1, 9, 14-15, 17-23, 25, 27-29, 31, 46, 65, 67, 106, 108-109, 112, 114, 118, 123, 127, 156, 158-159, 166-167, 175, 185, 188-189, 195, 197, 205, 216, 224, 228, 237, 241, 247, 257, 275, 278, 280, 282, 284, 292-293, 298, 302, 304-305, 311-312, 320, 322, 326, 335, 340, 343, 345, 347-348, 356, 358, 360-361, 364, 366, 372-374, 382-384, 386, 388
Home world, 1, 9, 14-15, 17-20, 22-23, 25, 27, 29, 67, 127, 159, 175, 188, 241, 278, 280, 282, 298, 302, 304-305, 335, 340, 343, 345, 347-348, 358, 360-361, 374, 382-384, 386
Homosexual, 98, 100, 241, 381
Hotel, 3, 5-6, 7, 17, 23-25, 27, 53, 67, 72, 77, 94, 101, 102, 109-110, 112-118, 123, 126-127, 156, 162-164, 166, 168, 172, 174-175, 182, 195, 197, 199, 203-205, 210, 212, 214, 220-221, 224, 226, 232, 235, 239-241, 247, 249, 280, 283-284, 286, 293, 295, 298, 300, 322, 324, 326, 336-337, 342, 345, 350, 363-364, 366, 368, 380

Identity, 5, 9-10, 12, 14, 19, 21, 29, 33-34, 36, 38-39, 41, 49-51, 53, 55, 57, 59, 61, 72, 78-79, 81, 96, 102, 104, 106-108, 112, 115, 118, 121, 123, 125, 127, 152-153, 155-158, 162, 164, 166, 169-170, 184-185, 187-188, 192-193, 210, 216, 218, 228, 230-231, 234, 241, 272, 275-278, 282, 284, 288, 290-292, 300, 302, 304-305, 334, 340-341, 343, 345, 347, 350-354, 358-361, 366-368, 370, 374, 376, 380, 382, 384, 387
Image, 15, 41, 47, 51, 53, 125, 153, 158, 170, 218, 221, 226, 230, 235, 241, 245, 247, 249, 276, 286, 297, 302, 306, 313, 316, 328, 374, 381, 388
Immigrants, 31, 55, 107, 127, 195, 336, 340, 341, 343, 347, 361, 380, 382, 386

Imperial measures, 10, 328, 359, 360, 384
In-group, 10, 112, 115, 127, 272, 345, 350

Jackson, Michael, 45-46, 239, 261, 322, 345
Japanese, 18, 77, 239, 241, 282
Judging, 197, 201, 231, 234, 324

Kinship, 6, 8, 72, 105, 271, 309, 343, 345, 370

Landscape, 19, 21, 34, 38, 47, 51, 57, 65, 72, 74, 76-77, 104, 152, 158, 161, 168, 173, 288, 290, 298, 362
Lefebvre, Henri, 47, 49, 64, 65, 355, 356
Legend, 96, 290, 364
Liminal, 79, 96, 99, 125, 177, 187-188, 210, 262, 298, 360
London, 25, 72, 76, 108, 152, 156, 215, 298, 378, 382

MacCannell, Dean, 15-17, 19, 21, 23, 33, 38, 173, 345-348
Majorca Daily Bulletin, 5, 206, 309
Male, 53, 74, 88, 90, 92, 98, 100, 109, 125, 159, 168, 170, 192-197, 199, 201, 204, 206, 208, 212, 214-216, 220-221, 226, 228, 234, 236-237, 241, 245, 251, 256-257, 259, 263, 265, 268, 271-272, 290, 304, 314, 316, 318, 322, 366, 376, 381-382
Man, 17, 23, 91-92, 94, 107-108, 111-112, 114-115, 123, 162, 164, 170, 172, 175, 198-201, 208, 212, 214, 218, 223, 226, 237, 241, 249, 251, 264-265, 268, 286, 288, 290, 306, 311, 313-314, 324, 332, 364, 378
Maps, 49, 64, 67, 72
Market, 10, 12, 14, 41, 72, 106-107, 116, 118, 120-121, 123-125, 127-128, 161, 172, 190, 216, 221, 231, 241, 272, 340-342, 368, 370, 372-373, 382
Mauss, Marcel, 38, 45, 261, 263, 279, 354
Meal, 89, 112, 210-212, 231, 292, 295, 298, 302, 320, 328, 336, 358
Meat, 5, 9, 226, 298, 302, 304, 306, 358
Men, 24, 72, 88, 100, 102, 128, 187, 193-195, 206, 208, 210, 212, 214, 241, 243-245, 251, 256, 259, 261, 264-266, 268-269, 306, 313, 316, 324, 328, 334, 360, 362, 366, 381, 386, 388
Merleau-Ponty, Maurice, 43, 263
Military, 31, 55, 66, 72, 74-75, 77-79, 81, 102, 115, 125, 152, 158, 282, 284, 335, 337, 359-360, 364, 384
Milk, 292, 309-311
Moral, 77, 203, 206, 208, 212, 362